"Mek Some Noise"

MUSIC OF THE AFRICAN DIASPORA

Edited by Samuel A. Floyd, Jr., and Rae Linda Brown

"Mek Some Noise"

Gospel Music and the Ethics of Style in Trinidad

TIMOTHY ROMMEN

University of California Press

BERKELEY   LOS ANGELES   LONDON

Center for Black Music Research

COLUMBIA COLLEGE   CHICAGO

University of California Press, one of the most distinguished university
presses in the United States, enriches lives around the world by
advancing scholarship in the humanities, social sciences, and natural
sciences. Its activities are supported by the UC Press Foundation
and by philanthropic contributions from individuals and institutions.
For more information, visit www.ucpress.edu.

Chapter 3 is adapted from "Nationalism and the Soul: Gospelypso as
Independence," *Black Music Research Journal* 22, no. 1 (Spring 2002):
37–63. Many thanks to the Center for Black Music Research, Columbia
College, for allowing me to update and revise it here. Lyrics from
"We Coming," "Ah Love You So," "Blessed Are the Elders," "Seeking
Is My Home," and "Anything" appear by permission of Sheldon
Blackman. Lyrics from "Nothing Is Impossible," "War," "You Dun
Know," and "Trendsetters," and music and lyrics from "Do You Know"
appear by permission of Sherwin Gardner (www.sherwingardner.com,
www.myspace.com/sherwingardner, www.flowmastersrecords.com).
Lyrics from "Waving T'ing" appear by permission of Andrew O'Brien.
Lyrics from "Gimmie Room," "Gospelypso," and "They Say" appear
by permission of Noel Richards. Lyrics from "Zion March" and "I Can't
Please You" appear by permission of Lyndon R. Sterling. Lyrics from
"Calm before the Storm" and "Fornication" appear by permission of
Ancil Valley and the Broadway Boyz.

University of California Press
Berkeley and Los Angeles, California

University of California Press, Ltd.
London, England

© 2007 by The Regents of the University of California

Library of Congress Cataloging-in-Publication Data

Rommen, Timothy.
  "Mek some noise" : gospel music and the ethics of style in Trinidad /
Timothy Rommen.
      p.   cm. — (Music of the African diaspora ; 11)
  Includes bibliographical references (p.   ) and index.
  ISBN: 978-0-520-25067-3 (cloth : alk. paper)
  ISBN: 978-0-520-25068-0 (pbk. : alk. paper)-
      1. Gospel music—Trinidad and Tobago—Trinidad—History and
criticism. I. Title. II. Title: Make some noise.
  ML3187.R66   2007
  782.25'40972983—dc22   2006023845

Manufactured in the United States of America

15 14 13 12 11 10 09 08 07
10 9 8 7 6 5 4 3 2 1

This book is printed on New Leaf EcoBook 50, a 100% recycled fiber
of which 50% is de-inked post-consumer waste, processed chlorine-free.
EcoBook 50 is acid-free and meets the minimum requirements of
ANSI/ASTM D5634–01 (*Permanence of Paper*).

For Kim and in loving memory of Callie

Contents

Acknowledgments

This book exists thanks, in large part, to the contributions and energy of people other than me. It is, first and foremost, a testimony to the love and friendship that my family and I have shared with Trinidadians from Port of Spain to Point Fortin and everywhere in between. Special thanks to my dear friend Roddie Taylor and to his family, who opened their home and their church to me during my initial fieldwork. Mt. Beulah Evangelical Baptist Church in Point Fortin was a fantastic home, and the warmth and generosity of that community enriched my fieldwork experiences immeasurably.

All of the musicians, radio DJs, and pastors with whom I had the pleasure of working during the course of my fieldwork gave a great deal of their time and energy to this project, and I single out a few here because of their extraordinary contributions. Many thanks to Noel "the Professor" Richards, Marilyn "Destiny" Joseph, Sherwin Gardner, Sheldon Blackman, Isaac Blackman, the Broadway Boyz, Anthony "Space" Williams, Jamie Thomas, Anthony Moses, Michael Dingwell, and Sean Daniel.

In addition to the many Trinidadian friends that made this book a possibility in the first place, I have benefited greatly from a series of wonderful mentors and interlocutors. Many thanks to Philip V. Bohlman, who offered me his constant support along with invaluable critique and insight throughout the writing process. Sam Floyd and Martin Stokes also challenged my thinking over the past few years. My colleagues in the department of music at the University of Pennsylvania, moreover, read, commented upon, and engaged with my work in extremely productive ways. Thanks especially to Carol Muller, Guthrie P. Ramsey, and Mark Butler for their interest in and valuable contributions to this project. Finally, Shannon Dudley, Gage Averill, and Greg Barz helped me to interrogate and nuance my arguments further—thank you all. The editorial process at the University of California

Press has helped me tremendously and I thank Mary Francis, Jacqueline Volin, Kalicia Pivirotto, and the external reviewers for their careful readings of my manuscript. Thank you for making this process a pleasure. A special note of thanks to Roger Grant, whose assistance with proofreading and indexing the manuscript was invaluable.

A series of institutions believed in this project and funded portions of the fieldwork and writing process. I am very grateful to have received the support of a U.S. Student Fulbright Grant to conduct fieldwork in Trinidad (1999–2000). The University of Chicago also awarded me two Lowell C. Wadmond research grants to conduct fieldwork trips to Trinidad (1998 and 2001). Thanks also to the Woodrow Wilson Foundation for awarding me a Charlotte W. Newcombe Dissertation Fellowship (2001–2). Most recently, the Center for Black Music Research awarded me a Rockefeller Resident Fellow Grant (2004–5) to continue writing the manuscript. Finally, the University of Pennsylvania generously granted me the research leave I needed in order to accept the Rockefeller Resident Fellow Grant. I could not have completed this book without the financial assistance afforded by these institutions. Many thanks.

The greatest share of my thanks, however, belongs to my family. My wife, Kim, has been a constant source of encouragement during this process. She has been interested and invested in the project and has read and reread the manuscript as it gradually took shape. Thank you, Kim. Thanks also to my daughters, Natalia, Arianna, and Anika, who have put up with my, at times, long hours and absences during the course of this project. Thanks for always making me smile. Thanks also to my father, who read and commented on the manuscript as it took shape, and to my mother, whose dedication to the musical lives of her children helped shape my own interests and even this book. I dedicate this book to Kim, who continues to embody in her own unique way the beautiful and generous personality of her mother, Callie, who was taken from us before she could see this book in print. Memory eternal.

Introduction

This book is about conviction. It is about believing and translating that belief into action. It is about the way that music participates in actualizing belief—but also about the ways that music convinces. This book is about people talking about people making music—that is, reception. But it is also about people making music in order to say something—that is, performance. In short, this book is about the ethics of style. This book is about Full Gospel Christians who want to live as and sound like Christians in Trinidad. As such, it concerns the place of Full Gospel believers in the nation and in the region—it is a book about memories and identities, about futures and possibilities. But mostly, it is a book that hopes to convey in prose a poetics of belief so delicate and intricate that I have often felt at a loss for vocabulary and syntax with which to discuss it.

The chapters that follow explore music and its roles in the lives of Full Gospel believers in Trinidad. They explore the ways in which the several styles of gospel music circulating in and around that community are seized upon and used (or rejected) in the hope of securing Full Gospel identity in the face of other religious traditions and within the nation at large. As such, the chapters that follow concern themselves variously with musical style, colonial and missionary histories, national and regional politics, media flows and migration, and aesthetics. The central and unifying thread running throughout the book, however, is *conviction*.

The pages that follow, then, constitute an extended meditation on the convictions—the ethical concerns—that motivate the creation and reception of style in Full Gospel Trinidad. This is the case because ethics is firmly entrenched at the core of communal discourse about the relative usefulness of given styles and because ethical considerations serve as a principal motivation for many artists' individual contributions to what gospel music

1

sounds like in Trinidad. This book is, therefore, largely about how to approach thinking in terms of the ethical dimensions of musical experience and, more specifically, about the opportunities and challenges with which ethics—embedded as it is in the creation and reception of musical style—confronts Trinidadian Full Gospel believers.

In order to approach at a closer range the convictions that drive gospel music in Trinidad, and on the premise that understanding and foregrounding the ethical dimensions of musical performance and reception will lay the groundwork for a reconsideration of the extent to which style participates in discourses of identity, this book develops a model that I call the ethics of style. The ethics of style focuses attention on the discursive spaces between individual and community (self and other) in order to come to a more nuanced understanding of music in its sociocultural contexts. It functions as an analytical model that investigates the process by which musical style informs identity formation for both artists and audiences; illustrates how style thus becomes the vehicle for a multifaceted communal discourse about value and meaning; and interrogates the process of personal identification or disidentification with musical style as a moment of ethical significance. The ethics of style thus works to recenter conviction as a valid site of analysis. By interrogating the creation and reception of a given musical style within specific communities (in this case the Trinidadian Full Gospel community), and by tracing the convictions and beliefs that the style's performance and the discourses surrounding it underscore, the ethics of style works to highlight the nuanced and highly contested means by which music participates in processes of identity formation. But the ethics of style also addresses itself to the various ways in which style itself can be conceptualized and interpreted. Accordingly, I use "style" in order to refer not only to a broad range of musical characteristics, but also to performance contexts, dress, dance, and language use. This allows me to consider the various registers at which convictions are being played out and negotiated within the broader context of musical performance.

The motivation for developing this analytical model stems from my own struggles with a representational challenge. Put somewhat bluntly, the vocabulary with which I approached my fieldwork, and the theoretical models that I was prepared to apply, are insufficiently nuanced to manage adequately the task of representing the musical dimensions of the Trinidadian Full Gospel community.[1] Some ideas, like oppositionality and resistance, do not easily apply in the expressly evangelical context of Full Gospel Trinidad. Other models, such as hybridity and mimicry, explain some aspects of Full Gospel experience quite well (especially with respect to musical style), but nevertheless fail to explicate the full weight of the community's struggle for identity. This is largely because the terms of the models' engagement with local particularities do not (and should not be expected to) take into consideration the community's own approach to living out these particularities as Full Gospel believers.

Belinda Edmondson, writing about the state of literary criticism in the Caribbean, puts her finger on this representational challenge as well, suggesting that the theoretical vocabulary so pervasively used in Caribbean studies is applied at some risk: "Words like multiculturalism, *mestizaje,* oppositionality, otherness, colonialism, neocolonialism, shipwreck, mimicry, metropole, [and] migration . . . *stand in for an entire discourse.*[2] She elaborates on her concern as follows: "The Caribbean that has developed in scholarly discourse over the past forty years or so sometimes seems to have a life of its own, at times bearing only a cursory relation to the events of today. Yet the words, ideas, and discourses of these archetypes of 'Caribbeanness,' if you will, have such power to shape the way that the region now imagines itself that they have become mythic: to invoke these archetypes to explain particularities in Caribbean life is often enough."[3]

Edmondson cautions that the discourse driving Caribbean scholarship at times dictates approaches to local particularities, potentially writing over subtle variations and new possibilities in the process. The ethics of style, then, represents my attempt to resolve (or at least address) this representational challenge by taking seriously—and at face value—the beliefs and convictions motivating and animating questions of identity, as expressed in and through musical style, within the Trinidadian Full Gospel community. In so doing, I also address another set of ideas—those ideas concerned with religious life in the Caribbean and, more specifically, with Christianity in the Caribbean experience.

Like their colleagues in literary theory, scholars interested in the religious dimensions of Caribbean life have resorted to a set of archetypal ideas, often focusing their inquiries on the region's multitude of syncretic practices and thereby illustrating great currents of creative resistance to the hegemony of Christian doctrine and practice. (Myalism, convince, Santeria, Vodou, and orisha are a few representative examples.)[4] This approach to the region's cultural and religious practices has resulted in a trend toward reading Christianity as something from which to escape, and Michel de Certeau offers an excellent example of this when he observes: "[Colonized people have] often *made* of the rituals, representations, and laws imposed on them something quite different from what their conquerors had in mind; they subverted them not by rejecting or altering them, but by using them with respect to ends and references foreign to the system they had no choice but to accept. They were *other* within the very colonization that outwardly assimilated them; their use of the dominant social order deflected its power, which they lacked the means to challenge; they escaped it without leaving it."[5]

Christianity is assigned certain roles within this metanarrative of escape. It might, therefore, make an appearance as the negative catalyst for a particular type of overt resistance (Yoruba religion, Rastafarianism). Alternaively, it may be characterized as a mechanism that, because of its artificially imposed nature, engenders syncretic, difference-making reaction to Christian beliefs and practices (Santeria, Vodou, Spiritual Baptists). And for those scholars studying the spectacular failures of Christianity in the New World, it is often—and accurately—exposed as the principal justification for the worst and most unconscionable types of violence inflicted by Europeans on the region in the name of religion (the *encomienda* system, *reducciones*, and the *requerimiento*).

Although all of these assessments of the region's religious life have their place and clearly constitute important contributions to the study of Caribbean histories, most succeed in occluding from view—or writing over—the very issues that I explore in this book. Drawing on the ideas of scholars such as Michel-Rolph Trouillot, and in the spirit of Belinda Edmondson's *Caribbean Romances*, this book re-sounds some of the "silences" that have, for one reason or another, remained unscripted in the scholarly literature on Trinidad.[6] Specifically, I address the complexities attendant to the musical life-worlds of Trinidadian Full Gospel believers who have chosen unequivocally to embrace Full Gospel Christianity rather than to resist it in one form or another.

I should pause just briefly and clarify the way that I am using the concept of the Full Gospel community and what I mean when I refer to "gospel music." I use the term "Full Gospel" to indicate what is, at best, a loose affiliation of several denominations and strands of Protestantism within Trinidad, most of which are Pentecostalist in orientation. The term offers the advantage of referring primarily to Pentecostalist and charismatic denominations (and, importantly, not to Presbyterians, Anglicans, or Catholics). In spite of the necessarily loose definition that the term affords, then, it does delimit in a useful way the Protestants with whom this book is concerned. As I will illustrate in the pages that follow, Trinidadians themselves use this designation to refer to their position within the nation in general and Protestant Trinidad in particular. They also use the term when organizing themselves into local Full Gospel associations. The content of this rather loosely defined concept, then, is policed by the members of the Full Gospel community themselves—a process I discuss in greater detail in chapter 1.

"Gospel music" is another rather murky term in the context of Full Gospel Trinidad. By way of comparison, in the United States, Protestant musical practices are generally broken down into smaller bits (i.e., Southern gospel, praise and worship music, urban gospel, inspirational, spirituals, Christian rock, etc.). Within the U.S. context, which actually maps race and class onto musical style in rather unsubtle ways, the term "gospel music" generally refers to an African American sacred repertory and range of performance practices. In Trinidad, however, the term "gospel music" generally functions as a catchall category for Protestant music, in effect reversing the North American trend toward compartmentalization. The term "gospel music," as used in Trinidad, thus privileges content over style—a usage that groups rather divergent musical styles under a larger umbrella by virtue of their shared content.[7] It is interesting to note, moreover, that questions related to race and class are also subsumed in this atmosphere, an issue that I explore in greater depth in chapter 4. A brief illustration of how gospel music is understood in Trinidad can be drawn from a concert I attended in San Fernando in 2000. Held February 26 at the Palms Club, the concert was called Nicole 2000.[8] What follows is a brief vignette, culled and edited from my field notes, describing the wide range of styles that shared the stage that night.

> I arrive early. Already several hundred people are milling about the grounds of the Palms Club. They are here because this will be one of the year's biggest concerts in the southern part of Trinidad and because, since this is a general admission show, they want to ensure a good seat or spot. An incredibly diverse lineup of artists is going to be performing tonight. There will be plenty of gospel dancehall, hip-hop, and R&B, but also a good deal of gospelypso, and there is even going to be a steelband performance. Nicole is herself a gospel singer, and she is best known for singing covers of North American gospel music and original compositions in that vein. It is not insignificant that all of these styles are able to share the same venue on the same night. What feels a bit like a type of bricolage to me is considered perfectly normal by the Trinidadian believers here this evening. What I think of as music generally separated by scene, social group, performance space, and so forth is understood as a unified category in this context. Gospel music in Trinidad includes all of these sounds by definition. . . . The evening's events confirm this idea. For example . . . Sherwin Gardner just performed a song called "Pick Me Up!" screaming, "Every time I'm down, Jesus always, always picks me up!" over and over and running back and forth across the stage in soca/dancehall style. . . . Noel "the Professor" Richards, dressed in a

black leather outfit and white T-shirt reminiscent of beatnik cool, sang a song called "Try Jesus" that is built around the piano-driven Fats Domino sound of the 1950s. . . . The Nazarite Steelband pounded out a medley of hymns, calypso style. . . . Nicole worked through a set of R&B-inspired gospel songs, pacing majestically across the stage in a white wedding dress. . . . Marilyn "Destiny" Joseph sang a tune called "Alabanza" that approximates a salsa feel, all the while encouraging the audience to wave their rags. All of these musical moments trace very different trajectories of style, but each is considered gospel music in Trinidad and referred to as such.[9]

While all the music I discuss in the coming chapters enjoys a life outside of individual congregations' worship services, church services themselves, nevertheless, remain powerful drivers and markers of legitimacy. The nexus of the ethics of style, then, can be located in discourses that emerge against the backdrop of worship services, for these gospel musics are continuously read against the worship practices of congregations. And yet, these normative practices are challenged—threatened, even—by the very presence of the various gospel musics in circulation. Musical change is occurring in the process of creating a dialogue between current gospel musics and normative practices within church services, and the ethics of style affords me a point of entry into the convictions of artists, into the reactions of the community, and into the uses to which these gospel musics are being put in service of identity. It also affords me an opportunity to consider the role that performance context plays in shaping the various registers of style, a process which then feeds back into the ways that style is configured in ethical terms through the community's discourse.

With these issues in mind, the following chapters turn to a thorough exploration of each of the gospel musics being performed in contemporary Trinidad. Chapter 1 traces the religious histories that have shaped the current context within which Full Gospel Trinidadians are negotiating their identity. The chapter also introduces the four principal musical styles circulating in and around the Full Gospel community—gospelypso, North American gospel music, dancehall, and jamoo—thereby setting the stage for the chapters that follow. In chapter 2, I develop in greater detail the analytical model that I so briefly introduced here, providing both theoretical grounding and methodological justification for its use within Full Gospel Trinidad.

Chapter 3 examines the emergence of gospelypso and its reception history in order to illustrate the themes of post-independence identity that lie close to the heart of the style. In chapter 4, I analyze the rise of North American gospel music in Trinidad. Significantly, the historical trajectory of North American gospel music was essentially contemporaneous with the emergence of gospelypso—a fact that affords me a wide range of comparative possibilities and opens an important window onto the ethical and political motivations for choosing one style over the other.

Chapter 5 investigates the music of gospel dancehall and hardcore soca artists and the issues that surround their performances, including the ethical and stylistic implications attendant to their active creation of new social spaces for worship. Chapter 6 concerns itself with the musical style called jamoo. Coined by Ras Shorty I (i.e., Ras Shorty "eye," formerly known as Lord Shorty), this idiosyncratic approach to gospel music offers insights into the possibility of other ways of thinking about music in Trinidadian Full Gospel contexts, and this not least because Ras Shorty I found himself entrenched in a space somewhere between the Full Gospel community on one hand and the nation at large on the other, becoming—quite literally—the "voice of one crying in the wilderness."[10]

Chapter 7 brings the discussion of the ethics of style full circle. I suggest several ways that musical change and musical practices themselves might be reenvisioned and rethought in light of the ethics of style by offering a close reading of a Baptist church in Point Fortin, illustrating how the tensions engendered by the local Full Gospel Association, the influx of Pentecostalist worship patterns, and the current range of musical options are being negotiated by this small community of believers.

I should offer a final preliminary clarification here. Although I present artists within chapters dedicated to individual styles, these artists are generally much more flexible in their approach to style than my organizational choice might make them appear. Many of the artists I discuss in this book thus adopt multiple styles over the course of their careers and, for that matter, even on individual albums and during specific performances. Sherwin Gardner performs hardcore soca just as freely as he does R&B and dancehall. Noel "the Professor" Richards certainly focuses his efforts primarily on gospelypso but has also written songs in the style of "oldies" from the North American pop charts of the 1950s and '60s. Marilyn "Destiny" Joseph is also primarily a gospelypso artist, yet one of her big radio and concert hits is a rockers-inspired song. Nicole Ballosingh performs North American gospel but also explores gospelypso. And Isaac Blackman, while very dedicated to promoting jamoo, also incorporates alternative, hip-hop, and dancehall sounds in his work. My reason for structuring chapters around discussions of individual styles, then, concerns my desire to focus on the overall discourses that each generates, and I do not mean thereby to suggest that artists are in any way identified, once and for all, with particular styles.

I conclude this introduction in anticipatory fashion with the words of the refrain from Sheldon Blackman's song "We Coming," for it illustrates perfectly the enthusiasm and commitment of the artists and believers who enliven the pages that follow:

> Generation, generation look the future resting in we hand.
> Generation, generation, wake up the future resting in we hand.
> Backward never, forward we going!
> This generation, make way, we coming![11]

1 Music, Memory, and Identity in Full Gospel Trinidad

As the scheduled time of the worship service draws closer, a small group of people begins to congregate in the sanctuary of Mt. Beulah Evangelical Baptist Church. The doors are open, inviting all those who wish to participate to join the group. The singing starts about fifteen minutes before the service begins in earnest. Yet this time is important, even crucial—a preparation for and anticipation of that which is to come. Any member of the group is welcome to lead out in song, and the entire atmosphere depends on spontaneous interaction. During this time of singing, people continue filing into the room, gradually adding their voices to those of the group and increasing both the volume and the general intensity of the activity. Immediately before the service begins, the singing comes to a close and is replaced by an invocation. A member of the congregation leads the invocation, but all join their voices in affirmation and agreement, causing the voice of the one to be lost in the collective voice of the group. The prayer straddles the time before the service and the beginning of worship, thereby stitching together nonritual and ritual time.

From the author's field notes, January 2000

Reading history against itself and delving into the ethnographic past, this chapter engages in a preparatory ritual not unlike that of the invocation I just described in a Full Gospel worship service.[1] The stitching that I explore here, however, is not between secular and sacred time, but rather between the past and the present. Michel-Rolph Trouillot, who points out that subjects "do not succeed a past; they are its contemporaries," articulates the necessity of teasing out the various ways that the past is embodied in and through the present.[2] In an important sense, this chapter parallels the function of an opening invocation, which serves not only to define the present but also the past(s) with which contemporary Trinidadian believers are sharing their present. By exploring the religious history of Trinidad, I am able to illustrate more fully the challenges with which the present Full Gospel community is faced and against which it is working toward securing its identity. By extension, this chapter also provides the context necessary for a thorough consideration of the theoretical basis for and the practical applications of the ethics of style in contemporary Trinidad. The second half of the chapter introduces the performance contexts and the individual styles that together shape the musical life of Full Gospel Trinidad.

INVOCATIONS: OF RELIGIOUS HISTORIES

The island of Trinidad played host to Europeans for the first time on July 31, 1498. That was the day that Christopher Columbus chanced upon the island and, on seeing three hills rising high above its southeastern coast, annexed to Spain a bit of the New World, christening it in honor of the Trinity.[3] The island then proceeded quickly to slide into a three-hundred-year period of colonial insignificance. Spain did relatively little to establish on Trinidad what Antonio Benítez-Rojo has called "Columbus's machine," for it was busy installing that machine in other, more lucrative locations.[4]

Relegation to the status of colonial afterthought did not, however, translate to an escape from the colonial encounter. In fact, Trinidad's Amerindian population was decimated during this period. Following the pattern of so many other colonial encounters in the New World, the Arawaks and Caribs fell victim to the ravages of newly introduced European diseases (especially smallpox) and warfare, both with the Spanish and with each other. As Kevin Yelvington points out, many Amerindians were also "exported as forced labour to other Spanish possessions."[5] So brutal was the colonial encounter in Trinidad that Bridget Brereton estimates the Amerindian population was halved within the century following Columbus's visit, "from around 30,000–40,000 in 1498 to 15,000–20,000 in 1592."[6]

Nearly a century elapsed between Columbus's initial visit and the founding of St. Joseph, Trinidad's first permanent Spanish settlement, in 1592. What followed, of course, was the installation of the principal institution of Spanish colonial power, the *encomienda*. The idea behind the *encomienda* was that conquest and Christianizing constituted two sides of the same coin. "The *encomendero* was granted a parcel of land, with the right to exact tribute (usually in the form of labour, or crops, or both) from the Indians living on the land. In return he was expected to Christianize 'his' Indians and protect them."[7] In practice, however, the first part worked very well, whereas the "in return" part became, at most, an afterthought. Dale Bisnauth points out the spectacular failure of the Christianizing intent of the *encomienda*. "At best the programme of christianizing and civilizing the indigenous peoples of the Caribbean achieved the most minimal results. By 1644, there were about two hundred and fifty Christian Caribs in Trinidad out of a total population of about four thousand."[8]

The low number of converts was attributed, at least in part, to the flight of the Amerindians away from the *encomiendas* and into Trinidad's interior regions during the seventeenth century—a further indictment of the abuses being perpetrated by the *encomenderos*. This state of affairs precipitated the installation of the second pillar of Spanish colonialism—the *mision* or *reduccion*. In 1687 Capuchin missionaries settled in Trinidad, established a number of missions, and set to work ensuring the success of Columbus's machine. Put otherwise, the missionaries seemed always to secure more labor than they did souls.[9]

The missionaries gained control over the labor of several thousand of the remaining Amerindians by organizing them into mission villages, but the missionaries' successful monopoly on the workforce soon engendered open resentment by the settlers, as well as violent revolt by the Amerindians (the Arena Uprising of 1699), and the missions were abolished in 1708.[10] By 1713 all of the missionaries had left Trinidad, and the Amerindians in the mission villages were entrusted to the settlers. Shortly thereafter, in 1716, the *encomienda* system was also abolished.

The decades following the withdrawal of the missionaries and the abolishment of the *encomienda* system found Trinidad thoroughly impoverished and lacking a viable economy. Trinidad was simply too far removed from the vital trading routes to warrant visits by Spanish trading vessels, and it was not until the 1770s that Spain, responding to the challenges posed by British colonialism and the currents of continental politics, began to make significant attempts at developing the island's economy. By 1776 it was apparent that Trinidad lacked the labor base for a profitable economy, and the decision was made to install the refined version of Columbus's machine—the plantation—on the island. Yelvington traces this development as follows:

> Responding in the eighteenth century to an increasingly aggressive British imperialism . . . the Spanish attempted to transform Trinidad into a profitable agricultural slave colony by opening up the island to Catholic foreigners from friendly nations. The *Cedula de Población* in 1783 was directed at French planters in the French islands formally ceded to Britain and those resident in the French Antilles as well. The former were suffering from severe political and social discrimination at the hands of British administrators, the latter from exhausted soils and plagues of insects. These planters were given grants of land and other inducements, receiving an amount of land commensurate with the number of slaves they brought with them: the more slaves the more land. Free coloureds received half the amount of land as whites.[11]

The influx of the French planters and their slaves and of free black planters and artisans quickly transformed Trinidad into an active plantation

economy. The island now exported cocoa, coffee, cotton, and sugar in sufficient quantities to make it a viable stop along the trading routes.[12] The
advent of the French Revolution in 1789 and the beginning of the revolution in Saint-Domingue (now Haiti) during 1791 provided additional political and economic impetus for French planters to immigrate to Trinidad, and
the result of this influx was a decided shift from Spanish to French creole
culture. As John Cowley points out, "With virtually all of the early slave
population having been born in the French islands, black culture . . . reflected this African-French-Caribbean bias, including the establishment of
patois (Caribbean French Creole) as a lingua franca."[13] The religious culture
of Trinidad was changing as well, for the rapidly increasing number of slaves
and free blacks upon whose shoulders the economy was being built brought
with them their West African spiritual heritages.[14]

Meanwhile, it did not take long for Spain to get caught in the intrigues of
continental politics. France forced Spain into the uncomfortable position of
declaring war on Britain in 1796, and the British promptly rose to the challenge, capturing Trinidad and its emerging economy in 1797. By 1802
Trinidad had been formally ceded to Britain, and the gradual Anglicization of
the island began.[15] Trinidad's move into Great Britain's political sphere naturally brought about the installation of the Church of England and would
eventually lead to the arrival of a wide range of Protestant denominations.

The influx of Protestant missionary activity in the nineteenth century
did not, however, emanate solely from England. In fact, new denominations
and their corresponding congregations were, more often than not, introduced and then pastored by intra-Caribbean, Canadian-, or United States–
based missionaries. The Anglican Church, which consecrated its National
Cathedral in Port of Spain in 1823, soon found itself sharing Trinidad's souls
with a wide range of other denominations. The Missionary Society of Grey-
friars Secession Church, Glasgow, established the first Presbyterian church
in Trinidad in 1836. In 1868 the Canadian Presbyterian Church sent missionaries to evangelize the growing East Indian community, and the Moravian Church, which had established a missionary presence in Tobago as
early as 1787, established missionary activities in Trinidad in 1890 as an
extension of its work in Barbados.[16]

None of these denominations, however, predate the Baptist presence in
Trinidad. Yelvington notes that "divergent groups of free blacks came to
populate Trinidad during slavery and afterwards. These included former
American slaves, slaves freed from foreign slave ships by the Royal Navy,
and immigrants from other Caribbean islands."[17] One of these groups con-
sisted of 781 former slaves who had fought alongside the British during the

War of 1812. In return for their services, they had been promised freedom and relocation. The British, honoring their promise and fulfilling one of their own needs in the process, settled the former soldiers in Trinidad between May of 1815 and August of 1816.[18] The first two groups were settled in the North, while the remaining six groups were allotted land in the uncultivated and sparsely populated southern interior of the island, where they were formed into six separate Company Villages.[19]

These former soldiers brought the Baptist faith to Trinidad. The northern settlers incorporated African as well as Catholic elements into their worship and eventually came to be known as Spiritual Baptists (or "Wayside" or "Shouter" Baptists). Teacher Hazel Ann Gibbs-DePeza has remarked, "The Spiritual Baptist Faith . . . can justly be described as the attempt of the Negro to establish bench marks for freedom, to fashion out of the religious elements in the community, something more fitting to the needs of the people, a worship more realistic."[20] The southern settlers, however, evolved a form of worship closer to continental Baptist thought in doctrine, if not in practice.

Practice would soon be at issue, for the London-based Baptist Missionary Society began work in Trinidad during 1843. Upon initiating contact with the Company Villages in 1845, the missionaries succeeded in creating a great deal of tension by ordering the local Baptists to submit themselves to London Baptist authority in matters of doctrine and practice. What followed was a classic case of what Dick Hebdige has called the "struggle for possession of the sign."[21] Some of the Trinidadian Baptists agreed with the missionaries and joined themselves to the London Baptists. Others, however, vehemently opposed this course of action and were consequently, and in a wonderfully presumptuous claim to authority, branded "disobedients" by the missionaries. Unfazed, these "disobedients" promptly reasserted their autonomy, referring to themselves as "independents" from that day forward.[22]

These three Baptist groups (Spiritual, London, and Independent) continue to thrive in contemporary Trinidad, and several of these incorporate numerous variations on a theme (amounting to some fourteen legally recognized denominations within the larger Baptist umbrella).[23] The Baptist Union of Trinidad and Tobago (London Baptists) continues to be distinct from the Independent Baptists, but these denominations, however divided they may be over certain doctrinal, historical, or ecclesiastical issues, are united in their desire to remain separate from and unrelated to the Spiritual Baptists, whose beliefs and practices they consider syncretic to a fault.[24] The nineteenth century, then, saw the arrival of the Anglican Church, of various Presbyterians and Baptists, and of the Moravian Church.

The sociocultural and religious geography of Trinidad was, however, only beginning to take shape. In a pattern that repeated itself across the Caribbean, Trinidad's plantation economy became entirely dependent on cheap labor once it was set in motion. The abolition of the British slave trade (1807), the first and second Amelioration Orders (1824, 1831), the prohibition on the importation of slaves from other colonies (1825), the emancipation of slaves (1834), and the apprenticeship years (1834–38), nevertheless, all signaled the gradual decommissioning of the current incarnation of Columbus's machine. By the 1840s many Trinidadian elites were facing the very real possibility of financial ruin and began to prevail upon the British government to sanction the importation of labor from India. Sanction was granted in 1844, and a second wave of exploitation and human tragedy—what Hugh Tinker has called a "new system of slavery"—was initiated in Trinidad.[25]

This new middle passage was in full swing by 1845 when the ship *Fatel Rozack* arrived in Port of Spain and was not brought to an end until 1917. All told, more than 144,000 people endured that "journey of seven seas," and the resulting East Indian community has since grown to comprise approximately 41 percent of Trinidad's current population.[26] Hindu and Muslim religious beliefs and practices were added to the growing number of religious systems in Trinidad, and the government's Population and Housing Census of 2000 states that approximately 28 percent of the population claims Hindu or Muslim faith.[27] Immigrants from China, Lebanon, Germany, and Portugal also made the journey to Trinidad during the nineteenth century, and by the beginning of the twentieth century, the cultural and ethnic dimensions of Trinidad were rather well defined and in place.[28]

The twentieth century, however, saw new patterns and nuances emerge, for New York, London, Toronto, and other locations throughout Europe and North America increasingly became destinations for Trinidadians seeking economic and educational opportunities. Importantly, the diaspora has become a source of exchange between the local and the global—a fertile ground upon which to imagine pasts, presents, and futures. These social and cultural movements and the geographies that they weave will figure heavily in the chapters that follow, not least because many contemporary religious trends are intimately bound up in the relationship between Trinidad and the growing Caribbean diaspora.[29]

Political independence from Great Britain was fought for during the middle decades of the century and won in full on August 31, 1962. But independence came with competing claims to authority and power, and the cultural politics of the post-independence years have engendered the black power movement of the 1970s, the attempted coup by the Muslimeen in 1990, and the rise to political power of the formerly disenfranchised East Indian community during the 1990s.[30] Meanwhile, political dependence on the United States continued to grow.[31] Not surprisingly, the religious life of evangelical believers also became increasingly oriented toward trends, ideas, and sounds from North America during this time. The role of North America has, in fact, become so significant that it arguably functions as the spiritual center of contemporary Full Gospel Trinidad. Pentecostalists in particular, whether of independent, Church of God, or Open Bible Standard affiliation, have been missionizing in Trinidad ever since the early years of the twentieth century, and they continue to attract large numbers of converts each year. A great majority of these missionary efforts have been fostered by intra-Caribbean initiatives or organizations based in Canada and the United States, and a brief sketch of some of the denominations that began work in Trinidad during the twentieth century illustrates these trends quite well.

In 1912 Rev. Batson brought the African Methodist Episcopal Church to Trinidad, organizing a congregation in St. James. Robert and Elizabeth Jamieson, independent missionaries from Canada, began working in Trinidad in 1923, setting the stage for the eventual affiliation of several independent churches with the Pentecostal Assemblies of Canada (PAOC) in 1926. By 1935 there was enough regional support to inaugurate the Trinidad Bible School, an institution that later became the West Indies School of Theology (1947). Within little more than a decade, this regional movement had grown large enough to separate from the PAOC, and 1958 saw the creation of the Pentecostal Assemblies of the West Indies (PAWI). But PAOC's formative role in the life of PAWI remains quite palpable even today, for the great majority of PAWI churches are pastored by graduates of the West Indies School of Theology.[32]

Mattie McCaullie, of the Church of God in Christ, arrived in Trinidad in 1927, and the beginnings of Church of God (CG, Cleveland) missionizing there date to the 1940s. These efforts came to fruition under the leadership of Edward D. Hasmatali, who chose to affiliate his independent congregations to that denomination in 1956. It was during 1955, moreover, that Open Bible Standard missionaries from the United States arrived in Trinidad and witnessed amazing growth. In fact, within less than two decades, the Trinidadian Open Bible Standard Church became independent (1972). Today, the Open Bible Standard Church is arguably the nation's largest Pentecostalist denomination (in terms of both membership and number of congregations). The Church of Christ was started through a local radio program hosted by Bob Brown, who hailed from St. Vincent. The effectiveness of these programs eventually led devoted listeners to invite Brown to lead the first gospel meeting of the Church of Christ in Trinidad in 1971.[33]

Trinidadian churches continue to benefit from funds, radio programs, cable television shows (e.g., on the Trinity Broadcasting Network), and other material assistance from their brothers and sisters in North America. North American assistance in the region has often been read in a decidedly negative light and has generated no small amount of aggravation and concern among those groups who are losing members to the Pentecostal churches.[34] The influx of North American financial and material assistance is, moreover, generally understood as a deliberate commodification of faith—as a means of gaining advantage and then capitalizing on the lack of resources available to the competing faiths. A typical example of this point of view is found in an editorial published in the e-zine *Hot Calaloo:*

> All over Trinidad a battle is underway. It is a battle for souls and is being waged by the US-based fundamentalist Pentecostal Church. . . . Although many converts are at the expense of traditional Christian churches, two-thirds come from T&T's Hindu Asian community. . . . Hindu religious leaders are upset and accuse the Pentecostals of conducting an aggressive disinformation campaign against their religion and spreading intolerance. . . . The Pentecostals even advertise for converts on TV. Hindu leaders accuse Pentecostals of using the American dollar to buy souls. They vow to fight back to retain their members, but they don't seem to stand a chance.[35]

Since Pentecostalists were listed as a combined group with 84,066 members in the government's 1990 Population and Housing Census, it was widely believed that the 2000 census would confirm Pentecostalism as the most rapidly growing religion in Trinidad. In fact, many believed that Pentecostalism would replace Anglicanism as the third-largest faith in Trinidad (behind Roman Catholicism and Hinduism). One of the difficulties in coming to an accurate figure of Pentecostalist adherents, however, is that many of the churches are independent, having been founded by individual apostles who do not claim affiliation with any larger organization. This is reflected in the 2000 census data, which actually shows a decrease in the number of self-identified Pentecostalists (from 84,066 to 76,327). Between 1990 and 2000 the number of individuals who self-identified with the religious category of "other," however, increased dramatically (from 98,936 to 120,666). It is, in any event, very difficult to ascertain the degree of growth in Pentecostal congregations, but the likelihood that the 2000 census category accurately reflects membership trends among these congregations is not high.[36] Natasha Coker, religion reporter for the *Trinidad Express,* sums up the statistical challenges as follows: "The exact number of these churches is difficult to ascertain. This is because the highest growth rate is occurring among the 'independent Pentecostal churches' as opposed to more established entities like the Pentecostal Assemblies of the West Indies (PAWI) and the Open Bible Standard Churches. Only a fraction of these independent churches are registered with the Association of Independent Ministers (AIM)—a group of independent Full Gospel ministers."[37]

Pentecostalists generally emphasize the work of the Holy Spirit in the believer and within the church to a greater extent than do other Protestant denominations. The gifts of the Holy Spirit—manifested through speaking in tongues, healing, and visions—are all considered signs of an empowered Christian life. Another hallmark of Pentecostalism is expressed well in a saying that Harvey Cox relays as follows: "The man with an experience is never at the mercy of the man with a doctrine."[38] Pentecostalism thus values the experience of God above doctrines or creeds, and Cox gets at this by suggesting that Pentecostalism is perhaps best understood not as "a church or even a single religion at all, but a "mood."[39] These attitudes toward the primacy of experience and the work of the Holy Spirit notwithstanding, Pentecostalists find themselves aligned with evangelical Protestants in many respects and consider themselves part of a larger community of believers—the global church.

NEGOTIATIONS

Of Protestant Communities

Steven Bruce points out that one of the consequences of the Reformation "was not a Christian church strengthened because it had been purified but a large number of competing perspectives and institutions."[40] As such, boundaries are fluid, more tenuously defined, and often blurred within the Protestant community. It should be clear from the preceding pages that Trinidad's complex religious geography finds Full Gospel believers quite keen to maintain clear distinctions between themselves and other religious groups. One means by which boundaries are maintained (policed) in Trinidad is by recourse to the local Full Gospel association. The logic governing the Full Gospel associations works politically to ensure that religious orthodoxy of a certain, member-defined shape is maintained. Pentecostalists, whether affiliated or independent, and Baptists, for example, do not generally consider Presbyterians and Anglicans to be faithful in teaching the full gospel. In fact, they are in many ways equated with the Catholic Church, whose excesses and failures are widely believed to have contributed to what my friend Pastor Roddie Taylor refers to as "a carnival and fete-crazy culture."[41]

By the same token, Spiritual Baptists, Jehovah's Witnesses, and Ethiopian Orthodox Christians are considered too far removed from the teachings of the full gospel to warrant membership in the association. Caught between laxity on the one hand and syncretism or heterodoxy on the other, the Full Gospel association works to reify and buttress the doctrinal positions of its members. The Full Gospel association also fulfills another function: it opens lines of communication between the pastors of its member churches, ensuring that pastors refrain from competing for believers who are already worshiping at other member churches, a practice that is derisively referred to as "sheep stealing." In other words, the association ensures that competition for human capital does not occur at the expense of any member churches. The rapid growth of the Pentecostal churches is, thereby, politically deflected away from the relatively few non-Pentecostalist churches that gain membership in the association.

Churches that gain membership in the Full Gospel associations throughout Trinidad, then, constitute a community that actively excludes Catholic, Anglican, and Presbyterian churches on the one hand and groups like the Spiritual Baptists on the other. While significant differences in practice and even doctrine exist among Trinidadian Full Gospel churches, these are not considered substantive enough to preclude fellowship. This is the case primarily because they do agree on several key doctrinal points considered essential for fellowship, including salvation by faith alone, the dual nature of Christ (fully divine and fully human), and the three-in-one nature of the Trinity. Full Gospel associations, furthermore, regularly plan joint events and work to model unity in spite of the inherent competition engendered by Protestantism.

Of Music and Worship

The service proper begins with more singing, this time led from the pulpit, as the few latecomers find their seats. This portion of the service can be led by an individual or, alternatively, by a worship team consisting of several members. These leaders fulfill a particularly important role in facilitating the singing of the congregation, for it is the worship leaders that create the proper atmosphere for the rest of the service, setting the tone and mood for the congregation. Between lines of song, they will exhort the congregation to sing "loudly," "with energy," "to the Lord," "with thanksgiving," and so forth. The congregation is expected to respond to this encouragement, and this dynamic relationship creates a sense of community, commonality, and unity. The singing can last anywhere from ten to twenty or thirty minutes and usually consists of up-tempo, energetic songs.

Several genres of gospel music are actively performed in contemporary Trinidad, and I should like, briefly, to outline their sounds and styles. I begin by drawing attention to those styles that find congregational and solo expression during regular worship services and then move beyond church services to discuss styles that are performed on the concert circuit but rarely find expression in Sunday worship services. In so doing, I hope to illustrate the geography upon which much of the discourse surrounding gospel musics plays out.

The musical staples of Full Gospel worship services in Trinidad consist of hymns and choruses. Depending on the denomination, these can include Wesleyan and Dr. Watts hymns sung in long-meter (lined out) style, revival hymns from the turn of the nineteenth century, hymns found in standard hymnals such as "Holy, Holy, Holy," or a combination of all three.[42] The choruses are often drawn from a body of Trinidadian songs known as Baptist choruses, but many choruses, like "As the Deer" or "Lord I Lift Your Name on High," are being incorporated from North American praise and worship traditions.[43] These choruses, many of which are published by North American companies like Maranatha! and Vineyard, have grown out of the pioneering work in the 1970s of musicians such as Bill and Gloria Gaither and Andre Crouch, who wrote choruses such as "Let's Just Praise the Lord" and "Jesus Is the Answer," respectively. African American spirituals are also sung on occasion, and their introduction to Trinidadian worship life has been traced to the Company Villages.[44]

In general, Pentecostal congregations tend to sing a combination of North American choruses and revival hymns, choosing not to sing long-meter hymns and only a select few, if any, Baptist choruses.[45] Baptists, however, tend to sing a bit of each of the styles during the course of any given service, although long meter is rapidly falling out of use. North American choruses are the most popular replacement for the long-meter hymns in Baptist services, a fact that is often a source of conflict between the older and younger generations within a given congregation.

This rich conflux of musics inevitably creates struggles for musical space within the churches, and the decisions that dictate which songs will be sung (and from which repertory) actively construct and reflect meaning and identity. In a very literal sense Full Gospel congregations throughout Trinidad *are* what they sing. The songs a congregation sings at the beginning of the worship service remind the worshipers of who they are, and the songs that they do not sing raise important questions about who they might be. These questions are partially addressed in almost every service. It is significant, moreover, that the range of hymns available to believers has been incorporated into Full Gospel identity by way of other places—and in the case of most Pentecostal congregations, virtually all of the music they sing is originally nonlocal in one way or another. And yet the repertory of songs claimed by the Trinidadian Baptists (the Baptist choruses) yields insights into the types of structures and meanings that are held most dear. I will return to both of these issues in chapter 3 but turn now to a brief introduction of North American gospel, gospelypso, gospel dancehall, and jamoo, styles which are generally performed at gospel concerts as opposed to church services. That said, however, North American gospel music serves as a bridge between worship services and concert halls because, unlike the other musical styles available to Full Gospel believers, it often (and more easily) finds a home in both the concert and the worship service.

> Once the initial time of singing runs its course, the pastor or one of the deacons may offer a few announcements, a word of greeting, or both. Testimonies are also often encouraged at this time. These activities are often followed by what is commonly referred to as "special music." Special music consists of a solo or group performance during which the congregation does not generally participate. It is, in effect, a moment during the service when the congregants move from an active, participatory role to a relatively inactive and passive position. Often the congregation will be exhorted to pay special attention to the lyrics or message embodied in the song in an effort to stave off a lull in concentration or interest. Of particular interest here is that the selection of the musical number is often an individual's choice. As such, this moment during the service provides a very interesting window onto the relationship between individual and community identity.

No more open-ended or potentially transformative moment exists in the musical life of a Trinidadian congregation than that of special music. An individual is, within limits, encouraged to choose a musical number that powerfully speaks to her and subsequently to share it with the congregation. In this moment, the members of the congregation are confronted with change—change that is often occurring even as their sister or brother performs. The styles that I discuss in the coming pages are not congregational per se. They are, rather, predicated on the presence of a solo lead singer and, with the exception of some of the refrains, not easily adaptable to congregational singing. On those occasions when they are included, they enter worship services as special music. And yet the styles I discuss in the following pages are, with few exceptions, considered incompatible or inappropriate for use during worship services—they exceed the "within limits" caveat and are, as such, relegated to the concert circuit and generally excluded from services.

This split along the limit line is, not surprisingly, often the root cause of heated debate and conflict within individual congregations and among Full Gospel believers in general, for legitimacy, validity, and significance are largely confirmed through the inclusion of a given style in church services—through their fitness for use during corporate worship. The chapters that follow are intimately bound up in interrogating the limits imposed on musical style, in considering the implications associated with the contexts within which a given style is performed, and in analyzing the discourses that develop around these limits and implications. The question of limits (and of performance context) is instructive not least because one style in particular—North American gospel music—has enjoyed far greater acceptance within worship services than have the others.

NORTH AMERICAN GOSPEL MUSIC

African American gospel artists such as Andre Crouch, Helen Baylor, Yolanda Adams, Kirk Franklin, Donnie McClurkin, Fred Hammond, Hezekiah Walker, Trinity 5:7, and Mary Mary have, since the 1960s, exerted a great deal of influence on Full Gospel believers in Trinidad. These artists perform across a wide variety of styles, including straight gospel blues in the style popularized by Thomas A. Dorsey, hip-hop, rhythm and blues, and urban dance. Today, it is not uncommon to hear a song from any of these artists performed during the special music portion of a worship service (although the songs chosen are almost invariably the slower ballads). Often performed to recorded accompaniment tracks (tapes and compact discs for any number of songs are sold by the artists' record companies), these songs are generally accepted and welcomed as an edifying and spiritually significant element in the service. The same songs also have a life outside of worship services, as they are frequently performed at concerts throughout the country. This dual functionality is unique among the other popular gospel musics circulating in Trinidad and raises questions related to cultural intimacy and the negotiation of proximity, issues to which I will return in chapters 3 and 4.[46] Trinidadian artists, furthermore, emulate the style of these North American musicians, writing their own songs and producing their own recordings.

GOSPELYPSO

At about the same time that North American gospel music was making inroads into Trinidadian worship services, the country was also coming to grips with newfound independence (1962) and with the responsibility of constructing a post-independence identity. One of the consequences of this atmosphere was the black power movement, which, on the heels of the civil rights movement in the United States, sent shock waves through the Trinidadian government and fostered a great deal of debate in the years around 1970.

Young believers thought that a Christian message should be brought to the nation during this formative period and sought ways to accomplish this. What they eventually seized upon was a style that they called gospelypso. The idea was that a specifically local and uniquely Trinidadian style was needed at this historical juncture. This concern was articulated in direct opposition to the growing market for nonlocal gospel music and then put into practice. The melodic and harmonic conventions of calypso, thus, became the vehicle for a Trinidadian expression of the gospel and for Trinidadian Full Gospel believers' participation in the nation.

Calypso's connection with carnival and bacchanal, however, was too strong to be overcome, and gospelypso continues to struggle for acceptance within Full Gospel circles. The nationalist drive to highlight local musical practice in the process of bringing a Christian message to the nation made gospelypso a perfect label for these younger artists' creative work. And yet the label's explicit etymological reference to calypso simply added to the controversy over using calypso as a means of conveying an evangelical message. Gospelypsonians have worked for thirty years to break this association, and they continue to pursue their goal of bringing local music to prominence within the church and the nation. Even so, and in spite of the inroads that have been made since the 1990s, it is rare indeed to hear a gospelypso sung during a worship service. The first commercially successful gospelypso was released in 1993 when Nicole Ballosingh recorded "Jump for Jesus." Since then, only Sean Daniel—who recorded "Pan in Heaven" in 1997 and "Waving Ting" in 2002 and who won the Young King Calypso Monarch Competition in 2006 with the song "True Government"—has even come close to a radio hit. With the exception of these four songs, the nation has taken little if any interest in the efforts of gospelypsonians. Gospelypso has found itself relegated to a neutralized middle ground, affecting neither the church nor the nation at large in the way intended by its pioneers.

GOSPEL DANCEHALL AND HARDCORE SOCA

A rather different scenario plays out among artists who perform gospel dancehall and hardcore soca. These artists are also primarily of Pentecostalist confessional backgrounds, and most consider their immediate task one of "kingdom reformation."[47] The musical styles they utilize find their basis in the techniques and sonic textures of Jamaican dancehall and North American hip-hop as well as hardcore soca and rapso. The lyrics are, in much the same way as gospelypso, directed toward evangelistic and edifying purposes.

It should come as no surprise that these artists, like gospelypsonians, find themselves enveloped in a critical discourse both from inside and outside the Full Gospel community. Theirs is a different approach to this community, however, because they do not desire to participate in worship services or work toward legitimizing their style in the same way (or to the degree) that gospelypsonians do. Rather, they create for themselves alternative sacred spaces, including the gospel concerts themselves, within which they worship in the manner that they believe is fitting for contemporary Trinidadian believers. In short, they take advantage of the spaces that exist within what Norman Stolzoff has called "dancehall culture" in order to overcome what they consider a lack of true worship within the church itself.[48]

Many of these artists believe that they are anointed by God to bring about a paradigm shift in worship and that the youth of the church is called eventually to supplant current practices by their example. Sincerely believing that they have insight beyond the wisdom of the current leadership—sight that transcends the myopic vision of the church—they believe that the contemporary Full Gospel community suffers from a spiritual malady. Convinced that they themselves have found a way of addressing this malady, their lyrics are often directed against the church itself and are of a more cataclysmic and oppositional nature than the lyrics of gospelypsonians.

JAMOO

A final style is known as jamoo, or Jehovah's music. This idiosyncratic style is local in that Ras Shorty I (formerly Lord Shorty), one of the creators of soca, coined the term and performed the style until his death in July of 2000. The style is a mixture of soca, calypso, jazz, and African popular musics. In addition, Ras Shorty I consciously continued the project he began in the early 1970s with his pioneering soca compositions, for he often incorporated East Indian materials into the already eclectic sonic texture of jamoo.

His family band, called the Love Circle, continues to write and perform jamoo today, and several aspects of the style warrant brief mention here. First, while Ras Shorty I did convert to Protestantism, he never affiliated himself with a specific denomination, choosing instead to remain the spiritual head of his household and to study the Bible independently. This deci-

sion fostered suspicion regarding the sincerity of his conversion—a suspicion that extended to jamoo as well. Second, he continued to foster ambiguity with regard to his spirituality by referring to himself as Ras Shorty I, by
characterizing his music as conscious, and by wearing togas, sandals, and
dreadlocks. Rather than clearing the matter up by making a definitive statement or by formally joining a congregation, Ras Shorty I chose to remain
firmly entrenched at the peripheries of both nation and church and somewhat of a mystery to both. This afforded him a unique opportunity to influence both in ways that would not otherwise have been possible. Third, until
very recently, no one else even attempted to perform in this style. Jamoo,
then, is a gospel music that seeks neither legitimation by the church nor
praise from the nation. It is, in this sense, a voice quite other among the
musics circulating in Full Gospel Trinidad, and yet it is arguably the most
local of them all.

BENEDICTIONS

The sermon, which frequently follows special music, is often considered
the central element in the worship service. It is the time when the pastor
offers insight into the "Word of God." Based on his understanding of
the congregation's needs, the pastor variously challenges, chides, and
encourages the people, teaching them through explicating the scriptures.
A typical sermon might last anywhere from thirty-five to ninety minutes, and the congregants generally follow along in their own Bibles.
The links between music and word are very close indeed, and the style
of delivery, somewhere between song and speech, links the sermon to
the surrounding songs and prayers. This portion of the worship service
is by no means a static one for the congregation, whose almost constant
vocal affirmations and exclamations of agreement constitute yet another
example of the communal aspect of the service. After a concluding few
minutes of congregational singing, this time led either by the pastor or
the worship leader(s), the pastor often challenges the congregants to remember their mission in the world. He may remind them that believers
have the responsibility of sharing the "good news" with those who have
not heard it and of living lives that reflect the impact of the gospel in
their own lives. All that remains before ritual time dissolves back into
nonritual time are a few announcements and a benediction. The benediction is the last pastoral action of the service, and it constitutes a bless-
ing for the coming week. After the benediction, the congregants are dis-
missed, and many spend another few minutes variously talking with
one another, hailing maxis [minibus taxis], or trying to get council from
the pastor. The time immediately following a service is interesting in
that it does not quite constitute nonritual time and is clearly no longer

a part of ritual time. Many congregants deliberately take their time in making the transition back into nonritual time, drawing out the benefits of ritual time by remaining physically within or around the building itself and spending time together as a community. Nonritual time will take over soon enough.

This chapter has considered the complex religious histories and sociocultural contexts that form the backdrop against which Full Gospel believers in Trinidad worship, work out their identities, and live out their faith. Their careful policing of Full Gospel boundaries should not, then, come as a surprise, but it does make the roles that music plays within that community very interesting indeed. Music represents both a balm and a threat to Full Gospel identity, and the following chapters explore these two sides of the community's musical life by focusing on performance and reception.

In order to situate these explorations of performance and reception, this chapter has also offered a general idea of the structure that prevails in a relatively typical service in Full Gospel Trinidad—within the normative performative context for worship. That said, individual congregations and denominational groups, of course, incorporate idiosyncratic materials and ideas into their worship services. It should also be clear that some congregations remain much more open to musical experimentation than do others. Jerma A. Jackson's meditation on the strands of "exuberance" and "restraint" within African American churches can also be kept in mind in this Trinidadian context.[49] This normative context for worship (the worship service), moreover, plays a major role in shaping the discourse surrounding the value of musical styles, such as gospel dancehall, gospelypso, and jamoo. The worship service, then, serves as a standard that has implications for the "other" contexts within which gospel music is performed. Style and context are, as such, linked not only through actual performance but also in and through Full Gospel discourse. The narrative I have incorporated throughout this chapter should, then, serve the heuristic purpose of pointing out some of the elements broadly shared among Full Gospel congregations throughout Trinidad. But the narrative is also contextually important because of the primary and legitimizing role that worship services play in the discourse about musical style within this community.

Along the way I have also offered a brief introduction to the four principal musical styles with which the remainder of this book is concerned— North American gospel music, gospelypso, gospel dancehall, and jamoo. Each of these styles occupies a very different place in the life of the Full Gospel community, and their positions vis-à-vis the community afford me the opportunity to raise questions of identity and to answer them in part through recourse to narratives of the past and dreams for the future. Before turning to an exploration of each of these styles, I will, in the following chapter, outline the ethics of style, the analytical model through which I interrogate the spaces and contexts of music, memory, and identity that confront the Full Gospel community in Trinidad.

2   The Ethics of Style

Throughout the course of this chapter, I outline the theoretical basis for and the practical applicability of an analytical paradigm that I call the ethics of style. This idea stems from my deep conviction that understanding and foregrounding the ethical dimensions of musical performance and reception will lay the groundwork for a reconsideration of the extent to which style participates in discourses of identity in Full Gospel Trinidad. This is because the ethics of style focuses analytical attention on the process by which style becomes the vehicle for a multifaceted, communal discourse about value and meaning. Tracing the shape of this discourse—paying it adequate attention—is, as I see it, crucial to generating sufficiently nuanced understandings of musical style in Full Gospel Trinidad.

I am increasingly convinced that belief, values, faith—that is, conviction—have been held for too long, to borrow from Sartre, in bad faith.[1] Belief—whether placed in institutions, theories, cosmologies, or markets—permeates our lives, and yet we often wear our beliefs quite uncomfortably. After all, when it gets right down to it, they configure themselves in terms of right and wrong, good and evil—in terms of ethics. Scholars have long struggled to and, at times, brilliantly succeeded in finding vocabularies that describe human interaction (community) in terms other than those of the ethical life.[2] One need only think about excellent ideas with names like oppositionality, hybridity, creolization, and mimicry to realize that these models unquestionably offer important means of engaging the particularities of the region's musical life. And yet it is my contention that these words also serve to mask (or at least fail adequately to engage) ethical considerations that, if foregrounded and taken seriously, could offer additional analytical possibilities.

This state of affairs, then, suggests that the unarticulated spaces of belief

27

and conviction—spaces which are kept at bay in bad faith and through good theory—might yield fruitful insights into the discourses surrounding the creation and reception of music (style) in Full Gospel Trinidad. So, for example, music production and consumption are linked to each other but often rendered problematic in Full Gospel Trinidad not primarily for aesthetic or political reasons, but as a result of the (mostly divergent) ethical subcurrents that inform the judgments of both artists and audiences—subcurrents that might best be described by what I call the poetics of conviction. The aesthetic and political register, while far more comfortable to live in (and write about), is nonetheless informed by the ethical lives of individual artists and fans. A short illustration at this juncture will help set the framework for the arguments that follow.

WHO I AM: "SUPPLEMENTING" THE YOUTH WITH SHERWIN GARDNER

Sherwin Gardner, one of Trinidad's most accomplished gospel artists and producers, often writes and performs gospel dancehall tunes. As I will illustrate in greater detail in chapter 5, this artistic choice is motivated out of a strong desire to bring the gospel to the youth of the nation (and by extension to the region). As Sherwin puts it, "God provides an anointed music for each age. Dancehall is the music of this age."[3] Nathaniel Howard, bassist for the Trinidadian band Melchizedek Order, elaborates on this idea, saying, "We want to reach the greatest number of people for Christ. Most people are listening to dancehall . . . so we play dancehall."[4] These artists are, of course, quite comfortable with the musical gestures and sounds of dancehall—they are aesthetically drawn to the style. And yet they choose dancehall over other stylistic alternatives as much for ethical as for aesthetic reasons.

In fact, one of the claims I make in developing the ethics of style is that ethics is prior to aesthetics in the case of Full Gospel Trinidad. Put otherwise, ethical considerations must be satisfied before aesthetic concerns are entertained. So, these artists' concern for their fellow Trinidadians drives their choice of style even as other factors play a role in determining the creative expression of that style. The generally skeptical and often aggressively negative attitude toward gospel dancehall expressed by many church leaders and pastors notwithstanding, these artists are convinced of the necessity of their choice. Instead of reading their musical choice only in terms of, say, subcultural style or as an oppositional response to institutional constraints on their freedom of expression within the Full Gospel community—both of which are legitimate and important ways of generating insight into the conflicts being played out in Full Gospel Trinidad—I augment these types of analyses with an exploration of the ethical concerns, the convictions, of these artists as well as those of their fans and detractors. This approach allows me to interrogate the discourse surrounding gospel dancehall not only in terms of the degree to which it illustrates the conflict between competing sections of the community but also in terms of the extent to which it facilitates (or threatens) an ethical project. The ethics of style, then, affords me the opportunity to explore the political and social issues at stake while simultaneously taking seriously the underlying ethical considerations—the poetics of conviction—that drive both choices and discourses about musical style.

The tendency of artists like Sherwin Gardner and Melchizedek Order to use instances of Jamaican patwah in their songs illustrates these claims quite well. Church leaders and pastors opposed to gospel dancehall use the idea of mimicry in order to invalidate this practice discursively. Rev. Vernon Duncan, for example, claims, "Every nation has its own language. If you don't use your own language, you are being deceptive, and that's the opposite of truthful."[5] The implication here is that the entire enterprise of musical appropriation is marked by a less-than-honest representation of self and is, as such, incompatible with evangelization.[6] The argument is framed in terms of how it is good to be, for example, truthful—it is freighted with an ethical content. But this charge is turned on its head by gospel dancehall artists, who turn to biblical principles in order to justify their musical and lyrical choices. Quoting Paul's words to the Corinthians, for example, artists will say, "I have become all things to all men, so that by all means possible I might save some."[7] If Paul could become all things to all men, then gospel dancehall artists are merely following his example. The countercharge is thus based on the ethical imperative of evangelization, an imperative that these artists are attempting to follow in part through their careful choice of musical style.

The words of Sherwin Gardner's "Do You Know," from his album *Who I Am*, illustrate both his conviction and his determination to continue along the path he has chosen. In this sense the lyrics are directed toward two audiences—those whom he is trying to reach with the gospel and the Full Gospel community. The music he uses as a vehicle for these lyrics, moreover, is firmly rooted in dancehall sounds and techniques. I have transcribed, in very schematic form, the first verse of this song (see example 1).

Example 1. First verse of Sherwin Gardner's "Do You Know."

As I see it, these lyrics require more than a political, social, or aesthetic reading—they are founded on conviction and require an analytical model that takes this foundation seriously.[8] The ethics of style is intended to accomplish this and, in the process, to explore and nuance the political, social, and aesthetic implications of gospel dancehall. According to Sherwin,

(continued)

his message will continue to go out despite resistance, even from people who "know theology," and Sherwin will let the "day of judgment" determine whether he gave the youth the "right supplement." These lyrics do, of course, offer plenty of room for analyses that highlight questions of power, aesthetics, and resistance. And while it is important to recognize that

Example 1 *(continued)*

Sherwin is signaling his resistance to the conservative leadership within the Full Gospel community, these lyrics simultaneously illustrate his deep commitment to the goal which that same leadership would claim motivates its own efforts—evangelization. The nuances that develop out of this type of friction in spaces that represent, in an important sense, shared ground are fruitfully explored through recourse to the ethics of style. This excursus is merely a brief example of the types of concerns that I am trying to address in formulating the ethics of style, but it suggests the potential rewards of mobilizing an analytical model that takes the ethical—the poetics of conviction—into account.

That said, I am very aware that ethical issues have not escaped notice in Caribbean scholarship. What I aim to achieve in formulating the ethics of style, then, is to reframe these issues in order to privilege the ethical over and against other modes of inquiry in an effective way. Put somewhat polemically, the ethics of style is a means of reinstating belief and conviction as significant and indispensable sites for the analysis of meaning, production, and reception in music. I am, as such, simply calling attention to a well-recognized but often undertheorized aspect of musical life in the Caribbean and applying it to a specific musical context—that of Full Gospel Trinidad. To that end, the following sections uncouple the two main concepts bound up in the ethics of style in order to explore at a closer range what I mean by each term. The concluding section of this chapter then reconstitutes the ethics of style in anticipation of the case studies that follow.

ETHICS

Ethics! At best a complicating mess of intentions and at worst the source of disabling and narrow moral positioning. There are, undoubtedly, more interesting things to think about and, certainly, more concrete issues toward which we might devote our attention. For better or worse, however, ethics permeates the creation and reception of musical style, and this is simply because human beings are engaged in these processes. This fact alone places ethics squarely within the realm of scholarly interest, and yet there is very little evidence of a sustained effort to explore the ethical dimensions of musical life. In my view, failing to interrogate the role of ethics in the creation and reception of musical style represents an attempt (however inadvertent or unconscious) to change the subject—to talk about something else.[9] I take encouragement along this line of thought from several other scholars' determination to defend the primacy of lived experience and moral intuition (ethics) within their respective disciplines.[10]

Charles Taylor's thought in particular offers the promise of a theoretical framework built on an alternative vocabulary.[11] At stake for Taylor is the importance of achieving a certain groundedness that arises from engagement with the meanings things have for us and from an emphasis on the existential aspects of life. What emerges from his writing is a strong commitment to meeting individuals and, by extension, communities at the point of their own discourse regarding their own values and ideas about meaning. In so doing, he also concerns himself in particular with the ethical dimensions of this endeavor. It is his version of "thick" description. Taylor's work is, in this sense, very closely aligned to the aims of ethnography but has the benefit of explicitly foregrounding ethics along the way. The ethics of style, then, represents my attempt to incorporate Taylor's thick ethical language into the process of interrogating musical style.

Another voice has recently provided good reason to persist in sticking to the subject, as it were—that of Geoffrey Galt Harpham, who argues that, try as we might, we cannot get away from our humanity, even in that most prized (sacred?) realm of language. In his book *Language Alone: The Critical Fetish of Modernity*, he spends a great deal of time illustrating that the language fetish of modernity can be understood as a way of avoiding something potentially painful: the necessary interrogation of our humanity (or the lack of it) and, by extension, our value(s). For Harpham, the subject—humanity—is always already embedded in the language we use in attempting to leave it behind.[12]

Taylor and Harpham thus both worry (in very different ways) that the philosophical and critical machinery that we are working with today is too "thin," and this primarily because of its bad faith relationship to other philosophical and critical possibilities. And this is the point at which Africana thought offers an important contribution, albeit one that continues to be relatively overlooked (silenced). Paget Henry and Lewis R. Gordon have both illustrated that the attempts toward achieving a project called Africana thought, black philosophy, or Afro-Caribbean philosophy continue to struggle against the terms of engagement instantiated and policed by colonial and neocolonial power. That the objects of study and the aims of Africana thought are directed toward ideas and issues that have not, in general, concerned continental philosophy makes the task that much more difficult. And yet it is clear that a tradition of thought has been fostered and maintained in spite of these challenges, one that powerfully suggests at least two good reasons for working toward recentering ethics within ethnography.

First, the underlying premises upon which Africana thought is built are founded on a concern for the ethical and existential aspects of life as it is worked out in community.[13] Community is, thus, central to questions of identity within Africana thought. There is, in other words, a sense of obligation to community within Africana thought that overrides (or extends beyond) the merely functional role that community obviously plays in the process of identity formation. Second, Africana thought acknowledges the need for—the primacy of—mythic thought, for there remains within Africana philosophy an openness to the primacy of the metaphysical, to the possibility of spirit.[14] And this is the ground upon which an ongoing engagement between continental and Africana thought might play out. This line of thought finds Paget Henry suggesting, "African existentialism reveals these modes of openness to spirit that have become hidden undersides of the modern ego."[15] In fact, African existentialism places the spirit in a central position that, if ignored or left misrecognized, leads to dehumanizing effects upon the individual. To be fully human, then, to negotiate adequately questions of identity, rationality, and community, an individual must recognize and allow for the role of the spirit or divine in her life. According to Henry, "This hierophanic approach amounted to a spiritual sociology or physiology that subjected the economic, political, cultural, and biological dimensions of everyday life to the spiritual domain."[16]

Turning once again to Taylor, we might say that any account that dismisses the metaphysical (with all of its attendant complications and problems, including our scholarly [dis]beliefs) represents a thin reading of ethics, and that Africana philosophy presents an opportunity for enriching—for thickening—these concepts. This openness to spirit, moreover, coincides quite well with Stuart Hall's sense that we cannot hope to understand the circum-Caribbean without a very real engagement with its spiritual dimensions. The process of identity formation in the Caribbean is, then, linked very closely to an ethics informed on the one hand by an openness to spirit and, on the other hand, by a communal approach to determining what identity might mean in the first place. Put otherwise, approaches to identity in the Caribbean participate in the overarching themes of African philosophy and Africana thought. And if this is indeed the case, then an important conclusion follows, for it becomes clear that ethics can be posited as an important—even an indispensable—site of analysis in Full Gospel Trinidad.[17]

In this connection, Stuart Hall and Paul duGay have argued very persuasively for a model of identity that recognizes the ways in which subjects are hailed by various subject positions but also acknowledges the necessary investment that subjects make to chain themselves into these subject positions (to identify with this or that subject position)—a process that they call articulation.[18] How to think about this relationship between subject and discursive formations? How to come to terms with these articulations where musical style is concerned? I suggest that the ethics of style can be an important tool in this endeavor. Before turning my attention to style, however, I should briefly clarify what I am *not* trying to do. I am not proposing utilizing ethics in order to ferret out some essentialist version of truth, value, or good. I am not trying to offer an individualized "politics of truth" of the order suggested by Alain Badiou.[19] I am not suggesting that the ethical dimension of art is somehow the driver of style or that the ethics I envision is in any way tied to universal or foundational narratives of value. I am not attempting to offer a backdoor to understanding intent. I am most certainly not suggesting a systematic ethics or attempting a properly philosophical treatment of the concept. My aims are much more modest.

What I *am* suggesting is that artists, audiences, and members of the Full Gospel community throughout Trinidad are highly attuned to discourse that centers around ethics—that ethics is indeed the focal point around which they construct their own discourses about the value and meanings that musics have for them. I am also suggesting that the musical creations and performances of these artists are considered meaningful in the richest sense of that word. Put another way, it is clear that musical style is put to use in order to achieve certain goals and that these goals are informed by overarching ethical concerns—by individuals' poetics of conviction. In the process of performance, then, the music becomes charged with the depth of life, touching upon issues related to politics, gender, ethnicity, and a host of other community-specific as well as extracommunal concerns.

STYLE

> Style is another word for the perception of relationships.
> John Miller Chernoff

The significance of musical style within my analytical approach relates to the powerful evocation of ethical positions (always already discursive) made possible through musical performance.[20] As such, style itself functions as discourse—hails subjects as a discursive formation—performatively instantiating both the positive and negative appraisals of its usefulness and meanings for both artist and audience (community). It might be useful to remember that the ways in which music functions as discourse have already been considered at length.[21] But the specifically musical instantiations of discourse traced by scholars like Nattiez are not the subject of my inquiry here. Rather, my interest in music and discourse takes the form of thinking more generally about how musical style calls subjects into a relationship with itself and, by extension, with other subjects. I am interested in the symbolic forms that music takes, then, only to the extent that I find it useful to think about the ways that music is able to "give rise to a complex and infinite web of interpretants."[22]

When this capacity for generating interpretants is contextualized within a community that has already delimited the boundaries of acceptable meanings, a community that has already come to a shared sense of what it values, then style can come to be controversial—subversive even—causing subjects to reevaluate their relationships in light of new discursive formations. It is in this sense that I am appealing to the ethical—it is not the musical event, but rather the act of interpretation and judgment that instantiates an ethical point of view, and as I understand it, style cannot be judged in this way in isolation from community. I am reminded here of a passage that Simon Frith penned while considering the ethical dimensions of music consumption and production, a passage that is part of a larger article discussing the role that music plays in shaping identities:

> Music constructs our sense of identity through the direct experiences it offers of the body, of time and sociability, experiences which enable us to place ourselves in imaginative cultural narratives. Such a fusion of imaginative fantasy and bodily practice marks also the integration of aesthetics and ethics. John Miller Chernoff has thus eloquently demonstrated how among African musicians an aesthetic judgment (this sounds

good) is necessarily also an ethical judgment (this is good). The issue is "balance": "the quality of rhythmic relationships" describes a quality of social life. "In this sense, style is another word for the perception of relationships."[23]

So Frith, following Chernoff, is very concerned with the merging of aesthetic judgment and ethical judgment. He is also keen to point out the role that relationships play in the process of coming to a judgment in the first place. A bit more from Frith on this point will help to situate my own argument:

> Identity is thus necessarily a matter of ritual, it describes one's place in a dramatized pattern of relationships—one can never really express oneself "autonomously." Self-identity *is* cultural identity; claims to individual difference depend on audience appreciation, on shared performing and narrative rules. . . . But what makes music special—what makes it special for identity—is that it defines a space without boundaries (a game without frontiers). Music is thus the cultural form best able both to cross borders—sounds carry across fences and walls and oceans, across classes, races and nations—and to define places; in clubs, scenes, and raves, listening on headphones, radio and in the concert hall, we are only where the music takes us.[24]

Musical style is, thus, a major and hopelessly complex site for identifications, and Frith makes it clear that individual identity is intertwined with, even subsumed into, communal identity. But this is the juncture at which I make a break from Frith's reading, for I suggest that a better perspective from which to analyze music in Full Gospel Trinidad is achieved when the relationship between aesthetics and ethics as presented by Frith is *inverted*. I suggest that, at least in the case of music in Full Gospel Trinidad, ethics is the antecedent of aesthetics. In other words, it would be nice if this or that sounds good, but if it *is* good then that characteristic will override aesthetic concerns. This does not mean, of course, that aesthetics is not enlisted as a form of argumentation or that aesthetics is unimportant in this context. I merely point out that ethical considerations take precedence over other modes of judgment.[25]

An insistence upon the primacy of ethics is important here because, as I understand it, style in this Full Gospel context presents its listeners (and creators) with an impossible choice. On the one hand, choose to identify with this musical offering and you will be changed forever. You yourself will be different in relation to the community of which you are a part. In fact, your identification with this style constitutes, at one level, your disidentification with a portion of the community and its values. On the other hand, reject it and you will pay a different price, asserting in so doing your disidentification with its creator(s). In the context of a community theologically committed to the pursuit of *unity*, this presents a very real problem. The process of articulation is, in this context, revealed as a profoundly ethical endeavor.

One of the reasons that style finds itself bound up in the ethical undoubtedly concerns the ease with which style crosses borders, for musical style carries with it into new context associations and discursive formations from other places. The Full Gospel community in Trinidad, however, is in the business of boundary policing, of excluding that which it is *not* and reinforcing its identity on those grounds. Full Gospel believers, then, must necessarily decide for themselves whether the tacit identifications that style instantiates are useful for the maintenance of their identity or if they in fact prove harmful, subversive, or otherwise useless to them. And this is the ground upon which musical reception plays out. These are most certainly struggles over ethical—not aesthetic—positions. Musical style is thus continuously hailing subjects (imagine yourself like *this*) while simultaneously being disciplined by the power of competing discourses (you don't want to be like *that*). There can be no doubt, therefore, that the styles in circulation in the Full Gospel community of Trinidad configure a series of potential identifications that force certain ethical consequences if accepted. Just how this process unfolds is the task to which the remainder of this chapter (and the book itself) is dedicated.

THE ETHICS OF STYLE

In coming to terms with this process, my thinking has been informed and enriched by the work of Jürgen Habermas and Emmanuel Levinas. While neither of these scholars offers a theoretical model to which I am unequivocally drawn or which I can use in an uncomplicated way, they are both, to varying degrees, quite important to my own development of the ethics of style. The following section, then, is a meditation on some of their ideas that brings the ethics of style into sharper focus.

From Communicative Action . . .

I would like to begin by thinking a bit about Jürgen Habermas's discourse ethics.[26] Discourse ethics may, at first, seem like an unlikely choice here, and yet Habermas himself made the following remark in an interview with Eduardo Mendieta:

I would not object to the claim that my conception of language and of communicative action oriented toward mutual understanding nourishes itself from the legacy of Christianity. The "telos of reaching understanding"—the concept of discursively directed agreement which measures itself against the standard of intersubjective recognition, that is, the double negation of criticizable validity claims—may well nourish itself from the heritage of a *logos* understood as Christian, one that is indeed embodied (and not just within the Quakers) in the communicative practice of the religious congregation.[27]

The connection between Habermas and the Full Gospel community, then, grows out of the primacy of intersubjective language and the need for generating consensus, and it is in this limited sense that discourse ethics affords me an important point of departure for opening the discussion onto the ethics of style.[28] I hope to show, however, that musical style operates in such a way as to transcend—in the fullest sense of this word—the bounds of discourse ethics, thereby pushing the possibility of achieving consensus through practical discourse to the breaking point and beyond.

I focus particular attention on two aspects of Habermas's discourse ethics. First, his approach to discourse ethics, articulated as it is within the broader framework of communicative action, provides a useful point of entry into the communal negotiation (through practical discourse) of concerns, values, and politics that prevails in Trinidad's Full Gospel community.[29] For Habermas, discourse ethics plays out in a public sphere of social equality within which each person is free either to assent or object. Before a norm can be accepted as valid, each participant in the community must agree to it (or at least be willing to accept the consequences of agreeing to it). Persuasive or justificatory speech, then, is the means through which communities work toward and, ideally, reach consensus.

Second, in working toward anchoring the importance of rational discourse (justificatory speech) within communicative action, Habermas makes an important distinction between ethical and moral discourse. Ethical discourse is, for Habermas, an intrinsically private activity that, furthermore, remains subject to irrationality. Moral discourse, by contrast, is a public enterprise based on intersubjectivity and, again for Habermas, is endowed with the potential for rationality. Habermas takes great pains to illustrate how rational thought works (you must be able to justify your point by offering reasons for your position that are acceptable to everyone involved) and to justify why it is essential for his principle of universalization. Put otherwise, justificatory speech falls squarely in the realm of moral, not ethical, discourse. And yet Habermas does acknowledge the ambiguity that can be introduced into moral discourse when an individual participant proffers an argument from an ethical position instead of as a moral question. How does a community deal with an instance where a participant offers reasons that are not, in fact, "reasonable" in the process of practical discourse—is it merely a case of poor communication, or does it indicate the emergence of ethical discourse?

In short, Habermas privileges the right, public, and universalizable over the good, private, and nonuniversalizable in his discourse ethics, and when the good encroaches on the right it personalizes the discourse and introduces a degree of ambiguity into the situation. William Rehg has summarized the difficulties that the process of this bleeding between ethical and moral discourse engender as follows: "Nonetheless, the fact that both moral and ethical discourses can involve the same material content certainly gives rise to ambiguities—in the heat of debate it is not so easy to distinguish moral and ethical questions. Thus it often occurs that one of the contested issues in a discourse turns on whether an issue is a moral one, with generally binding implications, or simply the particular perceptions of a single group presuming to speak for all."[30] While Habermas attempts to ground discourse ethics in a carefully argued and universalist approach to justice, his model is itself predicated on an procedural approach to consensus through communicative action whose susceptibility to the individual, personal, ethical thought-life of subjects is illustrated in the very ambiguity that often surrounds attempts at moral discourse. This ambiguity, however, provides a most useful juncture at which to situate some thoughts about the role that style plays in the process of moral discourse in Full Gospel Trinidad. But a few words about how discourse ethics might play out in a Trinidadian context are necessary first to contextualize these ideas adequately.

The Full Gospel community in Trinidad consists of many different congregations that are affiliated with numerous denominations, sometimes holding highly divergent views on certain doctrinal ideas and often competing with each other for resources (whether human or economic). All of this notwithstanding, however, this community continuously stumbles over a paradox that can be made to stand in for equality and freedom—the paradox of achieving unity in the face of denominationalism. Because unity is considered one of the principle manifestations of Christian love, there exists a certain amount of creative tension within each congregation and, by extension, between denominations. It is generally accepted that unity is an ideal toward which all must work, even though it may never be entirely achieved in this world. And yet Full Gospel congregants generally take this task seriously, by and large attempting to follow the instructions of Paul, who, in his epistle to the Ephesians, wrote, "Be completely humble and gentle; be patient, bearing with one another in love. Make every effort to keep the unity of the Spirit through the bond of peace."[31] The shapes that these efforts toward unity assume, however, are unique to each congregation. Some denominations are organized around a congregational structure, meaning that disputes are settled democratically. Each member has a voice in the matter at hand. Alternatively, some denominations and many independent churches are structured so that the pastors and leadership maintain a great deal of power to dictate the resolution of disputes. In these situations, the leadership style of the pastor determines the amount of input that is tolerated or requested from the congregation.

Ultimately, however—and this seems to me to be one of the key characteristics of Protestantism in general—individuals have the freedom to choose whether they will submit themselves to a given pastor's authority and whether they can in good conscience remain a member of a given congregation. I maintain that the combination of striving for unity as a community and the inherent freedom of individuals to leave one congregation and join another combine to engender an atmosphere within which discourse ethics is at least plausible. In other words, members of a given congregation are free to assent or disagree (in one form or another), and it is incumbent upon all to work toward unity. The trick here is that the line between moral and ethical discourse becomes even more ambiguous. I will return to this idea shortly.

An additional complication concerning the application of discourse ethics within a Trinidadian context is that evangelical Christianity itself operates in ever widening concentric circles, moving outward from the individual congregation to the denomination to the association and, finally, to the global church. It is important to consider the ideal of unity and the principle of freedom and the ways in which these impact upon (or are sidestepped by) the Full Gospel community in Trinidad. In the case of many congregations, making a connection to the global church (read North American church) is a tangible way of achieving a sense of unity and belonging without having to engage in the difficult task of local argumentation that lies at the heart of discourse ethics. They are able, then, to claim unity with the global church while simultaneously sidestepping the struggle of arriving at unity with associations or other churches within the Trinidadian Full Gospel community. I will address this issue, this virtual unity, in greater detail in chapter 4.

Similarly, it is often possible for individual congregations, and even for denominations, to remain deliberately isolated from and unmoved by the discourses that circulate throughout the local Full Gospel community. I am convinced, however, that it is not possible to remain outside the sphere of discourses related to the *musical* dimensions of Full Gospel life. The interplay among members from various churches, the vibrant gospel music circuit, and the mass-mediated presence of the musics on radio and television leave little room for inaction or passivity. I say this because the members of congregations throughout Trinidad are themselves heavily invested in and are attempting to ascertain the usefulness of the styles under discussion in this book. Sarah Thornton has penned the following observation on the subject of the media's impact on social groups: "Media are fundamental to processes of popular distinction because media consumption is a primary leisure activity and because they are leading disseminators of culture. Media are so involved in the circuits of contemporary culture that they could be conceived of as being part of the material conditions of social groups, in a way not unlike access to education."[32]

Viewed from this perspective, it becomes clear that congregations, denominations, and even the local Full Gospel associations have no choice but to face these discourses regarding musical style and to participate in them, for choices are available to individual believers, who are constantly being engaged (hailed) by the styles in one mediated form or another and in a variety of contexts. These members, moreover, are free to move from one congregation or denomination to another in pursuit of a satisfactory resolution to the tensions that the styles engender. In other words, the ethics of style is a pressing concern at the most personal and individual levels of Full Gospel life, and this concern permeates each subsequent layer of organization in Trinidad, leading to an atmosphere within which each person, as well as each organization, must answer yes or no to questions of musical style.

The difficulty for church leadership in Trinidad, a leadership that would love to see Habermasian discourse ethics work unequivocally, is that this approach to communication is continuously interrupted, undermined, and undone by musical style. This is the case primarily because of the dynamic I traced a bit earlier. Musical style in this context forces what amounts to an impossible choice within the Full Gospel community, leading to at least two difficult propositions. Either one identifies with the style (with all of the doctrinal and ethical implications that this decision implies) or one disidentifies with the style, marking difference and undermining unity within the Full Gospel community in a different way. This impossible choice is located in the discursive register and leads me to my final point. Style constitutes itself as a form of discourse within this Trinidadian context, embodying both the positive and negative appraisals of its usefulness and meanings for the church and individual believers through its performance in time-space.

The preceding pages have clarified some of the challenges facing discourse ethics in Full Gospel Trinidad but have also illustrated the need for consensus (unity) that makes this model appealing. They have, moreover—and I return here to the question of ambiguity between ethical and moral discourse—highlighted the personal character that pervades participation in this community. Two issues emerge in this Trinidadian context. First, the measure of truth, of norms, is rooted firmly in the metaphysical—in the ethical. Practical discourse is thus dependent upon the *ethical* for justificatory speech, which, as Habermas is right in pointing out, does not always result in reasonable arguments. Second, the basis for individuals' participation in this community is rooted primarily in their personal relationship with the divine and only secondarily in their obligation to the community within which they worship and live. I use "obligation" deliberately here, for I am preparing to introduce Emmanuel Levinas's ideas regarding the face of the other as a model that is perhaps more useful for thinking about the ethics of style.[33]

. . . To the Face of the Other

If Frith is right in following Chernoff toward a conflation of aesthetics with ethics in musical performance, and if I am not misguided in asserting the primacy of ethics in this Trinidadian context, then music as a discursive formation presents discourse ethics with a very sticky problem. As I see it, style addresses itself both to individuals and to the normative moral horizons of communities, collapsing the ethical and moral into each other in the process. In this sense, it is both ethical and moral in orientation, both rational and mythic. It is, in its very creation, open to the spiritual, to the metaphysical. It hails subjects through communities, posits both ethical and moral positions, and requires an individual response within a communal context, an impossible choice. This spells, to my mind, the moment at which a move beyond discourse ethics is necessitated, and in order to do so, I return briefly to Charles Taylor, agreeing with him that a better way to think about the moral domain is to consider ethical and moral discourse to be the same. In his introduction to *Sources of the Self,* Taylor makes the following argument:

> Much contemporary moral philosophy . . . has given such a narrow
> focus to morality that some of the crucial connections I want to draw
> here are incomprehensible in its terms. This moral philosophy has

tended to focus on what it is right to do rather than on what it is good to be, on defining the content of obligation rather than the nature of the good life; and it has no conceptual place left for a notion of the good as the object of our love or allegiance or, as Iris Murdoch portrayed it in her work, as the privileged focus of attention or will.[34]

Neither ambiguity nor conflict can be avoided. Nor can the private and public spheres of life be separated in any uncomplicated way. In fact, the principle of universalization founders when it is confronted by the ethics of the living, breathing subject. Conflicts about musical style, then, are not resolvable through a turn to the forum of discourse ethics. Rather, time (distance), economy, or location—something external to the style—finally provides a vantage point from which communities evaluate it again (anew).[35]

Musical style participates in an imaginative game. The subject is being hailed by the discursive power of the style because a Levinasian "saying/playing" lies behind it. The crux of the matter might be explained by turning to Levinas's articulation of the third party. The third party, according to Levinas, creates an environment within which justice can become a focus, where the subject's obligations—multiple, competing, and overlapping—are necessarily weighed and balanced against each other in coming to a course of action that takes all participants into consideration. I suggest that musical style, in its discursive hailing of the subject, acts not unlike a third party and places those who hear it under obligation to respond. It also forcefully brings to the foreground the other obligations that each subject is juggling as a member of the Full Gospel community in Trinidad and, in so doing, participates in shaping individuals' poetics of conviction. The proximity of the other, through whose face I am called to responsibility, opens a window, by extension, to the entirety of humanity. So, Levinas writes: "Everything that takes place 'between us' concerns everyone, the face that looks at it places itself in the full light of the public order, even if I draw back from it to seek with the interlocutor the complicity of a private relation and a clandestinity . . . the epiphany of the face qua face opens humanity."[36]

It is for this reason that I use Simon Frith's words as an epigraph to this section—style is, indeed, another word for the perception of relationships. But style is also more than merely perception, for the face of the other approaches in this case, commanding a choice regarding style—a choice that, as it turns out, affects the entire community.[37] Style, then, is an important vehicle through which individuals reaffirm or change (articulate) the status of their relationship to community.

The ethics of style is thus intended to focus attention on the process by which style becomes the vehicle for a multifaceted discourse about value and meaning, but also about identity formation. Performing gospelypso is, as I will illustrate in the following chapter, not only a statement of an artist's position within the larger discourse (a "saying"), but also an identification with other discursive formations (calypso, for example) *and* a restatement of the other subject positions that are held vis-à-vis the style. Hearing a gospelypso performance invariably calls to mind the fact that the listener must orient herself in relationship to the discourse surrounding it (the "said") in coming to grips with her response to the person behind the "saying."

From this perspective, it follows that style (and the discourse surrounding it) is a polarizing and insistent reminder of the impossible struggle for unity or, in Habermasian terms, of the struggle to arrive at the norm (consensus). Habermas and Levinas share a commitment to the centrality of language in adopting a moral point of view onto life. Taylor offers a real commitment to the thick description of the moral intuitions that drive this language (to the poetics of conviction). And the ethics of style provides a means for naming and then discussing the process of working these issues out in musical terms. Returning to the definition I gave in the introduction, then, the ethics of style focuses attention on the discursive spaces between individual and community (self and other) in order to come to a more nuanced understanding of music in its sociocultural contexts.

By way of conclusion, I should like to offer a few situating comments and caveats. First, the ethics of style is most fruitfully applied to instances where musical style is contested. This is an important delimiting factor for the ethics of style in that controversy regarding musical style brings to the surface discourse involving a range of possible ethical positions. Second, the ethics of style is most evident in contexts where communities are actively concerned with shaping or maintaining their identity. The greater the need for defining or protecting identity, the more visible the ethics of style will be. Third, I use the word "style" quite deliberately in order to keep the ethics of style as open to other forms of expressive life as possible. In this sense, fashion, art, and speech represent additional layers of and provide further nuance to musical style. I explore this in greater detail in chapter 4.

The ethics of style, then, offers an alternative vocabulary for engaging with gospel music in Trinidad—a vocabulary that highlights the particularities of the everyday musical life-worlds of Trinidadians and concerns itself with the struggles that the various musical styles engender as artists and fans work through the process of, following Stuart Hall, articulating their identifications. During the course of this book, I illustrate that the ethics of style, when coupled with and balanced by a careful application of several archetypes of Caribbeanness, provides a powerful approach to thinking about music in this Trinidadian context that clears space for analysis which takes seriously the importance of the divine in the lives of those searching for communion with one another.

3 Nationalism and the Soul

Gospelypso as Independence

What use will you make of your independence?

Dr. Eric E. Williams

The hard thing about gospelypso is that while things are coming around in some ways, it's still not accepted the way it should be.

Sean Daniel

I'm listening to Sean Daniel talk about his art. He is a young gospelypsonian who has been making a splash on the gospel music scene ever since he debuted with a song entitled "Pan in Heaven" in 1997. Sean has been performing in the carnival season tents for several years now, most recently with the Spectakula Tent, and creating no small amount of reaction among members of the Full Gospel community, who tend to see this decision either as confirmation of the style's complicity with carnival and bacchanal or as a sign that Sean Daniel is staying true to the original aims of the style's pioneers—trying to reach the nation for Christ, that is.[1]

It is the summer of 2003, and Sean is basking in the fact that his latest single, "Waving T'ing," did so well during the year's carnival season. In fact, "Waving T'ing" received quite a bit of local and regional airplay, and Sean has been busy keeping up with demand for his CDs. We are driving through the streets of San Fernando, discussing the state of gospelypso and making stops along the way to drop off CDs at various retail outlets. One of these outlets is the bookstore attached to and owned by the First Church of the Open Bible in San Fernando. He collects his money, drops off another thirty CDs or so, and we continue on our way.

Sean tells me, "This CD is really doing well! But it also shows that, while things have changed a lot, it's still a fight to make gospelypso work. All I can hope for is to recover the costs of recording plus a little extra for the next CD." And the struggle to which he refers exists not only at the level of the all-too-familiar seasonal economic challenges facing Trinidadian artists in general but is also embedded deep within the community of believers of which he is a part. Gospelypso, as he says, "is still not accepted the way it should be." Why? "Well, I try to explain it in 'Waving T'ing.'" He puts in a tape of his song to keep me company while he runs into a bank to deposit his earnings:

Oh aye yah yea, aye yah yea. Oh aye yah yea, aye yah yoh.
Oh aye yah yea, aye yah yea. Oh aye yah yea, aye yah yoh.
Question: Who started the waving t'ing? Who started the
    waving t'ing?
Who started the waving t'ing? Who started the waving t'ing?
Who started the waving t'ing? Who started the waving t'ing?
Who started the waving t'ing? Who started the waving t'ing?

Some people here in this country, doh believe waving come
    from God.
Say they believe this thing it unholy, it started in carnival.
So ah tell them . . .

Read yuh Bible, check Leviticus, or ask yuh Grandmother,
When she come in the church with the white kerchief and
    she wave it in the air,
And she giving a wave offering, wave offering, wave offering,
    wave offering.

Who started the waving t'ing? Who started the waving t'ing?
We started the waving t'ing! We started the waving t'ing!
Who started the waving t'ing? Who started the waving t'ing?
We started the waving t'ing! We started the waving t'ing!

Ah know you have yuh opinion, a personal conviction.
Aye some people holding on to religion, they stifling the
    spirit man.
But ah tell them . . .

Read yuh Bible, check Leviticus, or ask yuh Grandmother,
When she come in the church with the white kerchief and
    she wave it in the air,
And she giving a wave offering, wave offering, wave offering,
    wave offering.

Who started the waving t'ing? Who started the waving t'ing?
We started the waving t'ing! We started the waving t'ing!
Who started the waving t'ing? Who started the waving t'ing?
We started the waving t'ing! We started the waving t'ing!

Some think it was Iwer (No). He wasn't the author (No).
You think it was Super Blue (No). Boy doh let them fool you
    (No).
Read Exodus twenty-nine (Yeah). Read Leviticus ten (Yeah).
Read in the Gospels, read it up, read it up! Aye!

We started the waving t'ing! We started the waving t'ing!
We started the waving t'ing! We started the waving t'ing!
We started the waving t'ing! We started the waving t'ing!
We started the waving t'ing! We started the waving t'ing!

God tell Moses to start waving the sacrifices.
The enemy started using it for his own vices.

They use it to party and behave slack.
In Jesus' name we taking it back.

Oh aye yah yea, aye yah yea. Oh aye yah yea, aye yah yoh.
Oh aye yah yea, aye yah yea. Oh aye yah yea, aye yah yoh.[2]

These lyrics are illustrative of the tensions that exist between gospelyp-sonians and the Full Gospel community. Gospelypso is suspect. It is too closely related (if only etymologically) to the perceived evils of carnival and bacchanal. But Sean Daniel's song does not address itself to a new turn of events. Rather it restates—crystallizes even—a dilemma that has faced gospelypsonians from their very first explorations with the style some thirty years ago. Put somewhat crudely, the Full Gospel community has, by and large, refused to identify with gospelypso—to accept it as a valid, rep-resentative expression of Full Gospel identity.

The terms of this thirty-year struggle seem to turn on several ethical and religious questions produced when local expressions of faith in Trinidad intersect with a transplanted, North American, Pentecostal worship ideal. In order to explore some of the reasons for the ensuing struggle, I investigate the central place that gospelypso occupies in articulating these dilemmas, focusing attention on the ways that the ethics of style might shed additional light on the questions at hand. Because gospelypso came onto the scene at a particular historical moment and has, in large part, grown through the efforts of artists affiliated with Pentecostal churches, I should like briefly to rehearse a few key aspects of the political climate during the 1970s and to sketch an outline of the Pentecostal presence in Trinidad.

What might or should a Christian response to national independence sound like? What musical shapes can contribute a constructive, uniquely Christian perspective to a nation-building project? For that matter, how can music perform a redemptive task in a postcolonial, post-Christian society? These types of questions occupied the Full Gospel community in Trinidad during the drive toward political independence from Great Britain begin-ning in the 1950s and continued unabated after Dr. Eric Williams became the country's first prime minister in 1962. The ideological agenda mapped out by the black power movement of the late 1960s and early 1970s, fur-thermore, created an atmosphere within which these questions were trans-formed into issues that could be more broadly applied to questions of black nationalism.[3] Not that this was the only topic of conversation. But these questions formed part of the background noise that gradually came to the foreground as independence became a reality. Not surprisingly, musicians were among those most responsive to and concerned with these questions, and some eventually hit upon a style that seemed to offer some answers.

Enter gospelypso! Not that gospelypso was a brand-new innovation—far from it. Rather, it had been an unnamed register of musical performance within the worship services of the Full Gospel Community for quite some time. What changed was that the style was quite consciously *named*—called "gospelypso" for the first time—an act that refocused it and then posited it as a means toward answering many of the questions that concerned Trinidadian Full Gospel believers of the time. More to the point, it provided a vehicle that lent shape to a particular *type* of response to these issues, and this not least because some believers within the Full Gospel community were themselves engaged in a struggle for independence. Different in kind and degree from the national movement toward political autonomy, the discourse of the Full Gospel community nevertheless drew on nationalist themes and, by extension, found itself inextricably bound up in the political agendas of the 1960s and 1970s.

Political change was paralleled during this time by religious change, for Pentecostal missionaries had invited themselves into Trinidadian history during the first third of the twentieth century. Upon their arrival they introduced a new paradigm for thinking about and enacting worship. The missionaries preached a faith and practice that refocused and heavily emphasized the spiritual/metaphysical aspects of Christianity. In the most broadly inclusive sense, the importance that Pentecostalists placed (and continue to place) on spiritual gifts, healing, and the work of the Holy Spirit within the church offers the most striking evidence of this new emphasis. While these teachings were not wholly absent from the worship-life of the other denominations active in Trinidad, the Pentecostal message placed them on center stage, making that message a powerful and unique alternative to more long-lived paradigms.

Pentecostalists, however, not only challenged the practices of the members of other denominations, such as the Baptists, Methodists, and Moravians, but also necessitated certain equivocations and adjustments on the part of new converts, for North American Pentecostal missionaries were working in Trinidad when national independence from Great Britain became a political reality (1962). Moreover, the black power movement of the late 1960s and early 1970s forcibly articulated the need for and *right* to autonomy, thereby strongly influencing the thinking of Trinidadians.

Eric Williams himself, attempting to maintain the credibility of his party's political platform, put the following spin on the task at hand: "[The people] must, after more than four hundred years of being acted upon, act for themselves."[4] The ironies embedded in this statement notwithstanding, strong currents of national pride and cultural empowerment were indeed enjoying wide circulation even as missionaries were spreading their good news. Consequently, an overarching dilemma came to occupy local Pentecostal discourse about worship during the 1970s and 1980s—a dilemma focused on questions concerning the appropriate measure of national autonomy and the proper place of cultural identity within the Full Gospel community in Trinidad.

Within this religious and political context, music provided an expressive mode through which competing visions of Full Gospel Trinidad could be articulated and contested, and two primary musical responses came to occupy the discourse. On the one hand, artists who chose gospelypso concerned themselves with the local and with what a Full Gospel voice might mean (and sound like) in an independent Trinidad. On the other hand, some artists turned to North American gospel music, identifying with transnational dreams related to the global church and leaving nationalist ideas behind. Both of these styles presented the Full Gospel community with unique solutions to questions of identity, and both continue to draw artists and fans today. I will take up North American gospel music at length in the following chapter but turn now to an exploration of gospelypso's reception history.

> We were never meant to be a quiet, passive people.
> Noel "the Professor" Richards

Stuart Hall points out, "Precisely because identities are constructed within, not outside, discourse, we need to understand them as produced in specific historical and institutional sites within specific discursive formations and practices, by specific enunciative strategies."[5] With this comment in mind, we can trace the beginnings of modern gospelypso in Trinidad from the early 1970s. It was during this decade that pioneering artists associated with the Youth for Christ organization coined the term "gospelypso" and began to wield the style in direct, Christian response to the imperatives laid out by the black power movement—acting for themselves after four hundred years, as it were. Following the watchwords of Youth for Christ—"Geared to the Times, Anchored to the Rock"—artists worked to organize the first gospelypso concert at Greyfriar's Hall on February 5, 1972. The concert was deliberately planned to coincide with the height of the carnival season and demonstrated the commitment of Youth for Christ members to reaching their nation with the gospel. This then constitutes the historical site and moment within which artists chose their enunciative strategy—gospelypso.

What necessitated this new use of style? In order to approach an answer to this question, it is helpful to look more closely at the institutions within which gospelypsonians were at home. Trinidadian Pentecostalists had inherited a North American, intensely spiritualized, and by this I mean *gnostic*, faith that demanded surrender to the rightness and superiority of the cultural and aesthetic models the missionaries left behind.[6] In a discussion of the basic "turn within" that characterizes gnosticism, Philip Lee observes, "The concentration on self is a natural result of the passionate need to escape the world. Because no one can escape the real [physical] world except by death (suicide being the ultimate self-actualized escape), the only other solution is to effect an escape by withdrawal into the self."[7] Lee goes on to illustrate convincingly that Christians have historically approached gnosticism through the act of pitting the physical (evil) world against the spiritual (pure/good) world.

The problem with denying the physical, however, is that the physical world—along with attendant complications such as environmental concerns, social injustice, world poverty, and any number of other pressing issues—can be (and often is) written out of the agenda in favor of more pressing *spiritual* concerns. This approach to spirituality, moreover, is significantly complicated when it is put into play in Trinidad. This is the case not least because Trinidad's religious heritage includes Yoruba-derived practices (Shango) that make no clear distinction between the sacred and secular realms, and within which the distance between the spiritual and the physical world is configured much differently.[8]

Added to this is the middle ground that the Full Gospel community fiercely defends against religious laxity on the one hand and Spiritual Baptist and Shango heterodoxy/syncretism on the other. The sacred must, therefore, occupy a very specific, delimited range of possibilities, and this not least because the physical world is a bit too involved in the revels and rituals of the other religious groups to remain unproblematic for the Full Gospel community. Full Gospel believers in Trinidad are thus heavily invested in making these distinctions between the sacred (soul/spiritual) and the secular (body/physical) clear in the face of a culture that has historically conflated them in various ways. In the process, biblical passages such as "God is spirit, and his worshipers must worship in spirit and in truth" (John 4:24) are marshaled in order to support the idea that the Christian life is not found in the flesh. Put more polemically, one might even say that for many believers, the Christian's *life* is disembodied. By extension, this type of interpretation implicitly codes the physical world as evil, or at least inferior to the spiritual realm, which is understood to be good—the locus of *true* life.

It is therefore not coincidental that, in Full Gospel, missionized Trinidad, the local is today almost invariably conflated with the physical (body), whereas that which is not local is equated with the spiritual (soul). For example, if a Trinidadian congregation wishes to express joyful praise (physical, interpersonal, and centrifugal) during a worship service, then it is likely that a Trinidadian praise chorus will be used. (I will address this repertory in greater detail shortly.) If, however, that same congregation wishes to attain a worshipful (spiritual, personal, centripetal) atmosphere, then it is virtually guaranteed that a North American gospel chorus will be sung. The implicit inferiority of local cultural production is clearly illustrated in this repertorial tendency, and the gnostic imperatives linking spirituality with interiority are eminently observable in the closed eyes and subdued body movements of the congregants during these latter moments.

This hierarchical relationship between the physical and the spiritual dimensions of life is further codified through a designation commonly heard both in North American and Trinidadian contexts: "praise and worship" music. Praise and worship bears a coded hierarchy of value in its construction that can be broken down into the following two statements: praise is physical (and spiritual); worship is spiritual (and physical). Praise music is generally faster and more energetic (charismatic) and interpersonal in character than worship music. And when transferred to Trinidad, the local and nonlocal dimensions of musical life are also read onto this hierarchical construction. This, then, is the backdrop against which I find Philip Lee's reading of a gnostic escape into self so compelling. From this perspective, gnostic worship is primarily about individuals and their relationship to God while praise still opens onto the role of the interpersonal, to the sense of shared community that results from bodies working together toward a common goal.

Not surprisingly, some artists began to question the value of this spiritual inheritance and to look for ways of expressing themselves within (or in spite of) it, and I suggest that the turn to gospelypso constitutes, at least in part, a reaction against the gnostic paradigm of worship inherited from Pentecostal missionaries. The institutional site and discursive frameworks that led to artists' identification with gospelypso thus grew out of the Pentecostal church and its emphasis on the spiritual and, by extension, the nonlocal aspects of being a Christian in the world. Earl Phillip, one of gospelypso's foremost promoters and performers, articulates the dilemma as follows: "We have accepted both the message of Jesus Christ *and* the culture that came with it. We have not yet been able to split the message from the culture, [to] put what God give *us* with the message."[9] This realization, accompanied by the culturally local and socially empowering rhetoric of the black power movement—set as it was against the backdrop of national independence—provided a rallying point that had a profound impact on the imaginations of pioneering gospelypso artists such as Merle Tellersford, Ruth Graves, Vernon Clark, Leyland Henry, and Andrew Thomas.

> Don't expect me to write [hymns] like a European.
> Leyland Henry

Gospelypso did not, however, simply spring fully formed out of the mouths of singers like Merle Tellersford, Larry Harewood, and Nicole Rock. In fact, a genealogy of modern gospelypso reveals at least two antecedents, both of which are crucial to its development and subsequent reception. The etymologically and sonically obvious antecedent—calypso—provided artists with a stylistic model and a palette of sounds with which they were already intimately familiar. Little needed to be changed in terms of musical materials or performance practice, although significant modifications were made to the content and function of the poetry. The minor-key calypso (double-tone) and the storyteller tradition were easily adapted to the lyrical needs of gospelypsonians. The formulaic chord progressions of both the major- and minor-key calypsos, moreover, were readily appropriated and served as the framework for melodies that now were charged with carrying strongly evangelistic and edifying lyrics. A good example of this type of lyrical change is found in what many consider to be the first consciously created gospelypso song. Composed and performed by the Mystic Prowler in 1970, "A Man Is a Man When He Thinking Clean" was one of the models that gospelypsonians turned to in order to craft their own songs.[10]

The less obvious and more indirect antecedent is embedded within the body of song known as Baptist choruses, a repertory of communal songs that has circulated in the oral tradition of Trinidad since the early years of the nineteenth century. The links between Baptist choruses and Pentecostalist-driven gospelypso are not coincidental and provide a great deal of support to the ideas espoused by the style's pioneering artists. For starters, the values invested in and communicated through the Baptist choruses mirror the needs and ethical concerns that motivated the pioneering gospelypso artists—that is, they, like gospelypso, offer examples of musical performances wherein the local, the body, and the process of being-in-community are privileged. In addition, because Baptists have enjoyed a relatively long history in Trinidad, these choruses were widely known.[11] Thus, many Pentecostalists who had recently transferred their membership from other denominational affiliations were intimately familiar with these choruses.

Simon Frith has observed, "Music constructs our sense of identity through the direct experiences it offers of the body, time, and sociability, experiences which enable us to place ourselves in imaginative cultural narratives."[12] Using the three areas identified by Frith, I highlight in the following excursus the important ways through which the repertory of Baptist choruses supported, at least in principle, the development of gospelypso.

BODY

The Trinidadian choruses are generally performed in unison and incorporate a limited amount of heterophony, which is generated both by accompanying instruments and by the free improvisation of various members of the congregation. The principal accompanimental instrument is the tambourine, although guitars, keyboards, and other instruments are used when they are available. The tambourine is responsible for generating a steady rhythmic cycle consisting of one eighth note followed by four sixteenth notes and another eighth note, but performers have a great deal of freedom to improvise around this figure (see example 2).

This rhythmic cycle can be performed in a swing feel as well and is the most common and characteristic pattern performed on the instrument. It provides the rhythmic basis for almost all of the songs, generating congregational involvement in the process (generally in the form of hand clapping and dancing). It is in this constant movement that a striking characteristic of Trinidadian Baptist worship becomes evident. The bodies of the congregants become actors in the performance, simultaneously contributing additional rhythmic complexities to and signifying their own personal identifications with the songs.

What becomes significant in the context of the early development of gospelypso is that artists were able to point to a local repertory that engendered a positive and vibrant approach to embodied expressions of worship— a celebration of the body's spiritual capacity—that specifically counterbalanced the Pentecostal tendency to emphasize the spiritual (and hence nonphysical/nonlocal) aspects of being in the world. This body of songs explicitly celebrates the body as instrument, as actor, as performer, and the

Example 2. Tambourine rhythm often performed using a hard swing feel.

rhythmic content of the choruses provides the catalyst for this celebration. To put it another way, the experiences that these choruses offer of the body constituted a tangible confirmation of gospelypso's viability—a confirmation that was needed in the face of intense pressure to abandon the project.

I should be quick to add here that Pentecostalist worship is very "physical" as well. The body is certainly present—even charismatically so—and has been from the very beginnings of the movement at the Azusa Street revival. The question here, then, is not really about the actual presence or absence of physical bodies in worship, but rather the relative *value* that is assigned to that type of worship in the two traditions. The Baptist choruses essentially offered a way of legitimizing the body as the locus of worship, whereas Pentecostal worship aimed eventually to draw attention away from bodies and into meditation on the spiritual aspects of being in the world. Gospelypsonians, concerned as they were with reaffirming the intrinsic value of the body and, by extension, of the local in Full Gospel life thus found in this repertory a measure of confirmation that led them more strongly to pursue their own poetics of conviction.

TIME

The choruses are sung as many times as the song leader feels is appropriate. Thus, it is not unusual to repeat a chorus fifteen or more times, and there are even occasions when it becomes important to sing a particular song for more than ten minutes. This is especially true in processional situations. For example, a baptism can often involve a public procession that finds the entire congregation marching through the town on its way to the nearest body of water. Processional time is always filled with songs, as it is understood to be a public proclamation of faith, and at times a single song can serve this function. The flexible timeliness of the choruses is embedded in the structure of the choruses themselves, for many of the choruses are cyclical, leading straight back to the beginning of the melody and making it musically desirable to repeat the melody at least once (see examples 3 and 4). This cyclical quality is accomplished in a variety of ways—harmonically (ending on a half-cadence), melodically (ending on the dominant or super-

Example 3. "Way Jonah Gone?"

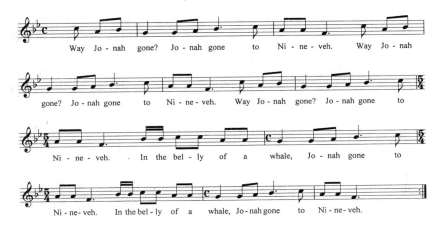

Example 4. "Go Down the Road."

tonic scale degree), rhythmically (by making use of upbeats), and, most commonly, textually (by structuring the text so that the end flows quite naturally back into the beginning).

In addition to the physical passing of time that occurs during performance, the texts of the choruses often deal with the mythical past or with the timeless future (which is equally mythic). For example, the song "We Shall Have a Grand Time" refers to a brighter future in heaven where believers will be "walkin' with the angels, singin' 'Hallelujah.'" Mythical characters are also activated in these choruses, as evidenced in "Way Jonah Gone?" Here we see the biblical character of Jonah mobilized for use during baptismal services (see example 3). The traditional typological interpretation of Jonah's experience in the belly of the great fish is that it prefigures Christ's own death and resurrection. The New Testament writers refer to the rite of baptism as the believer's identification with Christ's death and resurrection. Thus, the myth of Jonah is recovered here as a metaphor for the believer's death and rebirth into Christ. It also serves to connect the community with the timeless roots of its shared past.

A further type of relationship to time is found in "Something Deep Down Inside," a song that finds the narrator saying, "Something deep down inside, telling me to go on." In this case, the immediacy of the here and now is painfully present. The text—the narrator's confession—is articulated in direct relationship to the hardships of life. Furthermore, that "something deep down inside" is not particularly helpful in offering the singer a point in time when this "going on" might come to an end. This timeless ambiguity serves to reinforce the conception of life as pilgrimage.[13] A similar sentiment is in evidence in "We Will Meet Jesus By and By" (see example 5). Here, however, the ambiguity of time is stated in a more positive light, in a hopeful rather than doggedly determined manner.

On the most general level, this repertory of songs, by its very existence, constructs a sense of the legacy of Baptists in Trinidad. In other words, these choruses are believed to be a particularly Baptist form of expression and, as such, are considered the aesthetic property of those who participate in Baptist life.[14] Added to this sense of timeless or mythical past is that these songs have, almost without exception, been created by composers who remain anonymous, affording this repertory a kind of folk vitality while simultaneously serving to maintain a strong sense of community ownership.

I believe that the timeliness of the Baptist choruses provides a vital background link to the early development of gospelypso, a period during which artists were searching for a form of expression that would allow them to tap into the national sentiment. Here was a specifically Christian, relatively long-lived (at least by comparison with Pentecostal song repertories), and uniquely Trinidadian body of songs that could provide a historical link with the wider Full Gospel community while simultaneously referencing the history of the nation (and the Christian tradition in general). That said, however, I do not mean to suggest that gospelypso artists used the choruses in any *direct* fashion, but merely to point out that the artists could refer to these choruses as one of the roots upon which gospelypso was built. So, for

Example 5. "We Will Meet Jesus By and By."

We will meet Je - sus   by and   by.   We will meet Je - sus   by and

by.   We will meet Him by   the   way,   with a   ti-cket in   His hand.   We will

meet   Je - sus   by   and   by.

example, the texts of Baptist choruses did not translate directly into gospelypso lyrics, nor do the melodic structures of these choruses reappear in gospelypso settings. And yet, in a conversation I had with Leyland Henry, he made a point of repeatedly stating that gospelypso had been sung in the churches from "long time."[15]

SOCIABILITY

Trinidadian Baptists do not generally initiate the singing of these choruses with an instrumental introduction. Usually, the song leader begins singing and the guitarist or keyboardist (if available) spends the first two or three bars searching for the right key, joining the tambourine in accompanying the congregation once the proper chords are found. Relative pitch prevails, as the primary objective of the song leader is to start the song on a pitch that will accommodate the range of the melody within a comfortable tessitura for the congregation. The voices of the congregants are the most important element in the singing, a fact made clear by the structure of the singing itself. Instruments are secondary at best, and the function of the leaders is limited to starting the song and encouraging the singers. This approach to the act of singing goes a long way toward reinforcing a sense of community.

But the experience of sociability goes beyond the physical act of singing, extending to the texts and music of the songs themselves. Many of the songs in this repertory, such as "Way Jonah Gone?," are functional in that they are tied in a very direct way to specific events, such as conversion and baptism. The social dimensions of the choruses are, thus, also embedded within their texts. An excellent example of this type of chorus is "Go down the Road," which is often sung at revival meetings and at the time immediately following conversion (see example 4). The text of this chorus calls for the faithful to "Go down the road and sound the jubilee, tell them fire go burn them." It is at once a reminder of the fate from which the faithful have been saved and of the need to fulfill the great commission, that is, to bring the gospel to the whole world. In this one chorus, then, the common theological foundations of the community are made clear through an articulation of what the members are not and a simultaneous call to common action.

The song "Hallelujah Anyhow!" illustrates the role that encouragement plays in constructing experiences of sociability in Trinidad. Here we find the narrator urging the listeners to "never, ever let life's troubles get you down. When life troubles pass your way, lift your head up high and say, 'Hallelujah anyhow.'" The act of singing this song as a community provides powerful confirmation that individual members are enveloped in a network of relationships from which they can draw strength. "I am because we are" is configured here as a central pillar of being Baptist, and it allows each member access to encouragement from the group as needed during the course of performance. A final example of the sociability of these choruses is "Somebody Watchin' Me" (see example 6).

The worshiper is, in this case, understood to be in relationship with the divine. As such, the individual's relationship to the community is also intimately bound up in the personal relationship that each member of the congregation has with the divine. Sociability is achieved not only in such relationships but also out of the common spirituality that the individuals experience together. I suggest that gospelypso artists saw in the Baptist choruses a means of generating links to the broader Christian community in Trinidad, and the gradual movement of this repertory of Baptist choruses into Pentecostal worship services would seem to support this idea.

An important aspect of the sociability of these choruses is that they are considered the aesthetic property of the Baptists. Dale Bisnauth has commented, "The membership of the Baptist church [almost exclusively black] was responsible for that church's reputation that it was a 'poor man' church."[16] This reputation is expressed in more negative terms by Pastor Roddie Taylor, who points out that most other Christians believe that "Baptists are still in the bush."[17] I suggest that these choruses, widely perceived as the property of poor, backward Baptists, provided an encouraging parallel for gospelypso artists—a musical parallel to their own ultralocal and controversial poetics of conviction.

A final thought regarding time and sociability leads me to the words of Hollis "Chalkdust" Liverpool, who, in an attempt to trace the early history

Example 6. "Somebody Watchin' Me."

of calypso, notes, "Kaiso [calypso] . . . was enriched melodically by work songs and religious Yoruba music, particularly the Shango chants." He goes on to cite the linguist Maureen Warner-Lewis, who concludes, "Religious chants have survived to this day through the vitality of the Shango religion. And, their lyrics left behind, the melodies of some chants were co-opted by early minor-key calypsonians."[18] What remains significant here is that the Shango influence, like the Baptist choruses, dates from pre-1834—both of these religious traditions thus predate emancipation. While it is clear that Shango chants were significant contributors to the sound and style of what calypso eventually became, the existence of a contemporaneous, parallel Baptist repertory went a long way toward legitimizing gospelypso. Thus, gospelypso artists were able to claim that, by infusing calypso with religious lyrics, they were merely tracing the sources of kaiso from an alternative but equally ancient source, that the true roots of kaiso historically include (or at least do not preclude) a Christian perspective. This discursive strategy is captured by Leyland Henry and echoed in Noel Richards's assertion that "we've been singing kaiso in the church long time."[19] Connections to the sacred past, then, served as a means of validating a new use of style, providing justification not only within calypso circles, but also to the Full Gospel community.

Having briefly explored the antecedents of gospelypso, I now pick up the story in the year 2000 and work my way backward a bit. The song "Gimmie Room," performed by Marilyn "Destiny" Joseph, places its lyrical finger directly on the open wound of gospelypso's reception history (see figure 1).

> Well you know I'm a Trini, I'm a Trini to my heart, and I'll be a Trini till I dead.
> When it comes to praising, all I want is a start. Praising God does really get to my head.
> So when you see me dancing, when you see me prancing,

Figure 1. Marilyn "Destiny" Joseph in concert, Pointe-à-Pierre, Trinidad, 2000. Photograph by Timothy Rommen.

I don't want you think that I've gone astray.
If my behavior cause you worry, then my friends I'm sorry.
You don't have to join me, you don't have to agree!
All I ask of you is to clear the way.
Gimmie room! Gimmie room! Gimmie, room, people, just give me
    some space!
Don't you find this amazing, is my God I'm praising.
Push your chair up, gimmie room to praise![20]

This is a defiantly resigned song. "You don't have to join me, you don't have to agree! / All I ask of you is to clear the way. / Gimmie room! . . . give me some space." In this regard, Marilyn's song mirrors some of the sentiments expressed in Sean Daniel's "Waving T'ing." Throughout its thirty-year history, gospelypso has been actively resisted by the majority of Full Gospel congregations. While many Christians applaud the ethical decisions that foster emphasis on local cultural productions and consider gospelypso preferable to American gospel music in that regard, gospelypso still tends to be excluded from worship services in most churches and across denominational lines. The standard explanation, given by any number of pastors and laypeople, stresses that gospelypso is still associated with the perceived moral evils of carnival. It does not help matters that the Full Gospel community sees calypsonians such as Calypso Rose and the Mystic Prowler offer their own gospelypso albums for sale.[21] This trend reinforces the sense that gospelypso is simply calypso disguised for a day as something good but is ultimately never far from its roots in carnival.

Nicole Ballosingh knows about this struggle for respectability as well. In the first verse of her song "Jump for Jesus," for example, Nicole acknowledges as much, telling us that people accuse her of "acting as though [she were] still in the world."[22]

> Some folks say I'm crazy, some say girl, you're brave!
> To go on stage and sing at something and wave.
> Some say listen Nikki, you losing it girl!
> You acting as though you still in the world.

Hers is, in fact, a doubly coded confession in that it refers to two separate (if interrelated) failings, namely, musical and physical associations with carnival and a questionable spiritual life. Ironically, the association that links gospelypso with bacchanal—an association that casts gospelypso in an ethically and, by extension, spiritually suspect light—prevails in spite of the fact that almost everything that is sung or performed in services throughout the country relies on a base of rhythmic and textural materials that is understood and acknowledged as growing out of calypso. And here I am thinking not only of the Baptist choruses, but also of the hymns and North American gospel songs that are routinely sung to soca or calypso accompaniment. This irony is identified in Roddie Taylor's comment, "If they just hadn't called it gospelypso, everything would have been fine!"[23]

A genre born out of an intense desire to bring Trinidadian artistic expression to the nation, and to the Full Gospel community in particular, thus is considered ethically incompatible with Christian worship. And this is the moment at which I believe the ethics of style can usefully be brought into the discussion, because gospelypso artists see this style as a performative solution to the ontological realities and ethical dilemmas attendant to Full Gospel Trinidad. In other words, gospelypso is simultaneously seized upon as an effective response to those Pentecostal worship paradigms that marginalized local culturalisms *and* as a relevant, uniquely Christian intervention in the life of the nation. This attitude is amply illustrated in Noel Richards's song "Gospelypso":

> I said, Gospelypso is taking a bible passage and putting it in the
>   language,
> So that locals could get the message all in the village.
> It is bringing the bible to ordinary simple people, oh lady, that is
>   gospelypso.
>
> I said, Gospelypso is using what God give us to bring glory to Jesus,
> From the first verse to the last chorus, ask Lincoln Douglas, he could
>   tell you.
> The thing is a vehicle for reaching we people, oh lady, that is gospelypso.
>
> She said, Gospelypso is sweet gospel music, flavored with West Indian
>   lyrics,
> With a rhythm that's slow or quick you can take your pick.
> And I said, it is using we culture to present the scripture, oh lady, that
>   is gospelypso.[24]

The Full Gospel community, however, cannot see past the moral history of the genre itself and, consequently, rejects the efforts of gospelypso artists on ethical grounds. Each gospelypsonian's creative vision is, in short, greeted by an equally powerful discourse that seeks to discipline the artist's musical choices—her poetics of conviction. We thus see an entire genre rejected because of the associations that still link calypso and bacchanal in the public imagination. (E.g., Sean Daniel and Nicole Ballosingh are up there waving their rags just like Machel Montano would have.) Many recent gospelypsos narrate this rejection with a view toward correcting misunderstandings and misconceptions among fellow Full Gospel believers. Marilyn Joseph, for example, has remarked that "Trinidadians need a change of mindset" with regard to gospelypso.[25]

In a song entitled "They Say," recorded in 1995, Noel Richards spells out some of the more painful accusations leveled against gospelypsonians:

> They say that we causing trouble. They say that we causing bacchanal.
> They say we are crazy people. They say this thing isn't scriptural.
> They blame Nicole Ballosingh for starting the jumping thing.
> They say that she causing revolution.
> But what I want them to know, Jumping started long ago,

Cause it have a lot of jumpy people in the Bible.
And this is the example! And I tell them . . .

David danced for the Lord (I jumping for Jesus).
He was singing praise to God (I jumping for Jesus).
Israel used to celebrate (I jumping for Jesus),
When the Lord did something great (I jumping for Jesus).
You think they were wrong? (No!) To sing happy songs? (No!)
They couldn't stop the dancing, the feeling was strong.
We doing the same, man, why we getting blame?
We just want to praise His name and jump, and jump, and jump,
    and jump![26]

In light of these opposing discursive geographies, of the very different poetics of conviction highlighted in lyrics like these, it is significant that gospelypso artists have, for reasons related to theology and community, chosen to remain active within the institution that continues to reject their artistry—to continue to affirm their links with the very community that accuses them so bitterly of being worldly and "causing bacchanal."[27] And yet the church community does welcome them and offer them a home of sorts. They are simply expected to leave their baggage (their gifts) outside. By rooting themselves in this place in between, the musical style they perform is freighted with the ethical weight of the discourse and, by extension, becomes inseparable from it. Their decision, in short, makes visible to the community their poetics of conviction.[28]

This state of affairs presents an interesting challenge for individual believers, however, for they are confronted with what I referred to in chapter 2 as an impossible choice. They must either chain themselves to the discourse of gospelypso, thereby aligning themselves with that ethical project and placing themselves outside the normative boundaries of their Full Gospel community, or reaffirm their agreement with the prevailing interpretation of gospelypso as inappropriate for and even dangerous to Full Gospel identity. In either case, they are forced to reveal the seams that keep the fragile sense of Full Gospel unity together, and it is this process of articulation, this choice, this moment of decision in the face of the other and of others that the ethics of style addresses.

This process of articulation toward which I direct the ethics of style is further illustrated by what I call the negotiation of proximity. Answers to an inquiry regarding this or that aspect of gospelypso will vary depending on who is asking the questions. For example, local Christians are very quick to champion gospelypso as an example of Trinidadian faith and musical expressivity when speaking with visiting (nonlocal) Christians. Within the boundaries of Trinidadian practice, however, gospelypso is subjected to a much more rigorous standard, where the ethical imperatives of the Full Gospel community take precedence over stylistic considerations. I suggest that these trends are dictated in part by the peculiar logic of the negotiation of proximity.

We can get at this idea by thinking about the degree to which North American gospel choruses (of the type popularized by Bill and Gloria Gaither and Andre Crouch and, more recently, by publishing houses like Maranatha! and Vineyard) permeate worship services across the country.[29] These types of songs are readily accepted as appropriate for worship in most Protestant denominations but remain, no matter how closely they are currently tied to the Trinidadian Full Gospel landscape, fundamentally other. This distanced position creates an atmosphere within which firm statements about their moral and ethical content are easy to pronounce.[30] Thanks to their distanced point of origin, they are less bounded, more useful. Gospelypso, however, is situated far too close to home to remain unfettered and uncomplicated. It is implicated in the messiness of everyday life and is, as such, much more difficult to incorporate into the pristine landscape of gnostic spirituality toward which the Trinidadian Full Gospel community aspires. Earl Phillip articulates this idea from the opposite perspective: "Our music is doing well abroad, but in Trinidad we still trying to get it off the ground."[31] Another way of getting at the negotiation of proximity is suggested in Noel Richards's song "Gospelypso":

> Lady you know when them big foreign artists come down,
> We does pack up the Jean Pierre Complex and National Stadium.
> All Helen Baylor songs we know good, but we don't even know who is
>   Larry Harewood.
> Pop, Dub, and Reggae, we love to sing and then we criticize we own
>   thing.
> We never treat we own as we should till some foreigner tell we it good.
> Gospelypso, lady, is greatly misunderstood.[32]

I believe that this paradoxical relationship by virtue of which the far becomes near and the near far points to deeply embedded issues of what Michael Herzfeld calls cultural intimacy. "Embarrassment, rueful self-recognition: these are the key markers of what cultural intimacy is all about."[33] For what could look more traditional, less modern in the face of a transplanted, North American religious paradigm than a local music, and a local music associated with bacchanal at that? Like so many other culturalisms throughout the Caribbean and Latin America, gospelypso is talked up to outsiders but is embarrassing to insiders. By way of example, just think of the trajectories that Argentinean tango, Cuban rumba, Trinidadian steel pan, and any number of the region's authors and intellectuals have had to travel before gaining any measure of respectability in their own nations. Each had to travel far in order to become near, as it were. And even at that, there remains the uncomfortable thought that these journeys might not matter at all. Earl Lovelace voices this concern as follows: "They don't want to *hear* you. They just want to know they have a writer."[34]

The case of gospelypso is particularly interesting to me in this respect because it involves what might be thought of as a double embarrassment. First, it builds on calypso, which is a source of perennial embarrassment to the nation. Here I am thinking about the impact that the long history of the genre has had on the sensibilities of the state, because the various injunctions and laws passed with the goal of limiting or eliminating carnival and calypso point to some rather dark chapters of history—chapters linking calypso to slavery, dubious race relations, and class struggles, to name just a few.[35] These are hardly the modern images that a self-proclaimed multicultural nation-state wishes to incorporate into its international face.

Second, gospelypso is enunciated from *within* Full Gospel institutions, which is a source of perennial embarrassment to these churches. Just as the "nation-state is ideologically committed to ontological self-perpetuation for all eternity," the leadership within the Full Gospel churches in Trinidad is invested in maintaining a metaphysical link to North American, nonlocal musics and worship paradigms for all eternity (in every sense of the word).[36] This commitment is in evidence not only in the musical material that makes its way into the services, but also in the consciously adopted North American dialect that pastors and music directors use during services and in the suits that approximate the image portrayed by pastors on the North American–based Trinity Broadcasting Network. (I will address these trends in greater detail in the following chapter.)

And in the midst of this project, some of the church's own members are "causing revolution"; by drawing attention to the transplanted nature of Pentecostalism within Trinidadian culture, gospelypso artists simultaneously undermine and embarrass the leadership—and this principally through forcing the impossible choice which I have already mentioned. Put otherwise, because gospelypsonians refuse to separate themselves from the Full Gospel community and simultaneously refuse to bow to prevailing norms of musical acceptability within that community, they are (as is their music) a constant reminder of the ethical differences—the multiple poetics of conviction—that exist within that community and that these differences are the sites around which identifications are being articulated.

In choosing this difficult course of action, gospelypso artists have, since the 1970s, adopted a method of cultural (and ethical) critique that bears a strong resemblance to what Herzfeld calls social poetics. Herzfeld explains that the "specific task of social poetics is to reinsert analysis into lived historical experience and thereby to restore knowledge of the social, cultural, and political grounding—the cultural intimacy—of even the most formal power and the most abstract knowledge."[37] By introducing gospelypso into the performative history of the Trinidadian Full Gospel community, artists have reinserted analysis and, by extension, ethical critique into the fabric of both nation and church in a most visible and audible fashion. Gospelypso, then, can be understood as a means through which Trinidadian artists claim their place in the independent nation and their independence within the church. Conversely, gospelypso can be conceptualized as a discursive formation that is continuously hailing subjects, thereby encouraging them to articulate their identification with the local, the physical, and, by extension, the national and to work toward a more fruitful understanding of what it means to be a citizen and Full Gospel believer in Trinidad.

I should add here, however, that one of the fault lines that gospelypso's social poetics highlights concerns cultural politics within Trinidad. A large percentage of Trinidadian Pentecostal believers are of East Indian heritage, and just as calypso is problematic as a symbol of the Trinidadian nation, gospelypso presents a significant challenge to Pentecostal identity when it is championed as the quintessential local gospel music. This tension plays out along the same lines as does the national debate about what should constitute national culture. It is fair, then, to question what exactly should constitute the local in the first place. If it is a purely Afro-Creole version of Full Gospel Trinidad, as gospelypso seems to suggest, then that vision of the local simply does not reflect the diversity of the church in Trinidad. One of the most successful means of addressing this concern among Full Gospel believers who do not accept the cultural terms upon which gospelypso is built is to deflect the issue by embracing North American gospel music. I take this subject up in the following chapter.

Even so, many of the lyrics of recent gospelypsos continue to express the hope that the church community will come generally to accept gospelypso as a legitimate Christian art form. The last verse of Noel Richards's "Gospelypso" is a case in point. The lyrics narrate a conversation between Richards and a woman who is initially very skeptical of gospelypso's merits. By the end of the conversation (the last verse), however, Richards not only convinces her that gospelypso is a good thing but also makes her an evangelist for the style.

She said, young man, I appreciate what you've told me,
And from what you've said I see gospelypso differently.
No more will I ever criticize. What you tell me open up my eyes.
I see the thing as a ministry for reaching lost souls in this country.
But don't limit yourself to Trinbago, go sing a song for the world to
   know.
That the word of God could be spread through gospelypso.

Both the resigned tone of "Gimmie Room" and the overly optimistic
flair of "Gospelypso" narrate the position that gospelypso occupies in relation to the church. And while a strong desire to gain acceptance from the
leadership remains, gospelypsonians recognized early on that they needed
to provide an alternative forum for the performance and promotion of the
style. This situation led Youth for Christ consistently to stage rallies, to promote open-air meetings, and to rent venues such as the Greyfriar's Hall or
Spektakula Forum for concerts. From 1972 until 1983 these represented the
only avenues open to most gospelypsonians.

In 1983, however, the Petite Bourg chapter of Youth for Christ organized
and hosted the first Gospelypso Competition, complete with judges and
scorecards, in the yard of the St. John's Anglican Church.[38] Just as the first-
ever gospelypso concert was scheduled at the height of the carnival season
in 1972, offering Christians and non-Christians an alternative to the calypso
tents and fetes, so the Gospelypso Competition was designed to be gospelypso's alternative to the Calypso Monarch Competition. After several
successful years of competition, the national chapter of Youth for Christ,
under the leadership of Herman Brown, took up sponsorship of the event
and continued to sponsor the competition annually through 1997.

In 1999 gospelypso artists were provided with a new venue for performance. Under the direction of Earl Phillip, the Jubilee House Gospelypso
Tent opened during carnival season. The tent operated in 2000 as well but,
due to financial reasons, was not open during the 2001 season. Earl Phillip
had expressed the hope that both the competition and Jubilee House would
be opened again in 2002, but neither venue has been reopened since 2001.

These alternative performance venues all point to the difficulties that
gospelypso artists continue to experience in negotiating their relationship to
the larger Full Gospel community in Trinidad. Sean Daniel finally decided
that it was time to take gospelypso to the national calypso tents instead of
trying to create alternative, exclusively Christian performance opportunities. Since winning the Unattached Calypso Monarch title in 1999 with his
song entitled "One a Day," Sean has been performing annually at the tents.
He has been a regular with the Calypso Spectakula Tent in Pointe-à-Pierre

and, most recently, with Generation Next Kaiso Tent and continues to reap his share of criticism (and praise) from the Full Gospel community over his decision.

I believe that the continued search for performance venues illustrates the strong convictions that gospelypso artists hold concerning their music and their place within the church. On the one hand, they could simply capitulate to the will of the majority of church leaders and stop performing altogether. This is not, however, an acceptable option for most gospelypso artists. On the other hand, they could cut their ties with the church and discontinue their attempts to make inroads into Full Gospel worship. Yet this option is also unacceptable to most gospelypsonians. They deliberately maintain a strong connection both to gospelypso and to the church, seeking to find ways of bridging the conceptual gap and theological framework that makes their music so difficult for church leaders to accept.

Thinking through the connections among ethics, religion, musical style, and politics in Trinidad leaves me intrigued by the prospect of analyzing the music through the ethics of style. As I see it, the ethics of style highlights some of the crucial misunderstandings that fuel the discourse surrounding gospelypso's acceptability in the Full Gospel community. It illustrates both the ethical grounds upon which gospelypso was, and continues to be, created and the ethical grounds that are preventing its incorporation into Full Gospel worship. When combined with theoretical ideas such as the negotiation of proximity, cultural intimacy, and social poetics, the ethics of style adds an important register to the analysis of gospelypso. I remain convinced that, with so many people invested in the success (or failure) of gospelypso, the style has itself become synonymous with the rhetoric surrounding it, and the ethics of style addresses the deeply held convictions that drive that very discourse.

Indeed, success or failure continues to be a major concern, for one of the challenges facing gospelypso as a style is a lack of young artists willing to perform it. During the mid- to late 1990s, many of the performers were between forty and fifty years of age, and only a handful of younger performers actively continue to promote the genre. Sean Daniel is the most prominent of these younger artists. Today, it is much more fashionable to pursue local styles like hardcore soca or rapso than to sing kaiso. While this trend is bemoaned by the pioneers of the style, the desire of young artists to pursue other musical avenues should not be surprising, for it mirrors the reasoning that served as a catalyst for gospelypso itself. Leyland Henry has remarked that the early gospelypso artists were self-consciously attempting to "be hardcore and radical."[39] Nevertheless, there is widespread concern that soca will ultimately overrun the slower, storytelling style.

And what is to be made of the various other styles that are currently competing against gospelypso for airtime on the radio, space on concert bills, and sales in record stores? As Noel Richards says:

> All Helen Baylor songs we know good, but we don't even know who is Larry Harewood.
> Pop, Dub, and Reggae, we love to sing and then we criticize we own thing.

Having here illustrated the criticisms leveled against gospelypso, I turn in the following chapters to a closer exploration of the music of artists who choose to express themselves through the mediums of North American gospel music, pop, dub, and reggae. In so doing, I will continue to investigate the ways that questions of the local and nonlocal inform the identifications of artists and audiences within the Full Gospel community in Trinidad.

4 Transnational Dreams, Global Desires

North America as Sound

> We are all one family. . . . It doesn't make sense to reject something just because it isn't local.
>
> Rev. Vernon Duncan, pastor and musician

Vernon Duncan's statement succinctly encapsulates the concept that legitimizes an ideological and, by extension, ethically informed approach to the use of North American gospel music in Trinidad—family. This concept was expanded upon in a conversation I had while participating in a rehearsal of Michael Dingwell's band:

> When we sing songs like "I Love You Lord," we are bearing witness to a spiritual reality. . . . We are, after all, all brothers and sisters in Christ, no matter where we happen to live. . . . No, no, it isn't that we don't feel comfortable singing Trinidadian music. . . . Singing a song like "Lord I Lift Your Name on High" is simply a way of showing that we are part of something much bigger than Trinidadian culture or nationality. . . . I mean, Christianity isn't just Trinidadian, and we are only passing through this world, traveling to our spiritual destination, to a place where we are all going to be worshiping together. . . . I think it's a mistake to miss out on great worship music just because it happens to be written somewhere else.[1]

One of the core ideas expressed in both the epigraph and the conversation revolves around imagining "family" from the perspective of one's own participation in the invisible church, understood here in its fullest, most global sense.[2] The invisible church, as I use it here, can be understood as the sum total of believers everywhere, and many Trinidadian artists, believers, and pastors are thrilled to be able to illustrate the connections they have made with their brothers and sisters around the world.[3] It comes as no surprise that one of the most important and expressive ways that they imagine their participation in this community of the global sacred is by incorporating nonlocal—in this case North American—musical style into their worship services and concert repertories. I should also mention that the concept of the invisible church as it is understood in Trinidad bears a great deal of resemblance to the way that cosmopolitanism has tended to work. In other words, the global connections between people and places are reinforced, and this often at the expense of local instantiations of the same questions of solidarity.[4]

This chapter explores the development of North American gospel music in Trinidad, interrogating some of its connections to transnational and neocolonial processes and cosmopolitan dreams along the way. Throughout the chapter I illustrate that these processes, set in motion as they are within a sacred context, are freighted with layers of meaning that profoundly change their ethical and ideological frameworks. I write with the intent of nuancing the ways that transnational and neocolonial issues (and the ideal of cosmopolitanism) are often discussed with and through the ethics of style in order to demonstrate the powerful counterprocesses that Trinidadian Full Gospel believers put into play, both in discourse and through musical practice. To that end, and in order to provide a context out of which the remainder of the chapter will unfold, I should like first to trace the outlines of what is generally considered gospel music in Trinidad and then to offer three brief vignettes, each of which traces the fault lines of this chapter's central concerns.

As I indicated in the introduction, the term "gospel music" covers a great deal of musical ground in Trinidad, and I would like, briefly, to tease out some of the different musical styles that are included when it is invoked by Trinidadians. The most general definition includes *all* folk and popular music that is considered Christian in the Full Gospel sense of the word as well as music written specifically for services. This usage is considerably broader than it would be in the United States, for it includes styles such as urban gospel (by which I am referring to artists such as Trinity 5:7, Mary Mary, and Kirk Franklin), choral gospel (such as the music performed by the Mississippi Mass Choir, the Wilmington Chester Mass Choir, or James Cleveland), R&B-influenced gospel (like the music of Yolanda Adams and the BeBe and CeCe Winans), gospel blues (by composers such as Thomas Dorsey), spirituals, quartet and small ensemble gospel (by the likes of the Dixie Hummingbirds or the Blind Boys of Alabama), and any number of other styles that are appropriate in terms of lyrical content, including the music of southern gospel composers such as Bill Gaither, the worship songs of Andre Crouch and Alvin Slaughter, and the service-oriented choruses produced by publishing houses such as Maranatha! and the Vineyard Press.

This does not mean, however, that all of these styles regularly find their way into worship services. Rather, the primary staple in services is the repertory of choruses produced expressly for communal singing. Special selections can and often do draw on the other styles but are generally focused on ballad- or anthem-like songs, mass choir numbers, or meditative, R&B-influenced songs, and rarely (if ever) on styles such as urban gospel or hip-hop. North American gospel music is thus used selectively, and the boundaries of acceptability are measured by the same mechanisms of boundary policing that I explored in chapter 3. In other words, urban gospel and hip-hop, like gospelypso, generally fall outside the realm of acceptability because their associations with North American popular culture are made highly visible through media coverage in Trinidad, thereby rendering them threatening to Full Gospel identity.

Another important aspect of this range of styles is the conflation of what, in North America, are styles with distinctly racialized histories. I mention this because it is important to recognize that gospel music in Trinidad travels different routes through the racial imagination than it often does in the United States.[5] So, for example, a Trinidadian will refer to songs by both Bill Gaither and Thomas Dorsey as gospel music without making any sort of distinction between them. In the United States, however, a careful categorization is made—one, after all, is an example of southern gospel music (read white) while the other is a gospel-blues song (read black). I bring the racial imagination into this discussion because I believe that it goes a long way toward illustrating the machinery that drives the negotiation of proximity in Trinidad, a question to which I will return a bit later in this chapter.

By the early 1970s, then, Trinidadian artists were exploring the possibilities of reproducing existing North American gospel music for their own use but also experimenting with writing and performing in a style very much influenced by this repertory. Their efforts were roughly contemporaneous with those of gospelypso artists but were generally received much more favorably by the Full Gospel community. Some artists performed right in their own churches, creating the music for services and doing occasional concerts. Others managed to create a national reputation and to travel the country, performing at churches and in concerts. In general, then, artists who chose to pursue North American gospel music as a "sound" were afforded a greater measure of freedom and acceptance within the Full Gospel community than were gospelypsonians.

That said, however, the range of gospel music that is considered useful for worship services has since the 1970s remained somewhat delimited by the need for a moderate and conscious application of the styles to Trinidadian Full Gospel contexts. Some artists, such as the Apostles 5 (1970s) and Princess Camelia (1990s), have chosen to work right at the limits of that range, but, as I will illustrate in the pages that follow, these artists were met with very different reactions to their choices than were gospelypsonians. I turn now to three vignettes that illustrate the overarching idea that occupies the remainder of this chapter—the extent to which the Trinidadian Full Gospel community has come to identify with and explore North America as sound.[6]

UNITY RALLY

Notes: January 30, 2000, Open Bible Cathedral, Point Fortin

It is Sunday evening, January 30, 2000, and I am standing in the balcony of the Point Fortin Open Bible Cathedral. This event is the first pan–Full Gospel meeting that I've attended since arriving in Trinidad, and it is being sponsored by the Point Fortin Full Gospel Association. The Full Gospel Association is a local cooperative consisting of churches that adhere to the teachings of the "full gospel," a membership requirement that is deliberately ambiguous. As it happens, the members of the Full Gospel Association are the sole arbiters of membership. My friend Roddie Taylor is the president of the Point Fortin chapter, and he sees his appointment as an important step toward bringing the various church communities of Point Fortin together.

The difficulty here is the long-standing one of schism, and this primarily because no congregation wishes to deal with the true implications of the word "unity." As Steve Bruce points out, "The consequence of the reformation was not a Christian church strengthened because it had been purified but a large number of competing perspectives and institutions."[7] In the Full Gospel environment, unity becomes a concept to which most people appeal and an idea that affords congregations and denominations the ability to feel as though they are working together. In practical terms, however, talk of unity rarely contributes to actual unity. Put differently, ecumenism is always interesting to talk about but rather difficult to sell.[8]

The preacher for the evening, Bishop Emory Samson of the Bethel Pentecostal Church, receives rousing applause as he takes the podium. The applause, however, comes primarily from members of his own congregation. There is a certain lack of unity that grows out of the partisan nature of denominationalism, and I am not sure how the idea of fellowship, embedded as it is within the concept of unity, will ever be realized. Perhaps the members of the Full Gospel Association recognized this fact indirectly by naming the organization an association rather than a fellowship.[9]

The songs that we sing are almost exclusively North American choruses and standard Protestant hymns such as "Holy, Holy, Holy." The Pentecostal pastors all dress in business suits and emulate North American modes of speech, avoiding—somewhat studiously—the local dialect. The exact opposite seems to be the case with the Baptist preachers, who wear what they consider to be traditional African clothes and generally speak in a heavy local dialect.

Style is, in this instance, performed in the realm of fashion and language use, and I am interested in thinking about the ways through which these other registers of style function as discursive formations in their own right, at once illustrating their own powers of expression and broadening the ethical horizons of discourse about identity by taking their place alongside the use of musical style. These contrasting uses of fashion and language instantiate, in other words, another register within which the poetics of conviction are played out.

> I am somewhat unsure what to make of this Unity Rally. To begin with, the word "unity" does not even come up during the rally, a fact that adds to the uncomfortable sense that the surface sheen of the event—including banners and flyers—only diverts attention away from a general lack of community. To be sure, a mass choir does perform a number by Ron Winans entitled "Totally Dependent on You," and this choir does include members from several churches in the Association. But beyond that, the event itself does not live up to its billing. The choir rehearsal, which I attended the previous evening, had the feel of an uncomfortable reunion—everyone knows each other but no one has much to say.

All of this reminds me of another concept that looms large in the Trinidadian Full Gospel landscape—identity. Jonathan Boyarin puts it as follows: "What we are faced with—what we are living—is the constitution of both group 'membership' and individual 'identity' out of a dynamically chosen selection of memories, and the constant reshaping, reinvention, and reinforcement of those memories as members contest and create the boundaries and links among themselves."[10] Boyarin's remarks illustrate the appeal of imagining a unity with the invisible church precisely because congregations who do so are able, at least theoretically, to sidestep the uncomfortable task of facing the *visible* church and thereby also the task of contesting and creating the boundaries and links necessary for living with each other. And it is in this context that the transnational connections between Christians are articulated and reinforced.

NICOLE 2000 GOSPEL CONCERT

Notes: February 26, 2000, San Fernando

> The concert is a serious production, broadcast live on 94.1 FM and deliberately juxtaposed to the southern semifinals of the Calypso Monarch Competition, an event taking place about two miles from here in the same

city. Location: the Palms Club. It provides enough room for close to two thousand people, and it is indeed a packed show here tonight. The setup for the show is interesting. Two stages have been erected, one in the concert hall itself and the other outside. Ticket color determines which stage a given person sees live. The performances will alternate between the two stages, and video screens stand in for the artists at each stage. Thus, if a performer is onstage inside, the outside screen is on, and vice versa.

This setup provides several advantages, not the least of which is maximized attendance. In addition, even though each artist performs only two to three songs, this still allows the crews working each stage enough time to tear down and set up for the next act while the overall show continues via video. It also works much better for radio broadcast, as the performances are virtually seamless. Finally, it allows for two masters of ceremony—one on each stage. This affords the organizers the ability to foster a friendly rivalry between the two stages and, by extension, between the two audiences. Audience participation is maximized, leading to a greater level of intensity during the show, which is again great for the radio broadcast.

The concert starts at six and continues well past midnight. Most of the performers are relatively well-known artists in Trinidad. This is in contrast to the many gospel concerts that foster new local talent and most certainly influenced by the fact that the concert is being broadcast live. A constant theme of the evening is that of worship. Attendees are meant to understand one thing: Tonight is going to be a worship(ful) experience. Musically, the event is heavily influenced by North American styles. I am struck by the fact that North American sounds so dominate the concert. Even many of the songs composed in Trinidad are clearly written with these models in mind.

A very interesting exception to this is the Nazarite Steelband.[11] This group performs a calypso arrangement of a well-known hymn, "When We All Get to Heaven." More important than their repertory, however, is the response they generate from the audience. The previous performers, Christ Dymensions, had received a jubilant reaction. I venture to guess that two-thirds of the audience was jumping up (literally jumping and waving rags in the air) during their performance of a hip-hop–inspired song. When the Nazarite Steelband begins to play, however, the audience almost immediately draws back to the refreshment stands located at the rear of the facility. The number of people dancing? Maybe two hundred . . . maybe.

What does this reaction mean? I ask people about it during the performance and afterward. The steelband is the national instrument, and calypso is one of the most recognizably Trinidadian musical genres. Why the apparent lack of support? Is it another manifestation of the association with carnival that so plagues gospelyspo artists? Is it simply too familiar? Is it a lingering stigma attached to the origins of the steelband? Is it taken for granted? According to the people I ask, this is not the case. Yet they are unable to posit any plausible alternatives. One of my companions, Anna Delfish, mentions that it is easier to get into the music and jump up when there are words to mark the way. Most simply answer my inquiries with a shrug and "I don't know."

BENEFIT CONCERT

Notes: June 17, 2000, Trin-Mar Cricket Club

> Anthony Moses is setting up his equipment at the concert hall. I am sitting in with Michael Dingwell's band, playing a little guitar here and there and generally enjoying the opportunity to witness the concert from this vantage point. Anthony and I are engaged in a conversation about Fred Hammond's most recent release *(Purpose by Design)*. I haven't yet heard it, but Anthony is enthralled with it. He tells me that Fred Hammond is his favorite musician.
>
> The concert goes well, the audience is appreciative, and the band plays great. During the concert, Michael Dingwell performs songs such as "Ain't Nobody Do Me like Jesus," hymns such as "Blessed Assurance" and "My Jesus I Love Thee," and ballads like his popular song "Healer in the House." Michael Dingwell dresses in a suit and makes a point of speaking with an affected North American accent.

I am reminded here of the connection between language and place and wonder at the implicit association with North American cultural spaces that Michael Dingwell enacts in the process of his performance (see figure 2). He is performing his style in similar fashion to that of the Pentecostal preachers I mentioned at the Unity Rally. More to the point, he has matched his language and fashion with his musical choices, performing three separate registers of style in a powerful evocation of North America as sound (and look).

> I am also struck by the sheer breadth of the North American materials used in Michael's set. Some songs are nineteenth-century revival hymns, others, such as "I Love You, Lord," are choruses made popular during the 1970s by the Maranatha! Music groups. Still others are modeled on gospel-blues songs. It's an interesting conglomeration of materials, not least because most North American congregations would be hard-pressed to perform such a broad range of materials, even in what is commonly referred to as a "blended service."[12] Moreover, most North American musicians would not choose to perform all of these songs

Figure 2. Michael Dingwell in concert, Point Fortin, Trinidad, 2000.
Photograph by Timothy Rommen.

in a single concert. But Michael Dingwell considers himself a minister
and, as such, is intent on leading his audience in worship.

The preceding vignettes address a consistent set of concerns attendant to
gospel music in Trinidad. Acted out and discussed in private and public by
artists, pastors at church services, and audiences at gospel concerts, these
concerns all point to the idea of North America as sound. And this overarching idea finds expression in the combined force of at least four emergent
themes: the importance of North American musical style in Full Gospel
Trinidad; the continuous stylistic interplay with other North American cul-

turalisms such as language and fashion in articulating individual poetics of conviction; the difficulties posed by issues of unity and diversity within the Full Gospel "family"; and finally, the care that is taken to identify sacred music as *worship* without regard to place or space. During the remainder of this chapter, I will explore each of these themes in turn, thus tracing the ways that Trinidadian Full Gospel believers envision (revision) North America as sound.

"HE'S GOT THE WHOLE WORLD IN HIS HANDS": THE IMPORTANCE OF NORTH AMERICAN GOSPEL MUSIC IN FULL GOSPEL TRINIDAD

As I pointed out in chapter 3, gospelypso was not the only option available to artists of the early 1970s. In fact, North American gospel music was the primary, mainstream, and most accepted style among the various local, regional, and transnational choices available to the musicians. I am convinced that the appeal of North American gospel music is tied, albeit indirectly, to the ethical challenges I outlined in chapter 3, for it represents the road more frequently traveled. Gospelypso artists were seriously troubled by the general lack of attention to local styles and culturalisms, whereas other artists found no such tension in the situation. While gospelypso artists sought to add a distinctly local, Christian voice to the newly independent nation and were inspired by (if not necessarily in agreement with) the empowering discourse of the black power movement, many other artists found in North American gospel music an equally satisfying means of expressing their Christianity in Trinidad.

The ethical questions that presented themselves so forcibly to gospelypso artists, then, were answered in quite different ways by these other artists, for they were imagining themselves as members of a community that reaches beyond the nation to incorporate the world—they were performing their membership in the invisible church. This concept (cosmopolitanism?) is not a new one, and scholars have long recognized the role that religious ideology plays in creating links that extend beyond national and regional borders. For example Ulf Hannerz, in his essay "A Polish Pope among the Maya: On Community and Globality," makes the following observation: "As the Pope flew in and out, it now seemed as if the road from the tribal village of Tusik, by way of the peasant village of Chan Kom, the town of Dzitas, and through Mérida continued on to Rome, eternal city and global city."[13]

I am inclined to equate the shapes of this journey described by Hannerz with the frequent visits to Trinidad by North American gospel artists such as Andre Crouch (1976), Helen Baylor (1980s), Kirk Franklin (1999), and Donnie McClurkin (2000), to mention just a few. While Jacques Derrida might prefer to call the entire project one of "globalatinization," I am more concerned with the ways through which local Full Gospel believers have approached this imagined/invisible community/church and created a set of meaningful and useful links that find expression in a Trinidadian context.[14]

One of the most frequent complaints lodged by gospelypso artists against those musicians who choose to perform North American gospel music can be paraphrased as follows: They are abandoning their own heritage and artistic language and exchanging it for another's. But this complaint is countered by an important idea that finds expression in Philip V. Bohlman's thoughts regarding the role of music in religious practice. "Music enhances the everyday aspects of religious practice, thereby localizing it. . . . Music combines with religious practice to look *inward* in order to specify meaning rather than outward to determine its connections to globalized constructs of meaning."[15]

Bohlman's thoughts, then, offer an intriguing alternative to thinking about North American gospel music in Trinidad. Gospelypsonians such as Earl Phillip tend to see the emphasis on North American materials as a grave sign of cultural imperialism and of a lack of confidence in local production on the part of their fellow Trinidadians. He maintains, "We have accepted both the message of Jesus Christ *and* the culture that came with it. We have not yet been able to split the message from the culture, [to] put what God give *us* with the message."[16] What Bohlman is suggesting, however, is that the use of North American gospel music in a Trinidadian context is an indication that it has in fact already been localized (at least to some degree). While it is clear that North American gospel music is not local in style, it has clearly been judged as having a certain level of applicability to the Full Gospel community in Trinidad. The disproportionately greater amount of North American gospel music performed in services and concerts vis-à-vis other styles is in itself a strong indicator of the attractiveness that North American style holds for the Full Gospel community.

That said, I suggest that North American gospel music is in fact localized in terms of its usefulness within the community. And—irony notwithstanding—when considered from this perspective, it is no stretch to suggest that North American gospel music is more local(ized) than gospelypso. The concept of the invisible church, then, serves its own, very specific function within the landscape of the Trinidadian Full Gospel community by providing the legitimizing discourse with which to defend the use of a music that has become such a centrally important component of Trinidadian spirituality. Put otherwise, the concept of the invisible church works to legitimize the performance of North America as sound in Full Gospel Trinidad. And this is precisely the discursive approach that Trinidadian gospel artists bring to any discussion related to the ethical dimensions of musical style in Full Gospel Trinidad.

The ethics of style is, I believe, quite usefully applied here, for a reversal of the general trends of transnational and neocolonial power structures is clearly in evidence. But this reversal is not accomplished by way of more commonplace measures of resistance such as sabotage, subversion, or deflection. Rather, it is through an evaluation and subsequent adoption of the music itself that the style is made local. This usefully local version of style, moreover, is not identical to the original, for it is infused with a heavy dose of calypso and performed with the realization that it is an import product. It is possible, of course, to read the pervasive application of calypso's rhythmic base to North American gospel music as a form of resistance, as an instance of the hybrid at work, as it were. Even so, I find it more useful to think of the antecedent processes that created the space for North American music in the worship life of the Full Gospel community in the first place. Put otherwise, this music works in the community, and it is only after this usefulness has been established that the process of localization infuses the style with calypso and soca rhythms.

This then is another excellent example of the ways through which the ethical takes precedence over the aesthetic in Full Gospel Trinidad. Significantly, however, it is the very "importedness" of North American gospel, its distanced proximity to Trinidadian Christians, which makes it so useable, so applicable. I am, once again, working with the idea of the negotiation of proximity, attempting to illustrate the appeal it holds within a gnostic system of spirituality. In order to illustrate the usefulness of North American gospel, I offer the following excursus on North American choruses in Trinidadian worship services.

North American Choruses in Trinidadian Worship

I am struck by the practical and performative dichotomy that exists between Trinidadian and North American choruses in worship services. When a music minister wishes to get the congregation involved and excited (praise), she will almost invariably draw on the Trinidadian repertoire. But when it is time to become truly meditative, spiritually attuned, and serious (worship), then there is virtually no substitute for North American product. There are, I believe, several factors involved in this. In chapter 3, I explored the implications of approaching these two bodies of song by connecting the physical and the local and setting them against the connection between the spiritual and the nonlocal. My aim here, however, is to illustrate the practical uses to which these two bodies of song lend themselves. These practical uses are partially rooted in the musical characteristics that tend to prevail in the two repertories, particularly in terms of tempo and rhythmic intensity. A Trinidadian chorus is, with few exceptions, more likely to incorporate a great deal of syncopation, tends generally to emphasize percussive elements over harmonic materials, is quicker in tempo, and lends itself to infinite repeatability. (See chapter 3 for more detailed descriptions and examples.) Once begun they are not easily brought to a close. In fact, once in motion, no natural endpoint, save the end of the lyrics, is in evidence, which causes some Trinidadians to comment that they have to "stop the song" rather than end it.

North American choruses, by contrast, are generally slower in tempo and do not exhibit cyclical qualities to the same degree.[17] Martin Nystrom's song "As the Deer" exhibits some of these characteristics but also reveals others. It unfolds over sixteen measures that are divided into four-measure phrases; these phrases can be represented as A−A^1−B−A^1. The most adventurous rhythm in this song of moderately slow tempo is the dotted quarter note. But the song is more concerned with harmonic motion than most Baptist choruses. The A phrases are performed in a major key, while the B phrase moves into the relative minor and ends on a half-cadence in the relative minor before returning to the major and reinforcing the tonic in the closing section. (So, when performed in C major, the B phrase moves into A minor and closes on an E^7 chord before returning to C major again.)

In addition to these musical characteristics, I suggest that many North American choruses convey or develop a sense of something akin to the sentimental, both lyrically and in their overall musical effect. Many of these songs, in fact, focus very specifically on an individual's spiritual experience and, in this sense, are perfectly suited for use as meditative songs. Representative examples of these types of songs include Martin Nystrom's "As the Deer," Laurie Klein's "I Love You Lord," Andy Park's "Only You," and Jeffrey Peterson's "Secret Place."

In this context, it is significant to remember that sentimentality is generally characterized by a displacement of feeling, memory, or desire onto an object of interest that is not ready at hand. Put a bit crudely, we generally wax sentimental when we long for loved ones who are far away. The very idea of homesickness, to continue this line of thought, presupposes that home is not near at the moment of our affliction. And, in the case of Full Gospel Trinidad, the yearning of the believer for an unseen—but felt—God is amplified by expressing it through a style that references someplace else.[18] The musical characteristics of the two bodies of song, then, are such that each fills a particular function within worship services, and this is the first sense in which North American gospel music becomes useful in a Trinidadian setting.

A second sense in which North American gospel music (and especially the choruses) is useable in Full Gospel Trinidad relates to the fact that it generally provides a rather stark stylistic contrast to the Trinidadian choruses. Its nonlocal origin, moreover, provides an additional degree of separation from the local choruses. The juxtaposition of these two bodies of song, then, provides a perfect context for the application of what Michael Herzfeld, following Peirce, has called "iconicity." He defines his use of the concept as "the way in which meaning is derived from resemblance: as a portrait 'means' its subject," and goes on to assert that "iconicity does not exist; it is called into existence."[19] I suggest that this categorizing of styles serves just such an iconographic function. The congregation hears a North American chorus and immediately knows the general mood (and place) that the music minister is invoking. Likewise, it is not difficult to respond to a Trinidadian chorus out of a sense of its overall emotional purpose within the service.

"LET'S JUST PRAISE THE LORD": THE SIGNIFICANCE OF NORTH AMERICAN CULTURALISMS IN FULL GOSPEL TRINIDAD

One of the consistent themes attendant to Trinidadian Full Gospel life is the conscious emulation and enactment of certain North American culturalisms, including styles of dress and language use. Jacques Derrida has pointed out, "In these times, language and nation form the historical body of all religious passion."[20] I am convinced that this is indeed the case in Trinidad, and that a great deal of this play with culturalisms is in fact a play with signs that are usefully read against the concept of "playing mas." In other words, I am intrigued by the disfigurations that are put into play when Trinidadians apply themselves to emulating North American Pentecostalism. In the pages that follow, I suggest that, contrary to the subversive implications often generated by discussions of concepts such as mimicry and masquerade, Trinidadian Full Gospel believers are engaged in a qualitatively different project.

Hollis "Chalkdust" Liverpool points out that the masquerade has generally provided a forum for subversion of one type or another: "By subtle use of cultural codes expressed through costumes, masqueraders in Trinidad up to 1962 revealed their hidden transcript: they insinuated meanings that were accessible to the lower classes especially, and, in some cases, opaque to the upper class. The evidence suggests that the poor and powerless used the

Carnival to express their accumulated resentments against the Colonial Government and the rich elites, as well as to indict social injustice wherever it existed."[21] The Trinidadian Full Gospel project is, nevertheless, at heart not (or at least not primarily) a subversive one. Emulating dress and language is, in this case, not designed to undermine or resist the authority of the North American models. Given the importance of the concept of the invisible church, articulated as it is from within Trinidadian churches themselves, it would be cynical to focus analytical attention only on mimicry and masquerade.

I suggest, therefore, that a bit of both genuine solidarity (the ideal of cosmopolitanism) and mimicry is constantly reshaping the surface of the visible church in Trinidad. That said, the authorizing discourses are at times emanating from North America and, at others, from Trinidad. As an example, let me offer the liner notes of one of the first long-playing gospel records produced in Trinidad. Released in 1976, it features the group the Apostles 5 and contains a broad range of musical material, incorporating tracks influenced by soul, funk, and Caribbean musics, including references to the very new sounds of soca. (See chapter 6 for a more detailed discussion of soca.) The liner notes, originally printed on the back of the album sleeve, offer a ringing endorsement of the project, a portion of which reads as follows: "Here is an album with a difference. The music is alive and commanding, depicting a kind of joy and happiness found only in Jesus Christ. The arrangement and presentation are certainly professional and, this album reveals, among other things, that the Apostles 5 must be one of the dynamic musical groups in the Caribbean today. Good for the name of Jesus, don't you think?"[22]

These words become much more interesting when it is revealed that they were penned by Walter and Ruth Nealy of the First Church of God in Christ, Brooklyn, New York. The endorsement, thus, comes from voices believed to carry the added weight of North American authority. A counterexample comes from a conversation I had with Jamie Thomas, who was one of the afternoon drive-time disc jockeys for the country's first Christian FM station, called Love 94.1. He has since moved on to host his own radio shows at Isaac 98.1 FM and, more recently, a gospel show on FM 195.5.[23]

During our conversation I mentioned that he had, for several weeks now, been playing a particular track, "Shackles (Praise You)," from a recently released album by Mary Mary at least twice a day, and I also noticed how often he had been entertaining requests to air the song.[24] "Oh, yeah, it's a great album and has several sweet tracks on it. 'Shackles' is way hot, but if I didn't want to play it, or just didn't like it, it wouldn't get aired and it wouldn't get big down here. Space [another DJ] and I are hit makers and you can see the sales at the record shops when we push something."[25]

Some might object to Jamie's claim, pointing out that Sony and other major industry leaders have already predisposed him to finding "Shackles" appealing—that they have, in fact, created a market and are now simply following channels in order to reap the harvest of their labors (the newest incarnation of indirect government?). While this might well be the case, I am more interested in that Jamie considers it his choice. Whether his freedom of choice is ultimately revealed as a chimera created by the gospel music industry, he has still evaluated the song and found it useful for the Full Gospel community in Trinidad. Furthermore, I believe that this is a strikingly important nuance to keep in mind when considering transnational flows because it points to the multivalent and multidirectional nature of these processes and also because it reminds us that identities are deeply implicated in these processes. It is often the individual person—that one radio disc jockey—who is imagining identity beyond the boundaries of what can easily be theorized and categorized as mimicry, neocolonial patterns, or mediascapes.[26]

Stuart Hall frames this as follows: "Identities are . . . points of temporary attachment to the subject positions which discursive practices construct for us. They are the result of a successful articulation or 'chaining' of the subject into the flow of the discourse."[27] The ability of individuals to chain themselves into differing discursive practices in imaginative ways is thus a personal—even intimate—means of self-making. Furthermore, the discourse surrounding gospel music in Trinidad is generated from multiple sources, both local and nonlocal. And while I do not wish to belabor the point, the invisible church introduces slippage into the conceptualization of space and place, making the local at times seem nonlocal and vice versa.

These discursive practices are, of course, not limited to the flow of migrants and visits to Trinidad by well-known North American artists and preachers. Rather, the mass mediation of religious material is such that a steady diet has been commonplace among Trinidadian Full Gospel believers since the early 1970s. And the mass mediation of gospel music and religious programming has indeed become part of the material conditions of Full Gospel believers in Trinidad, and this especially since the early 1990s, when Trinidad's telecommunications sector was opened up to allow for private broadcast licenses. However, not all are pleased about the impact of the media on the region. I need only bring to mind the words of Rex Nettleford, who considers this process nothing less than an attack on the peoples of the Caribbean. He writes: "The claim to national and cultural identity is not surprisingly made by some to appear to be a threat to peace, development and security, when it is, in fact, overriding, pugilistic hegemonic ambitions that constitute the real threat to national and cultural identity. The hijacking of the region's media, the invasion of the Caribbean people's intellectual space, and the cultural bombardment of the entire region by every means possible from North America are the 'weapons of war' used by those who would wish to save the region from itself."[28]

Contrary to Rex Nettleford's rather negative (but certainly justified) assessment of the role that mass media play in the larger transnational and political landscape, I suggest that the religious dimensions attendant to Full Gospel Trinidad cause a significant shift in the ways that media are consumed, interpreted, and redirected—a shift that might in fact have positive (or at least useful) consequences for individual Christians and congregations alike. Because Trinidadian Full Gospel believers consider themselves part of the invisible church, they also see the mass mediated forms of religious programming as a very natural means of participating in that community. Most important, the mass media provides a touchstone from which point they can chain themselves into this larger Christian discourse, both individually and collectively. In this context, then, it is not surprising to find music, fashion, and speech marshaled in order to evoke North America as sound and, more important, to create a sense of participation in the invisible church.

"OUR GOD IS AN AWESOME GOD": VISIONS OF UNITY AND DIVERSITY IN FULL GOSPEL TRINIDAD

The third theme I explore in this chapter concerns the concept of unity versus diversity within the Full Gospel community in Trinidad. It is encapsulated well by the heading of this section, which, in the space of one little phrase, can be read as conflating all Protestant communities into one group.[29] It is of course also a beautifully ambiguous reference, and some very difficult questions follow on the heels of this expression of solidarity. Catherine Hall poses them as follows: "In the late twentieth century questions about cultural identity seem to have become critical everywhere. 'Who are we?' 'Where do we come from' 'Which "we" are we talking about when we talk about "we"?'"[30]

In order to think about these questions of individual and community identity, I should like to revisit the Unity Rally I attended in Point Fortin, for the ironies are multiple and shed light on the complexities surrounding the idea of the invisible church. I have already indicated that, across most Protestant denominations, unity is an important doctrinal principle. The gospels include accounts of Jesus praying for unity among his disciples, and the epistles of the New Testament are clear on the importance of this characteristic to a Christian witness in the world. That said, it is also clear that schism has devastated the "one, catholic, and apostolic church" since well before the Reformation, and with increasing intensity since that time.[31]

This state of affairs makes it considerably more difficult for Full Gospel Christians to come to terms with what is meant by unity. It strikes me as particularly interesting that a unity rally is staged in Point Fortin, but that those in attendance are able to express more unity toward their North American brothers and sisters in Christ than they often do toward the siblings standing right next to them. I remain convinced that this ironic chaining of identity to—this identification with—that which is invisible and nonlocal is tied to the difficulties attendant to the negotiation of proximity. The prevailing situation in Trinidad is best understood as a power struggle, as a competition for membership and revenues (for material and capital). As such, it is extremely taxing to engage with these types of issues, for there is no escape from their immediacy.

It is in this connection that the invisible church comes to play such a crucial role in Full Gospel Trinidad, for it provides a measure of relief from these issues. Returning once more to a working definition, the invisible church is the sum total of all believers around the world. If the invisible church is considered the "true" body of Christ, however, then what is to be made of the *visible* church? For the two do not necessarily generate an equivalency. In other words, if the invisible church contains all *true* believers, then the visible church might—and probably does—contain nonbelievers. This concept is supported by biblical passages such as Jesus' parable of the sheep and goats (Matthew 25:31–46) and conjures images of the enemy within.[32]

Not surprisingly, we are presented with an eschatological context wherein spiritual disposition takes precedence over physical position. However, if this relationship between invisible spirituality and visible humanity is refracted through a gnostic lens, then the relationship can be broadened to the extent that the metaphysical is always already privileged over against the physical. I suggest that this is, in fact, often the case in Full Gospel Trinidad and that this allows the invisible church to assume a more powerful position than that of its local, physical manifestations (congregations). The slippage that the invisible church introduces into the conceptualization of space and place, furthermore, is crucial to the legitimizing and authorizing discourses surrounding the use of North American gospel music in Trinidad.

The invisible church, then, provides an end around for local Full Gospel believers that allows Trinidadian Full Gospel churches to assert unity without having to provide confirmation of this outside the walls of their own churches. There is, nevertheless, a sense in which feet of some sort or another must support the weight of this assertion within those walls and for the members who gather therein—the claim to unity must, in short, find some form of concrete expression in Trinidad. I suggest that North American gospel music constitutes the primary expression of this identification with the invisible church and simultaneously provides a common body of song that affirms unity among individual congregations in Trinidad. Along with dress and language, it performs a useful task, for it deflects attention away from the lack of unity within the Trinidadian Full Gospel community, focusing attention instead on the links that have been established with North American artists, preachers, and styles. Participation in North American gospel music, then, becomes the focal point of Full Gospel unity and stands in place of any actualized unity between congregations and denominations within that community. The negotiation of proximity is thus an exercise in deflection and disfiguration whereby the near is made far and the far becomes immanent and useful.

Taking this line of thought one step farther, I suggest that the lack of local unity extends to cultural politics within Trinidad as well. As such, choosing North American gospel music effects another kind of deflection from disunity within Full Gospel Trinidad—a deflection that allows believers to avoid some of the very sticky questions related to East Indian/Afro-Creole cultural politics in their nation and their congregations. By privileging North American gospel music, Trinidadian believers are singing into silence questions such as the one Catherine Hall has posed: "Which 'we' are we talking about when we talk about 'we'?" By turning to North American gospel music, Full Gospel believers are able to instantiate a type of unity that does not beg questions related to these very real, local concerns.

The concretized expression of unity through North American gospel music, however, is predicated on a clear sense of what is and is not included in this identification. This need for boundaries drives the community to delimit what styles are useful. A discrimination between, say, Ron Winans's worship ballads and Mary Mary's urban gospel songs is crucial to the successful articulation of identities between North American and Trinidadian communities. It should come as no surprise, then, that artists have, since the 1970s, occasionally found themselves struggling with the boundaries laid out by their community. The Apostles 5, for example, wrote and recorded excellent examples of gospel music with funk-, soul-, and R&B-influenced sounds. I should point out that it is significant that they were engaged in this process when Lord Shorty was writing songs such as "Endless Vibrations" and solidifying soca as a style worth pursuing in calypso circles. But unlike Lord Shorty, who initially endured a great deal of controversy over his change of style, the Apostles 5 found themselves, from time to time, at or beyond the acceptable limits of use in the Full Gospel community but not beyond acceptance within that community.

That said, an important point of distinction between the efforts of gospelypsonians and artists such as the Apostles 5 is found in the relative ease with which the latter artists were able to move inside and outside these boundaries. In fact, Rev. Duncan recalls that there was "surprisingly no controversy" over the musical choices that the Apostles 5 made during the 1970s.[33] Its thorough connection to North America as sound, a sound that drove most of the band's musical material, was sufficient to avoid the kinds of associations with which gospelypsonians struggled. Gospelypsonians, then, were stigmatized for their efforts, whereas artists who pursued North American gospel were never quite beyond the pale, as it were, even if they sometimes went too far in their experiments with style.

A final thought grows out of a statement penned by Theodor Adorno, who points out, "Distance is not a safety zone but a field of tension."[34] I am intrigued by this formulation because, as I understand it, there is in this Trinidadian case also an inverse proportion at play whereby a lessening of distance generates greater tension. Put differently, the more that the distance between self and other is narrowed, the greater the tension filling the remaining space becomes. This translates easily to the Full Gospel context, where a given group, music, or culturalism that is near is much more difficult to process and live with than are similar people, objects, and styles that hail from other shores. This escalation of tension will factor heavily in my analysis of local negotiations of the regional as it relates to music and language in chapter 5.

"EL-SHADDAI . . . EL-ELYON NA ADONAI":
WORSHIP, NO MATTER WHERE

What becomes rather more complicated in a Trinidadian context, however, is the *location* of the invisible church and, conversely, of its visible members. One reading of the conversation I had with Anthony Moses and Sean Friday (excerpted at the beginning of this chapter) points to the possibility that they do not consider themselves truly rooted in any cultural sense of the word. Put differently, that they are just traveling through this world makes them part of the invisible (read culturally North American) church. Ulf Hannerz makes this interesting observation: "Our imagination has no difficulty with what happens to be far away. On the contrary, it can often feed on distances, and on the many ways in which the distant can suddenly be close."[35]

With this in mind, I suggest that musicians like Anthony and Sean are imaginatively placing themselves outside of (far from) home, identifying with tropes of spiritual pilgrimage and with the far-off in order to create a useful and meaningful revisioning of the physical spaces that they inhabit every day. Interestingly, this revisioning accomplishes a double erasure. On the one hand, Trinidadian Full Gospel believers erase the divisions that the North American racial imagination has reified into categorical differences. Thus, a Bill Gaither song is considered gospel music in the same sense as an André Crouch song. On the other hand, by focusing energy and time on these North American musics, Trinidadian artists are effectively able to erase (or at least deflect) their own difficulties with regard to the racial imagination and cultural politics in Trinidad. In other words, instead of having to deal with the thorny and heated issues currently facing the nation regarding the proper place of East Indian culturalisms within the national sphere, Full Gospel congregations are able to sing a Kirk Franklin song in harmony.[36]

As this section's heading makes abundantly clear, there is plenty of room to move beyond North America when thinking about place (and culture or history). This section's heading is the title of an immensely popular North American chorus composed by Michael Card in 1981. The Hebrew words represent, I suggest, Card's reimagining of himself as part of something larger than North American Protestantism—the invisible church. Significantly, this song is rather popular in Full Gospel Trinidad as well, a state of affairs that finds Trinidadians imagining Card, imagining Israel, and all imagining the invisible church as being physically located somewhere else.

While the idea of place is clearly a major touchstone for my interpretation of the usefulness of North American gospel music in Trinidad, I should like, in the next few pages, to focus on the performative spaces that this music inhabits. The vignettes have introduced these spaces already, and these can loosely be grouped into three categories: the concert, the church service, and the space of individuals. Throughout much of this chapter I have focused primarily on music that might be performed in worship services, but there are some types of North American gospel music that find expression primarily on radio broadcasts and in concert settings. The urban gospel song "I Sings" by Mary Mary and Hezekiah Walker's "Let's Dance" are good examples of this latter type of song.[37] I have already indicated that some of the music of the Apostles 5 from the 1970s also enlivened spaces other than worship services. More recently, another stylistic variant that is rarely heard in church services is up-tempo, R&B-influenced gospel. What is significant regardless of performance space, however, is the sense that the artists and audiences are in the business of "worshipping," no matter where they happen to be or what style of gospel music is being performed.

We are not just musicians; we are anointed for the ministry.
                                                    Anthony Moses

An excellent example of R&B-influenced, Trinidadian-composed gospel music is a song entitled "Nothing Is Impossible." Composed by Sherwin Gardner and performed by Princess Camelia, this song has a strong bass line and a solidly constructed groove. The harmonic structure is built on an alternation between B minor and F# minor 6/4, which allows the bass line to move back and forth between B and C#. Low and high registers predominate in the instrumentation (cymbals, upper-register keyboards, bass, and drums), leaving the middle register essentially open for the vocalist and backup singers. This type of instrumentation, so important to the sound of hip-hop and recent R&B releases, creates an enormous amount of space, a hollowing out, that Princess Camelia proceeds to fill with vocal flourishes and embellishments. In addition, the vocals are the most prominent element in the mix, creating a very intimate, personal atmosphere. The lyrics are directed toward edifying and encouraging Christians rather than winning converts, a fact that strengthens any argument suggesting that this song could inspire worship. The lyrics follow:

> [Backup vocalists:] Nothing, nothing is impossible
> [Princess Camelia:] For you my Father, no, no
> [Backup vocalists:] Nothing, nothing is impossible
> [Princess Camelia:] Sweet Jesus, nothing, nothing.
>
> He can move the highest mountain
> He can part the deepest sea.
> He turned water into wine
> When I was down He made things fine.
> So I'm gonna praise Him all of the time.
>
> He's the reason for creation
> He can work in all situations.
> He's the reason for life
> I'm talking about Jesus Christ.
> Times when I thought things won't change
> My life He re-arranged.

Lord, all I want to do is trust in you
Cause you never leave me sad or blue.
I give you my heart, Lord
I give you my life.
'Cause nothing is impossible, no, nothing is impossible
Nothing, no
Hallelujah
Nothing, nothing, nothing, no.
I'm sure that you can testify that nothing is impossible.
He has seen me through.[38]

Lyrics aside, however, the song is too closely tied to sound ideals associated with the secular R&B industry, widely heard in Trinidad thanks to television and radio programming. As a result, Princess Camelia's song is not readily incorporated into Full Gospel worship services. Whether it can be called a worship song, however, is an argument that will continue throughout the remainder of the book, for this issue is not unique to the case of North American gospel music. It finds its way into discourse about other musics such as gospel dancehall and jamoo as well.

One of the most striking aspects of "Nothing Is Impossible" is Princess Camelia's emulation of North American dialect. There is a very deliberate attempt at authenticity of sound in both language use and musical materials, and in the process of pursuing this identification with North American models, Princess Camelia illustrates that Trinidadian Full Gospel believers are very attuned to trends in the North American entertainment and gospel music industries—to North America as sound.

A final observation about the spaces that North American gospel music inhabits in Trinidad is that it represents the only music that successfully negotiates the divides separating the private, the service, and the concert (if only in certain forms). I have already illustrated that gospelypso has struggled to gain entrance into the spaces where services are held. In the chapter that follows, it will become clear that the same holds true for regional sounds such as reggae and dancehall. I suggest that entry into the spaces where services are held is more heavily policed by processes related to the negotiation of proximity and to the ethics of style. I am even willing to go one step farther and suggest that North American gospel music gains entry into these sacred spaces because the spaces themselves have been revisioned as North American places. North America as sound is thus grounded in Arima Pentecostal Church, Trinidad and Tobago. More dramatically, Arima Pentecostal Church has revisioned *worship* as North America's sound.

THE ETHICS OF STYLE: TRUE WORSHIP
AND NORTH AMERICA'S SOUND

The four themes explored in this chapter all contribute to the Trinidadian conceptualization of North America as sound. North American styles are welcomed, fashion and language embraced, unity reinterpreted to refer more immediately to the invisible church, and place conflated to the degree that the far becomes near and the near, far. I am convinced that these themes all depend on the negotiation of proximity as it is played out through the logic of the invisible church. The usefulness, the localized meaning, of North American gospel music can, furthermore, be understood in terms of the ethics of style. Gospelypso artists take exception to the prevalence of these musical expressions inside and outside of the churches they attend. Yet a counterdiscourse, hinging on at least the four themes explored in this chapter, pulls North American gospel music from afar and in so doing reenvisions the face of Full Gospel Trinidad. This counterdiscourse is, I believe, fruitfully analyzed with recourse to the ethics of style in that Full Gospel Trinidad is conflated with North America and reimagined, producing a newly located Trinidad–North America as sound that would not have been possible in the absence of a musical style that could bear the weight of this discourse. In the process of reimagining Full Gospel Trinidad, North America's sound has also been made to stand in for worship.

The ethics of style, then, offers a means of thinking about the process through which Trinidadians make a deliberate identification with the nonlocal, an identification made through recourse to North American gospel music (articulation) and anchored in their desire to participate in the global sacred. This powerful poetics of conviction, moreover, translates into the production of a very strong interpretive context in relation to which other sounds and styles are read. And it is in this connection that the ethics of style becomes an especially valuable analytical tool, for the reception histories of gospelypso, gospel dancehall, and jamoo—along with the discourses that continue to swirl around these styles—are informed by (or at the very least affected by) a poetics of conviction that privileges the musical and stylistic identifications I have highlighted in this chapter. As such, North America as sound becomes a significant part of the comparative machinery that is marshaled in discussions of other musical possibilities. The ethics of style, then, has become useful in perpetuating a particular vision of "the good" in Full Gospel Trinidad, a vision that is particularly North American in both substance and sound.

5 Regionalisms

Performances beyond a Boundary

> We want to reach the greatest number of people for Christ. Most
> people are listening to dancehall, . . . so we play dancehall.
>> Nathaniel Howard, bassist, Melchizedek Order

> God provides an anointed music for each age. Dancehall is the music
> of this age.
>> Sherwin "the Intellect" Gardner

I have, to this point, focused attention on two styles that have enjoyed a relatively long history in Trinidad, at least by comparison to the music that
occupies me in the chapter at hand—gospel dancehall. While gospelypso
and North American gospel music have been a part of Full Gospel Trinidad
since the 1970s, dancehall has found its way into the community more
recently. Part of this trend among younger gospel artists has been driven by
the growing popularity in Trinidad of Jamaican musics, especially during the
1980s and '90s. Trinidadian gospel musicians have, for example, noticed that
artists such as Beenie Man, Bounty Killer, Capleton, Sizzla, and Lady Saw,
to name only a few, have since the 1980s become as ubiquitous year-round
as are Sparrow, Super Blue, Machel Montano, and Destra during carnival
season.

They are not the only ones aware of this pattern. For instance, an editorial printed in the *Trinidad Express* newspaper in February of 1997 laments,
"At the height of the carnival season a reggae song—'Living Dangerously'
by Barrington Levy and Bounty Killer—is the most requested music video
in Trinidad and Tobago."[1] Citizens complain about being subjected to dancehall in the maxis and taxis; pastors issue proscriptions to their congregations, making listening to or purchasing dancehall taboo for true Christians;
government officials at the Ministry of Culture express concern regarding
the pressures that regional musics exert on local genres and artists. Nevertheless, the wild popularity of dancehall and other reggae-derived styles in
Trinidad has led to an exciting and, at times, controversial range of musical
responses by Trinidadian artists. It should come as no surprise, then, that
since the late 1980s, and with increasing intensity during the 1990s and into

the new millennium, Trinidadian gospel artists have also been drawn toward experimenting with various ways of incorporating these styles into Full Gospel contexts.

The Full Gospel community has not suffered from a lack of examples. The South Africa–based artist Felicia Marion dominated the playlists of Love 94.1 FM for much of 1998 with the rockers-inspired hit "Drink."[2] More recently, the former dancehall storyteller Lieutenant Stitchie released his first—and eagerly anticipated—postconversion album, *Real Power*. Several singles from that release dominated playlists at Love 94.1 FM during 2000, and the album remains a favorite of DJs and listeners alike. His latest release, *Kingdom Ambassador* (2004), has also generated a great deal of airplay. Other Jamaican artists, such as Papa San and Carlene Davis, also regularly contribute new material that makes the playlists and stimulates the creativity of Trinidadian gospel artists.

This chapter, then, investigates the ethical discourse surrounding the performance and reception of regional musics in general and dancehall music in particular within the Full Gospel community in Trinidad. In order to provide a context for the chapter, I trace the cultural and political trajectory of dancehall from the marginalized spaces of lower-class, black Jamaica to Full Gospel Trinidad. In so doing I pay particular attention to the criticisms directed at the artists and fans of the music, thus allowing for an exploration of the ways that the politics of power, while present in both contexts, are shifted to address quite different concerns in the Trinidadian context.

THE LOUDEST ISLAND IN THE WORLD

"If I had my way I would ban music. And dancing. Make it a crime. Six months for every record you play. And hard labor for the reggae. Jane, I'm serious. This is a country that has been destroyed by music. You just have to think of what is going on right now on that beach. And think how lovely and quiet it would be, eh. None of that reggae-reggae the whole blasted day."[3] V. S. Naipaul places these words in the mouth of Harry de Tunja, a wealthy businessman and landowner of European heritage whose family has been part of his country's oligarchy for generations. In so doing, Naipaul puts squarely on the table the cultural and political debates that continue to swirl around Jamaican popular music to this day. These words encapsulate the power struggles that have defined Jamaican discourse about class and race for centuries. Moreover, Naipaul makes explicit the underlying catalyst of these struggles for control (whether political, moral, or cultural)—fear. Gage Averill's thoughts about power and politics provide a poignant reminder of what is at stake in Jamaica (as well as in Trinidad): "Power is far from being the property of the powerful; it is a pervasive quality that adheres to every action and interaction. It is sought, undermined, despised, ignored, resisted, and negotiated. In contrast to the term 'power,' 'politics' might best be viewed as the strategies and tactics for gaining, maintaining, and increasing power, especially (but not exclusively) in its more formal and public dimensions."[4] In the following pages, I illustrate the strategies and tactics for gaining, maintaining, and increasing power that are currently circulating in the discourse about dancehall culture within Jamaican society. This will provide the context for my exploration of dancehall music in Full Gospel Trinidad.

In his study of dancehall culture in Jamaica, Norman C. Stolzoff offers the following characterization of the dilemma:

> For the lighter-skinned middle and upper classes, glossed as *uptown* people, opposition to dancehall has galvanized their sense of cultural superiority—hence, their right to govern—because they think it demonstrates black lower-class cultural inferiority and lack of morality. For the most part, these uptown Jamaicans hear dancehall as obnoxious noise, which they often refer to as "boom-boom music," and they feel threatened because of their inability to control dancehall practitioners. However, for the black lower classes, glossed as *downtown*, dancehall is a symbol of pride in the ghetto, in black identity, and of African culture. For downtown people, especially the youth, the dancehall provides a medium through which the masses are able to ideologically challenge the hegemony of the ruling classes and state apparatuses. Dancehall is thus a marker of a charged cultural border between people of different races and class levels.[5]

This passage illustrates the prevailing uncertainty among the middle and upper classes regarding the continued stability of the social order and power structure—a structure that they consider to be under direct threat due to the uncontrollable nature of dancehall culture. Their attacks on the lack of morality and the inferior quality of the music, then, are strategies designed to militate against this fear and uncertainty—they are tactics calculated to maintain (regain) the upper hand.

Belinda Edmondson pursues these tensions from a different perspective, illustrating the complexities attendant to the installation of a Trinidadian-style carnival in Jamaica in 1990. She argues convincingly that the overwhelming support given to the event—and by extension to soca—by the middle and upper classes is a vehicle for undermining the cultural capital that dancehall artists and proponents have accumulated.[6] According to

Edmondson, the Jamaica carnival is in essence a countersubversion, designed to wrest political and cultural control from the hands of the black lower class. One of the principal (and ultimately paradoxical) means through which this is attempted is by making soca the positive foil against which the carnality of dancehall can be cast in a negative light: "The redefinition of the 'bad' carnality of dancehall to the 'joyful' carnality of soca and carnival reroutes the middle class's discomfort with the social and racial meaning of dancehall into an easy division between violence . . . and order . . . [between] the immorality of 'slackness' lyrics versus the playful erotic suggestiveness of soca lyrics; the vulgarity of ostentatious ghetto gold chains versus the 'colorful' carnival pageantry."[7]

Edmondson goes on to suggest that carnival and soca are useful in Jamaica precisely because, stripped of local political complexities, they provide a means through which the brown and white middle classes "may avail themselves of the associative images of an African-descended ritual without having to recognize its political dimensions as a product of poor, black culture." A benefit that she terms "accessibility without contamination" and which I think of as the negotiation of proximity.[8]

There is ample justification for concern among the middle and upper classes, for dancehall culture has indeed become a powerful and acknowledged social and political force in Jamaica. In a newspaper article from 1994, Jean Fairweather illustrates the point, observing, "For the first time, Jamaican popular music far outweighs the combination of church, politics, and the educational system in power and influence."[9] This flow of power from uptown to downtown crystallizes around several of the functions that dancehall culture performs in Jamaica, and Stolzoff structures his analysis of the cultural space of dancehall accordingly. First, he explores dancehall as a force of generation, mediation, and reproduction. Second, he illustrates the ways that dancehall constructs an alternative sphere—a space outside of the dominant racial and economic politics of the nation. Third, he investigates dancehall as a site of clashing. In the following section, I use these three categories as points of departure for an exploration of the divergent uses to which dancehall is put in Full Gospel Trinidad.

Before making the leap to Trinidad, however, I should briefly clarify my use of the term "dancehall." Much like Stolzoff, I conceptualize dancehall as a constellation of related musical practices extending from ska and rocksteady through rockers and on to dub and ragga. Like Stolzoff, I believe that these musical practices, while different from each other in important ways, nevertheless grow out of the cultural space of the dancehall. Thus, while I develop and analyze examples cutting across several of these styles during the course of this chapter, the term "dancehall" serves as a metacategory in the discussions at hand.

"MI NAH GO BOW DOWN": GOSPEL DANCEHALL, POWER, AND THE POETICS OF CONVICTION

I-n-I will hail, hail Emmanuel!
Jah, who guide and protect I from going down to hell.
I say hail, hail almighty Jah on di throne!
Jesus ney fi leave I alone.

Sherwin Gardner, "Hail"

As I noted earlier, the dominance of dancehall in Trinidad has not gone unnoticed. Criticism has come from diverse sources, including the press, government ministers, and artists. By way of example, Ronnie McIntosh, the well-known calypsonian and owner of Mc D Knife, a record label devoted exclusively to Trinidadian music, had this to say in a 1999 interview:

> Local singers are being hurt by the emphasis on Jamaican influences in our music. . . . That's the view of popular calypsonian Ronnie McIntosh, who declares himself "not too impressed with the direction of our music of today." McIntosh added: "I think the direction which the people with the power are directing the youths in is encouraging them to put more Jamaican influence in their music. *Even the Jamaican accent is in the music.*" Local singers are treated with contempt, he suggested. "When you take your music to the stations, for some reason, local entertainers have to be scanned by security, from there to an office, then someone has to listen to it first and then decide if to play it or not. But not so with the Jamaican artiste, especially if they singing so-called soca. If we were to get the same amount of rotation as the foreign artistes, we will do better."[10]

Interestingly, McIntosh is concerned about the role that dialect plays in this war of influence. I will come back to this theme a bit later, but suffice it here to say that dialect and language use (style) within popular music continues to be a major marker of place and, as such, figures heavily in the discourse surrounding dancehall in Trinidad. Another significant trend made explicit in his comments is that Jamaican artists are given more immediate access to airplay, even (and according to McIntosh "especially") when they are performing soca. While McIntosh has a great deal invested in the success of local artists and genres, his observations are nevertheless important in that they point to processes that I believe are driven by cultural intimacy.

The *musical* issues facing Ronnie McIntosh and other local calypsonians such as David Rudder, as well as local bands like Xtatik, are the subject of a constant stream of discourse among calypsonians and in the media. The moral dimensions of dancehall, however—divorced as they are from local Jamaican discourses and politics—do not tend to figure prominently in the general debate.[11] But this has not meant that the moral qualities of dancehall entirely escape investigation and criticism—merely that the debate is picked up by different voices. As young Christian artists began to take advantage of the evangelistic opportunities they saw in dancehall, the Full Gospel community quickly stepped up and began debating this issue with great regularity, both in the media and among themselves. What follows is a rather typical example of the type of polemic that finds its way into print:

> Somebody ought to speak out against the worldliness (i.e., the music and the dress code) that has infiltrated the church, the ecclesia, the bride of Christ. The music is at its worst. Here is one of the reasons being given for allowing this type of music (dub and rock) in the church— we are taking back what the devil took from us. I ask this question, did the devil take rock and dub from us? These types of music and others are born from the heart of Satan and the result of it is rebelliousness and disobedience. . . . You might say that music came from God. I agree. But any time there is a genuine thing there is always a counterfeit. . . . God does not want borrowed music from Satan to be part of our worship to Him. When we do this we are worshipping Satan. He is after worship too, you know. . . . Let's repent and turn away from sin and worldliness before it is too late.[12]

This author, who signs the opinion letter "believer in Christ," effectively sketches a mirror of Jamaican middle- and upper-class criticism of dancehall. The music "is at its worst" (read "boom-boom music") and the dress code is "worldly" (read "slack"). Yet the polemic in this letter continues on to a destination located far beyond the politically expedient moralizing of its Jamaican counterparts. What we have here is a war waged on the stage of Full Gospel theology and based on a moral code drawn from scripture. It follows that standards of behavior and, by extension, acceptability are raised to new heights in the process.[13]

Consider another more measured response to dancehall. "I have my reservation about the wholesale application of so-called pop music to evangelism," Rev. Frederick Coombs, president of the Council of Evangelical Churches, says. "Already the young people associate the dub beat more with the sensuous than with the spiritual. You have to draw a line somewhere. I don't think you should just have a wholesale acceptance of every type of beat and rhythm to convey the message of the gospel."[14] With these comments as a critical backdrop, I now step through Stolzoff's three categories in order to illustrate the uses to which dancehall is put in Full Gospel Trinidad.

Dancehall as Generation, Mediation, and Reproduction

> I still sing R&B . . . but more reggae, because I believe that it is needed in the church. Because it is really dominant on the outside.
>
> Sherwin Gardner

Since the late 1980s, dancehall has become an increasingly popular stylistic choice for gospel musicians. Not surprisingly, Youth for Christ was involved in the earliest experiments with dancehall. The organization, always keenly interested in reaching young people with the gospel, has never been reticent to risk controversy in order to achieve that goal. Accordingly, in October 1991, the organization initiated an evangelistic initiative revolving around dub music. The resulting musical group, called SWAT (Special Witnessing Agents Team), traveled around the country singing and evangelizing. Of particular interest here is the connection that Lincoln Douglas, the national director, drew between the coup attempt of July 27, 1990, and the formation of SWAT. "The coup attempt made the organisation realise . . . that the Church had failed youngsters by not challenging them or giving them enough responsibility. . . . We hadn't given them a cause to live for and to die for and they need something aggressive, very challenging."[15] Thus, a serious social upheaval is once again a catalyst for action on the part of Youth for Christ—in the 1970s it was black power; in the 1990s it is the attempted coup. The imagery conjured by the group's very name—SWAT— is also crucial to understanding the place of dancehall within Full Gospel Trinidad. The connection it makes to the role of actual SWAT teams makes explicit themes of violence and battle (now spiritual) that come to characterize the lyrics of many artists.

While SWAT disbanded after a few years, it did set a precedent, and many artists followed suit. The mid- and late 1990s saw numerous new groups and artists emerge, among whom Sherwin "the Intellect" Gardner and the Conversion Crew, Mr. Mention and the Power Generation, Tiko and Gitta (a.k.a. Royal Priesthood), Melchizedek Order, the Broadway Boyz, and Christ Dymensions are only the most prolific and best known. Upon the release of its first album in 1999, Melchizedek Order received this glowing review:

> In the Holy Bible, Melchizedek was a priest and a king who is first mentioned in the book of Genesis. In present day Trinidad, when the name Melchizedek is mentioned, thousands of young Christian fans know it refers to only one thing—the hippest gospel act on the local scene. . . .

Their message is decidedly urban and their music is driven by the hard-core reggae dancehall beats and rhythms that secular youth their age—19–23—party to constantly across the land. The lead singers of the 11 member group, Darryl and Jason, have vocal delivery that is comparable to any dub chanter. But unlike their dub counterparts from Jamaica, these guys sing it straight from the Heart of Jesus every time.[16]

What strikes me as significant in the case of almost all the gospel dancehall performers is the voice that the style gives to aggression, both lyrically and musically. No other style available to them is suited to channel the types of sounds and lyrics that these younger artists are producing. Themes previously underexplored, such as war between good and evil, descriptions of hell, and eschatological and prophetic messages based on materials from Revelation and Daniel, have become the Full Gospel complement to gangster and rude-boy dancehall.[17] Consider, for example, the refrain of the song entitled "Soul Taker" by Spiritual Ninja:

> I'm more than just a warrior
> 'Cause I'm a ninja for Jesus.
> Will destroy Satan like a fungus
> With the Bible as my apparatus
> All demons gonna bite the dust.

The imagery conveyed through these lyrics is clearly derived from the gangster/gunman ideal of dancehall artists such as Bounty Killer and Ninjaman. The object of aggression is shifted to evil (in this case Satan and his demons), and the spiritual badman is born. It is also not entirely coincidental that Curtis Miller chose "Spiritual Ninja" as his stage name. In some ways, he is continuing a practice often followed by young DJs in Jamaica, who "take on names that make reference to their 'father,' that is, to the DJ who most inspired them or first encouraged them to become involved in the dancehall game."[18] In a conversation I had with Curtis, he explained, "My favorite artists before I was saved were Bounty Killer and Ninjaman. Once I had the opportunity to start singing with [Lion of] Judah Sounds I just called myself Spiritual Ninja."[19]

Another example of the increased freedom to explore these types of lyrical themes is found in Tiko and Gitta's song "Zion March":

> Ruff road, tuff road, nuff load
> Me give that to Jesus because his love it nah corrode.
> It nah gwaan wash away
> God's love it nah erode.
> Me tell you Satan have fi get trampled like a toad.
> Me say Babylon go shut up and hush

Like some lint off ah me garment you have fi get brush.
You're underneath me heel next thing you get crush.
You there a toilet bowl very soon you get flush.
Hush, hush!
Your pastures me nah rush no mind them green and them lush.
They are difficult to chew and might give I man thrush.
Ah Babylon system Royal Priesthood nah rush.
Mount Zion
Well that's the exodus, hey![20]

I should point out that the refrain of this song is built around the melodic and textual materials of the well-known hymn "We're Marching to Zion" by Isaac Watts, thereby juxtaposing their new lyrical approach to a Dr. Watts classic in the course of the song.[21] But artists have also taken this lyrical freedom one step farther. For example, one of the biggest radio hits of 1999 was the song entitled "War." Written and arranged by Sherwin Gardner and featuring Mr. Mention, the lyrics of this song illustrate further the thematic possibilities opened through recourse to dancehall style:

It is a war yuh want, war yuh goan get
Cuh when yuh check it out, Jesus never fail me yet.
Ey boy mi is a killa, big exterminatah
Mashin up di walls of satan di hatah.
But when yuh check it out, Jesus Christ is di fathah
Love you and me now and forevah.
No matter what di enemy fi try
Mi beg up Jesus Christ, di addonai, di rulah on high.
Boy, ey, mi doh want yuh know
Mr. Satan, mi hold on to my God and never never let him go.
Every night some pestilence one that may come again?
Well religion yuh next in di church yuh are fake.
Oh man don't cause problem or we will tear down yuh bus
and we will tear down yuh fence upon di devil kingdom.
Execute di judgement now shut up, now let up, now keep silent
Cause di battle getting hot and di war is ragin'
And releasin' Mr. Mention and di youth culture.[22]

Aggression is here targeted at another spiritual enemy. In fact, the church itself comes under attack for being "fake," or hypocritical. Sherwin, however, is not alone in targeting the Full Gospel community itself with this type of invective. Another good example of this explicit "calling out" of the Full Gospel community is found in Tiko and Gitta's song "I Can't Please You."

I can't please you
I can't please you

I can't please you and you and you.
I can't please you
Me in ah no man pleasing crew
But unto Jesus Christ me ah go stay true.
God alone me please
Excuse me please
Is not to man, but Jesus Christ me ah please.
God alone me please
Tell the Pharisees
It seems like them infected with religious disease.
Them nah like how we look, neither how we talk.
We preach the gospel to save them from the fiery ground.
God sanction this, so why you say we wrong?
Upon the gospel we stand up firm and strong.[23]

These types of lyrics could not have found a home before dancehall and, not surprisingly, cause their share of consternation and frustration among church leaders. One "concerned believer in Christ," responding directly to Lincoln Douglas during the days of SWAT, had this to say: "I wonder if Brother Lincoln Douglas knows the meaning of the word aggressive. It means 'offensive or disposed to attack.' I would like to ask Brother Lincoln Douglas if aggressiveness should characterize a follower of Christ."[24] If the lyrics of artists such as Spiritual Ninja, Tiko and Gitta, and Sherwin Gardner are any indication, then the answer to that question is and emphatic "Yes!" Sherwin Gardner's song "Yuh Dun Know" is another example of this aggressiveness:

Babylon system
True me go burn dem
True me go done dem
In the name of Jesus a run dem.
Wan cause we problem
Christ could a solve dem
And you dun know there is none above him.
So let me tell yuh truth not lie
Christ him reign on high.
Yagga yuh ya ya ya yea!
So have no fear
Christ is always there.
All a my Christian people throw your hands up inna di air.[25]

A final example of this newfound textual and thematic freedom comes from a band called the Broadway Boyz. Their song "Calm before the Storm" invokes the book of Revelation and images of Armageddon in an attempt to exhort their fellow Christians to live in a visibly Christian fashion.

This is di calm before the storm
Youth and youth be warned.
Can't you feel di place waxing warm, yo.
This is di time fi prepare
brethren beware.
Who have ears to hear dem
let dem hear (blow on). [horns]
Scientists and dem versed in philosophy
Project that in di future there will be nuff cause fi worry.
Economists see di downfall of economies
Inna di East Africa, India, inna di West Germany.
America stockpiling fi Armageddon.
No matter if dem doctrine is of Lincoln or of Lenin
Nuclear arms still in mass production.
Di new world order lurks di background with its evil intention.[26]

Assuming the role of prophets who are "chanting down Babylon," many of these gospel dancehall artists are able to speak to issues of evil, spiritual warfare, eschatology, and Christian commitment in powerful fashion. As such, gospel dancehall has in fact provided a significant space within which generation, mediation, and reproduction are being stretched to include new musical sounds as well as new lyrical themes and issues.

Dancehall as an Alternative Sphere

What we do is reaffirm the cultural identity
of the young people.
                Lincoln Douglas, Youth for Christ

This fascinating statement reveals a great deal about the meaning of dancehall in Full Gospel Trinidad. I should say, first of all, that the word "culture" is here used merely to denote the milieu within which young people circulate and interact day-to-day. It follows that the statement should not be read as a claim to substituting Jamaican culturalisms for Trinidadian ones. Nevertheless, the culture/milieu that Douglas refers to does create an alternative sphere—a sphere that is separate from the nation and the church. The performances of gospel dancehall artists and their fans are thus beyond a boundary in several important respects.

The alternative space created by gospel dancehall finds expression on the airwaves and takes shape in CD, tape, and MP3 collections. But it finds its most important performative and communal expression in the gospel concert. For the gospel concert provides the physical space within which gospel dancehall fans and artists come together and construct both an alternative understanding of worship and a vision of the future. In order to provide a bit of background and to introduce some of the unique challenges inherent to the gospel concerts, I sketch a few of my fieldwork experiences.

CHURCH-SPONSORED GOSPEL CONCERT, AUGUST 8, 1998, POINT FORTIN

The event scheduled to take place later this evening is the musical equivalent of a track-and-field invitational. The gospel concert is a tradition among Full Gospel churches in Trinidad. Sponsored and organized by one church, the event is open to all churches across the country that are able to participate. Gospel concerts have two primary functions—evangelistic outreach and edification of the faithful. As such, a successful concert depends heavily on the cooperation of local churches and on an audience that consists of both "the faithful" and "nonbelievers." In this particular case, the concert is being organized and sponsored by Mt. Beulah Evangelical Baptist Church.

The preparations for tonight have been months in the making. Roddie Taylor, the church's pastor, has assembled a list of performers, rented the assembly hall of the Point Fortin Senior Secondary School, arranged for proper advertising, contacted other local churches to solicit their help with promotional tasks, and hired a soundman. All that remains is to set up the hall and test the equipment. I was informed of my role in the concert just yesterday. I am part of the band that will provide accompaniment for the performers. The band consists of a keyboardist and myself on guitar. I am uneasy. I have no set list; in fact, there is no set list. I have a poor instrument. Nevertheless, I am excited.

An earlier conversation with the keyboardist, Anthony Moses, has given me some idea of what to expect this evening. The performers, most of whom need live accompaniment, will literally start singing. It is then left to Anthony and myself to recognize the song and provide accompaniment in the appropriate style and key. Anthony is part of a small circle of individuals who are good enough at what they do to be quite well known in Trinidad and, by extension, to be in high demand. He fulfills a function not unlike a DJ at a club, seeking to establish and maintain the right mood for the concert. As the concert unfolds, I occupy various spaces within the event. Several performers bring accompaniment tapes while others play for themselves. During these performances, I am at liberty to leave the stage, a privilege that affords me the ability to witness the same event from several different perspectives.

Standing at the back of the assembly hall, I find myself intrigued because this concert is at once a display of Full Gospel unity and a clear illustration of the differences between the various communities involved. Broad similarities exist between the groups, but each of them is also localized to the point of maintaining unique taste and meaning boundaries and a strong sense of identity in the face of the other Full Gospel groups. The concert hall is a site that makes possible multiple intersections of cooperation and contestation, of unity and diversity, of border making and border crossing. In other words, it provides a space within which the built-in tension between theological unity and ontological difference, between the "body of Christ" and the "bodies" of the various congregations, is enacted, explored, and negotiated.

The concert ends at 12:45 A.M., and the hall empties as people variously board waiting maxis, start walking home, or flag down taxis. The following morning, while I am standing in Mt. Beulah Evangelical Baptist Church singing a particularly "Baptist" long-meter hymn, I find myself wondering what might be going on at the Open Bible Church just a few blocks down the road.

Church-sponsored concerts are very common during the summer and winter holidays, and many congregations throughout the country sponsor a standing annual gospel concert. Church-sponsored concerts are usually attended heavily by local churches, which generally translates into a wide age range (young children to elderly deacons). Moreover, since many of the performers hail from local churches, significant numbers attend from each church in order to support their talented brothers and sisters. This serves to highlight the divisions between the various churches, as most of the members of a given congregations wind up sitting together. The problem of denominationalism within a theoretically unified body of Christ, then, is a central concern that plays itself out in visible fashion during church-sponsored gospel concerts. (In this regard, these concerts deal with very similar concerns as did the Unity Rally I discussed in the previous chapter.) Church-sponsored events are a major source of the gospel concert activity throughout the year, although the prevalence of these concerts has dropped off considerably in recent years. Two other types of concerts also provide a forum for dancehall artists and their fans.

ARTIST-SPONSORED GOSPEL CONCERT, JULY 2000, ARIMA PENTECOSTAL CHURCH

The concert is called Consecrated and Anointed and is being sponsored by Mr. Mention and the Power Generation and Lion of Judah Sounds. They have even secured Jamie Thomas from Love 94.1 FM to serve as the host for the evening. I am traveling to Arima with Christ Dymensions, a band that hails from San Fernando (about an hour's drive away) [see figure 3]. I will be sitting in on their set tonight and have attended a few rehearsals in preparation for this concert. The members of Christ Dymensions have been conveying their excitement about this concert over the past few days, and even now, cramped into the maxi taxi with our gear, they are enthusiastic about the night's events. All of the participants tonight are young, up-and-coming dancehall and R&B artists. The concert, it seems,

Figure 3. Christ Dymensions and the author before the concert at Arima
Pentecostal Church, 2000. Photograph by Timothy Rommen.

is going to cater to a young audience. By extension, it provides a chance
for the artists to spend time evaluating each other's performances and
enjoying the company of their peers.

We arrive a bit early and find out that the power is out at the church.
There are small groups of people variously praying for the power to return, setting up food stands, and milling about outside. It is immediately
apparent that the median age of the audience is around eighteen to
twenty. In fact, with the possible exception of the deacon who is super-
vising the use of the building, I might very well be the oldest person
in attendance. The electricity returns, and the concert gets underway
at about 8 P.M.

The concert is initiated with a time of praise and worship. The rhetoric coming from the stage designates this evening as a time of worship, as a time to turn our attention to God. "Come on, we are going
to worship God in spirit and in truth tonight! Lift your hands to the
Father on high and worship Him with your whole heart, and mind,
and soul, and strength!" What follows is an exciting concert, with Jamie
Thomas acting as a human transition piece between the various bands,
each band performing between two and five songs. Nevertheless, the
rhetoric of worship continues to thread its way through the entire concert, leading me to think that this is a whole new way of conceptualizing
"church." The concert ends after midnight, and by the time I get back
to Point Fortin, it is 2:45 A.M. I wonder what the primarily middle-aged
people of Mt. Beulah Evangelical Baptist Church would have thought
about the concert–worship service?

The artist-sponsored concert draws a much more homogeneous audience and promotes greater uniformity in the types of musical materials that

are performed. It also tends to diminish the visibility of issues related to unity and diversity within the Trinidadian Full Gospel community. In addition to the focused peer group and rather uniform musical fare, the idea of the concert as worship contributes to the conceptualization of an alternative sphere within which participants are able to think about spirituality and community in new ways and formulate and reinforce an alternative poetics of conviction. It becomes possible to conceive of church as located in a different space and circumscribed by ethical and aesthetic borders considerably different from those in place at their local congregations. This is, I believe, one of the most important aspects of the artist-sponsored concert. A final type of concert deserves mention here.

CORPORATE-SPONSORED GOSPEL CONCERT, JUNE 26, 2000, JEAN PIERRE COMPLEX

I arrive at the Jean Pierre Complex with camera and video gear in hand. The concert, sponsored by Love 94.1 and several area churches, promises to be excellent. Donnie McClurkin and his band are headlining the show, and five or six local artists will be performing opening sets, including the Pierre Sisters, Rev. Peter Regis, and Sherwin Gardner. This is a nationally advertised and media-driven concert. There are perhaps five such events a year, including the annual Pilgrimage concert, which featured Felicia Marion in 1999 and Stitchie in 2000.

The audience consists primarily of younger people, but the appeal of Donnie McClurkin's music to thirty and forty year olds has drawn a good number of audience members from this demographic group as well. The weather has been poor all day, and the attendance mirrors the weather. There is little conversation among the audience members and even less milling about. (Tickets are assigned for specific sections of the stadium.) The concert begins on a rather sluggish note. In many ways the concert feels less like a gathering of community (as in the case of the first two types) and more like a necessary part of seeing Donnie McClurkin in person.

About half an hour into the concert, it becomes painfully apparent that the concert will not sell out. At this point, security begins allowing greater access to the floor of the stadium. During the course of the next few minutes, more and more of the younger audience members make their way to the foot of the stage. As they crowd around the stage, the atmosphere begins to change and the concert picks up both in energy and degree of artist-audience interaction. Even though the attendance is poor, I am sure that there are more people in the stadium than at any of the other church- and artist-sponsored concerts I have attended. The crowd at the foot of the stage must comprise roughly a thousand people by the time that Donnie McClurkin takes the stage, and there are another two thousand people or so enjoying the concert from the relative comfort of the stadium seats.

These three types of gospel concerts all contribute to the creation of an alternative sphere for gospel dancehall adherents, but each to different degrees. Thus, while church-sponsored concerts usually illustrate the difficulties of interdenominational politics and do little to encourage solidarity among the gospel dancehall artists and fans, they do provide opportunities for the (primarily) younger generations to see the challenge of Full Gospel unity for what it is. These are experiences not easily lost on most of the artists or fans, and they contribute some fuel to the fire expressed in lyrics such as the following, sung by the Broadway Boyz, "Bring in the day of cross-denominational brotherhood and end this cold night of wrong."

In artist-sponsored concerts, by contrast, the solid peer group fosters a great deal of social interaction and also goes a long way toward generating a sense of community that transcends both congregation and denomination. This is, I believe, the first step toward coming to terms with gospel dancehall as an alternative sphere. Community is, thus, redefined as gospel dancehall. And if gospel dancehall is community, then it follows that it could also serve as church. This is precisely the logic that governs the rhetoric about worship at these types of concerts, and it also helps to construct an alternative poetics of conviction among gospel dancehall artists and fans. These experiences make the lyrics that I just mentioned by the Broadway Boyz seem all the more pressing. These concerts in fact go a long way toward indicting the larger Full Gospel community for failing to strive for unity, and this precisely because the gospel dancehall community feels that they are able successfully to address this issue during these events. The ethics of style is here revealed as having a contextual as well as a musical dimension.

The corporate-sponsored concert, for its part, allows for a moderation of the idea of community and worship. This type of concert is, first of all, much less local in terms of attendance, thus mitigating the visual keys marking denominationalism. Second, it is usually held in a large venue, with greater numbers in attendance, which allows peers to gather in the front by the stage and, in essence, isolate themselves from the rest of the audience. The ironies implicit in this logic notwithstanding, this type of concert fulfills an important role by providing a forum for the largest gatherings of the gospel dancehall community in Trinidad. If the headlining act is an artist such as Stitchie (as was the case at Pilgrimage 2000), it almost automatically reduces the number of older attendees, leaving primarily younger people at the concert. Consider, for example, the reply I received from one of the over-forty-year-old members of Mt. Beulah Evangelical Baptist Church upon asking if she would be attending Pilgrimage that year: "You mad or what?" She went on to explain that the concerts are far too loud and that "the youths make too much ah fete."[27]

Dancehall culture, as it exists within Full Gospel Trinidad, then, is grounded in significant ways in the experiences afforded by these three types of concerts. Church-sponsored concerts allow young gospel dancehall fans to see the divisions that exist in the Full Gospel community, while the larger, corporate-sponsored events help to flesh out the national dimensions of their alternative community. It is at these concerts that fans, who ordinarily listen to the music in the privacy of their own homes or with a few good friends, are afforded the opportunity to see just how far their imagined community extends.

The most important of these concerts, however, is the artist-sponsored event, because it is in this context that the alternative sphere of Full Gospel dancehall is manifested most completely. Among peers, away from church, young Full Gospel believers are learning to think about their spirituality in a different way. The sense of solidarity generated during these concerts leads to comments such as the following by the DJ Anthony "Space" Williams: "We are now in a generation where the young are leading the old. The young men are having visions and teaching the old the way."[28] It comes as no surprise, then, that many gospel dancehall artists and fans are beginning to criticize the church itself for what they perceive as its lack of spirituality and general lack of piety. This battle over music/aesthetics and spirituality/ethics is beginning to make its way from the press and the concerts into the sanctuaries and services of the Full Gospel churches around Trinidad, and this not least because young Christians, encouraged by their participation in the alternative sphere of dancehall, are increasingly emboldened to articulate their concerns and opinions—their poetics of conviction—to members of their church communities.

Dancehall as a Site of Clashing

> We're changing our mentalities
> Reformation to the Kingdom of God.
> Melchizedek Order,
> "Kingdom Reformation"

Stolzoff uses dancehall as a site of clashing to discuss the ritualized sound system clashes, the rampant competition between individual DJs, and the violence at times attendant to Jamaican dancehall culture. Because there is relatively little outright clashing among the Full Gospel dancehall artists in Trinidad, I bend this category to a new use here, focusing instead on the discourse that swirls around the genre and illustrating the ethical themes that emerge from it.[29] I do this by exploring the politics—the various strategies and tactics for gaining, maintaining, and increasing power—of dancehall.

WORLDLINESS

> We can see the effects of the world's dub music on our youths today, which makes them rebellious and it affects their ability to study at school and yet we say that we are using this dub music to promote the gospel!
>
> *Trinidad Express*

The most common criticism leveled against gospel dancehall artists is that their music is worldly—that it constitutes nothing more than a concession to the world.[30] This criticism also serves to affirm the suspect position that dancehall music is considered to occupy with regard to morality. In other words, while it is politically expedient to turn a moralizing gaze on dancehall in Jamaica, it is theologically necessary to do so in Full Gospel Trinidad. Gospel dancehall thus suffers in similar fashion to gospelypso. Yet, while the discourse surrounding gospelypso focuses on the immediate associations that calypso and carnival engender in Trinidadian imaginations, criticism of dancehall is forced to rely on the once-removed discourse surrounding Jamaican dancehall culture. Instead of referencing dancehall as it is (and has been) practiced among Full Gospel believers in Trinidad, pastors and concerned laypeople speak of dancehall's reputation, its origins, and the moral looseness of the culture surrounding it. Thus, rather vague allusions to slackness, poor dress, and rebelliousness are marshaled against gospel dancehall, whereas a more powerful discourse rooted in direct experience of the perceived moral excesses of carnival and calypso is called upon to defend against gospelypso.

What strikes me as very interesting here, however, is that gospel dancehall artists in Trinidad are all highly sensitized to issues related to morality and, accordingly, take precautions in order to avoid exactly these kinds of accusation. In fact, many artists illustrate their own concerns with the moral dilemmas facing their peers in their music, writing songs expressly warning against the very issues that so concern church leaders. Consider, for example, the refrain of the song unsubtly entitled "Fornication" by the Broadway Boyz, which warns listeners of the evils of extramarital sexual relations:

> Youth man, hear my cry!
> Stay away from di fornication!
> Would lead to tribulation and nuff frustration.
> Well nah man, now feel di condemnation.[31]

Another example of this concern for "righteous living" among artists is the song entitled "Beware (Strange Woman)" by Melchizedek Order:

> Beware! Of the Strange Woman.
> Cause yuh might just end up inna fornication.

This song goes on to detail the biblical story of Joseph and Potiphar's wife in Egypt (Genesis 39) and makes reference to passages from Proverbs about the temptations of women. The flip side is developed later on in the song (third verse). Here young girls are cautioned against strange men for fear that they might wind up in prostitution. In light of these very pointed lyrics, it can hardly be suggested that dancehall music in its Full Gospel contextualization promotes or participates in behaviors that could be considered "slack" or non-Christian.[32] Rather, the lyrics are consistently combative of these behaviors and tend to offer rather straight (in all senses of the word) readings of morality.

Nevertheless, many conservative believers continue to take issue with the perceived loosening of dress and dance codes within the gospel dancehall scene. While it is clear that the younger generations are no longer following the dress codes of their grandparents or even of their parents in this regard, there can also be no doubt that their dress is still very conservative by any standard. The bare-as-you-dare outfits so characteristic of the Jamaican dancehall scene and of Trinidadian carnival celebrations are entirely absent from Full Gospel expressions of dancehall culture. In this regard, the attire worn to gospel concerts is decidedly countercultural in terms of its modesty. The same can be argued with respect to the dancing that the gospel concerts engender. Winin' and grinding are absent, as are dance moves that are deemed sexually playful or suggestive. Couples are rarely seen dancing together, and much of the energy of the dancers is directed toward the stage. Even so, criticisms flow uninterrupted from pen and mouth. The following passage illustrates quite well the type of criticism that is leveled against the prevailing atmosphere at dancehall concerts, raising some interesting questions in the process:

> Dancing in the Spirit is fine but don't tell me that you are pleasing Almighty God when you rotate your waist in a perverted way and jump in a frenzy all over people, mashing some and bouncing some; that is of the flesh. . . . Someone told me that the reason why I, like many others was offended was because calypso and jumping up and getting on is part of Trinidad's culture, and so I was too conscious of this and so I felt bad about it. It's true to an extent but remember that it's not part of Christian's culture so to speak. We have a right to be offended; it's not part of being a true Christian and it never will be.[33]

This passage brings into focus one of the more interesting dilemmas facing Full Gospel believers in Trinidad. Darryl Ramdhansingh, author of this opinion letter, reminds his readers that the gospel dancehall struggle is not really about morality, dress, or dance at all, but about deciding—and having the power to identify and dictate—what is of the spirit and what is of the flesh. And this is the precise point at which the ethics of style once again becomes helpful in negotiating the gnostic tendencies inherent in the Full Gospel churches of Trinidad.

I suggest that this process works along the following lines. First, there is a general lack of physical evidence that the music, lyrics, or atmosphere (including dress and dance habits) of Full Gospel dancehall is morally "slack." Second, many church leaders and concerned members of the Full Gospel community, when faced with this critical void, immediately begin filling it by resorting to a criticism of the spiritual efficacy of gospel dancehall. Thus, while the dancing at concerts is, as Darryl Ramdhansingh rightly points out, offensive to many Full Gospel believers, and this primarily because of processes related to cultural intimacy, he is more concerned that dancing of this type (perverted) is not a part of Christian culture. His argument finds its terminus in the happy assertion that dance of this type along with dancehall music itself are invalidated in a Christian context. The difficulty with this line of reasoning, however, comes at the point where the physical meets the spiritual. It is easy for Darryl to proclaim a spiritual truth (perverted dancing is non-Christian), but quite a bit more complicated to see that truth worked out to his own satisfaction (what kind of dancing would be considered nonperverted). I believe that something deeper is at stake here.

The manifestation of the spiritual is, of necessity, the job of physical bodies. Thus, the mark of any true believer is rooted in the way that she lives her life. And I do not believe that I overstate the case when I suggest that Full Gospel dancehall artists and their fans are keenly aware of what it means to live as "salt and light" in their world.[34] I have illustrated that, in the case of gospel dancehall music, the authorizing discourse surrounding the spirit and flesh is directed at an audience that is already heavily invested in living righteously. The standard attached to the discourse, however, cannot possibly be matched to the satisfaction of church leaders unless gospel dancehall artists and fans were to declare their alternative sphere (and the music with which they fill it) anathema to Christian faith.

I believe therefore that this elusive, unachievable standard, by which dancehall artists and their fans can always be made to appear spiritually wanting, betrays the prevailing uncertainty among church leaders and the more conservative believers regarding the continued stability of the church community and its power structures—structures that they, just like their middle- and upper-class counterparts in Jamaica, consider to be under direct threat due to the uncontrollable nature of dancehall culture. In other words, when young gospel dancehall artists begin directing their critical gaze at the church, claiming, "Oh man don't cause problem or we will tear down yuh bus/and we will tear down yuh fence upon di devil kingdom." Trinidadian Full Gospel believers experience what the middle and upper classes in Jamaica have been feeling for some time now—fear.

LANGUAGE USE

Another approach to dancehall criticism focuses on the use to which language is put in gospel dancehall. Rev. Vernon Duncan summarizes this critique as follows: "Every nation has its own language. If you don't use your own language, you are being deceptive, and that's the opposite of truthful. God is Truth and we are supposed to be spreading the Truth. How can we expect to reach people with the gospel if they are constantly aware of our untruthfulness?"[35]

It strikes me as particularly interesting that Rev. Vernon Duncan does not apply the logic of this particular argument regarding language use to the North American gospel music that he himself sings with regularity and for which he adopts a particularly North American dialect. This is not, then, intended to be a universally binding criticism (though it is made to sound as such). It constitutes a special criticism, reserved expressly for gospel dancehall and the Jamaican patwah that accompanies it. I am intrigued by his statement precisely because of the way that language is already tied into power structures in Jamaica—a situation of which Rev. Duncan is keenly aware.

In her incisive meditation on orality, gender, and the vulgar in Jamaican popular culture, Carolyn Cooper makes a very effective case for moving beyond the politicized and historicized patterns of discourse surrounding patwah in Jamaica.[36] Her excellent essays close the distances between the oral and scribal modes of communicating and, by extension, between popular (Jamaican) and academic (English) modes of writing. One of the ways she does this is through recapturing, or "colonizing," the academic sphere by writing a large portion of a chapter in patwah (which she refers to simply as Jamaican).[37] In doing so, she strongly criticizes the patterns through which Jamaican patwah has historically been cast as decidedly inferior to the Queen's English—a sleight of hand that has enabled the middle and upper classes in Jamaica effectively to shunt off all who use patwah as inferior by association.[38] Cooper articulates this idea as follows: "Jamaican, the preferred language of orality, assumes the burdens of the social stigmatisation to which the practitioners of afrocentric ideology in Jamaica are continually subjected."[39]

The politics of contamination by association involved in enlisting language as a means of criticism thus go far deeper than mere dislike or aesthetic reservations. I suggest that Trinidadian critics of gospel dancehall who choose to point to Jamaican patwah as evidence of its inferiority are participating in this very project. More to the point, the spiritual dimensions of language use are also put into play, allowing for statements about truthfulness or the lack thereof on the part of Trinidadian musicians. This slippage enables a shifting of the focal point of the discourse, making it possible to call into question the spiritual character of a given artist in addition to casting doubt on the merits of the artist's language use.

THEOLOGICAL AMBIGUITIES

Further complicating the use of dancehall style in Full Gospel Trinidad is the connection, made explicit through language use, between dancehall and Rastafarian thought and ideology. This is the case not least because artists are consciously working toward recontextualizing the linguistic cues of Rastafarian spirituality and then putting them into play in Full Gospel dancehall. The process of combining or masking religious symbols, which has been a hallmark of Afro-Caribbean religious expression through centuries, is guarded against most carefully within the Full Gospel community. In fact, as I mentioned in chapter 1, there is much at stake in distinguishing themselves from the more syncretic religious expressions such as those of the Spiritual Baptists, Rastafarians, and orisha devotees. Yet gospel dancehall artists have nevertheless chosen to incorporate the power of word-sound, as it is understood among Rastafarians, into their lyrics. John P. Homiak makes the following observation about word-sound: "Words must be used judiciously and precisely because, in Rasta ontology, 'word-sound' *is* power. Word-sounds, moreover, are conceptualized in a fundamentally African way as 'vibrations' which have the power to impact directly upon the material world. Thus, when the Rastaman says that Rasta comes to 'destroy powers and principalities not with gun and bayonet, but wordically,' we gain a better sense of how the Rastafari conceive of the agency behind words."[40]

The resurgent popularity of "conscious" reggae in recent years has caused many young Christians in Trinidad to gain an appreciation not only for the values and ideology of Rastafarianism but also for the power with which Rastafarians use language. While I do not mean to suggest that gospel dancehall artists are seeking to invest their lyrics with the power of word-sound, I do believe that they are deliberately accessing a vocabulary (I-*ance*, Jah, Lion ah Judah, Babylon, etc.) freighted with a palpable gravity. Paradoxically, this very gravity has been conferred on the vocabulary by a religious system that, irony notwithstanding, was articulated in direct opposition to Western Christianity. This trend has caused a great deal of concern among church leaders, many of whom consider it borderline syncretic. Roddie Taylor puts it this way: "Jah-Jah, the clothes and platts, the colors . . . all that's missing is a 'Haile Sellasie' and you have a conscious reggae artist. Sherwin [Gardner] and Melchizedek [Order] are crossing over the line."[41] Mikhail Bakhtin has observed that words lead a "socially charged life," and the tension surrounding the Rastafarian elements in Full Gospel dancehall provides an excellent case in point.[42]

I remain convinced, however, that the appropriation of these relatively few words and concepts into Full Gospel dancehall music is calculated to add social depth, "consciousness" of a specifically Christian persuasion, and a certain weightiness to the lyrics. Identification with conscious Rastafarian ideology, moreover, enables gospel dancehall artists to imagine themselves as introspective, prophetic, and philosophical by association. And yet none of the artists would consider themselves "conscious" in the Rastafarian sense of the word. In fact, many of these artists' lyrics level heavy charges against Rastafarian ideology and belief, paradoxically invoking the language and sound of Rastafarianism in order to do so. Gospel dancehall artists have, in short, recontextualized this vocabulary for Full Gospel application and are imagining themselves as agents of radical change within the Full Gospel community in Trinidad.

SERIOUS THING, MAN! SOME FINAL REMARKS

In concluding this chapter, I would like to suggest, following Jacques Attali, that Full Gospel dancehall—the noise of Full Gospel Trinidad, the boom-boom music of Jamaica—makes new sense and alternative meaning. I believe, moreover, that the middle and upper classes in Jamaica as well as the church leaders and conservative believers of Trinidad are deeply concerned about this "noise" for good reason, for they sense in the surrounding atmosphere a frightening possibility—one that Attali committed to paper as follows: "A network can be destroyed by noises that attack and transform it, if the codes in place are unable to normalize and repress them."[43] I am reminded again of Anthony "Space" Williams's words: "We are now in a generation where the young are leading the old."

The criticisms leveled against gospel dancehall artists and their fans are designed to sound grave, to imply lack, and to suggest inferiority of both moral and spiritual character. Gospel dancehall artists and fans, however, actively promote precisely those values and theological concerns that the leadership and conservative believers hold dear. Furthermore, most artists do not attempt to defend their music or behavior by engaging directly with criticism, preferring instead to let their music, lyrics, and behavior speak for them. "I don't take them on!" is a common response to my inquiries regarding their lack of response.

That the means by which these spiritual goals and values are achieved is a point of contention and that dancehall is itself a source of conflict within the Full Gospel community is quite clear. Not as readily apparent here are the subtle undercurrents of the critical discourse surrounding gospel dancehall. My analysis thus far has suggested that the rhetoric concerning spirituality and morality reduces in its final analysis to a struggle for power rather than to the moral and theological battle that it is made out to be. The ethics of style, then, traces, in the case of gospel dancehall, neither a discourse about morality nor even about spirituality, but rather a discourse about the will to power.

I should point out that this is strikingly different than the discourse surrounding gospelypso or the poetics of conviction that makes North American gospel music so very appealing within the Trinidadian Full Gospel community. In contradistinction to gospelypso, which directly threatens the actual ethical boundaries set in place by the community, gospel dancehall is understood as a direct threat to the order of things. Once-removed from the moralizing of middle-class Jamaica, that discourse is used here as well but to different ends. In the case of North American gospel music, the reasons for appealing to this style are multiple and driven primarily by questions related to negotiating the biblical mandate to strive for unity in the face of a fractured denominationalism. Connecting to a stream of discourse from North America is, thus, much easier than dealing with local complications. Gospel dancehall does not offer these kinds of connections, but it does threaten the authorizing discourse of North American style (whether language, sound, or fashion) by illustrating in concrete fashion that other possibilities exist. Gospel dancehall artists are chaining themselves to a very different stream of discourse (along with its fashion and language use), and in so doing, they are highlighting the strategic use of these very techniques in the pursuit of North America as sound.

What becomes most uncomfortable as this line of reasoning plays itself out is the implication that church leaders and conservative believers may themselves be found to be disingenuous at some level—that they are becoming (morally and spiritually) what they so broadly indict gospel dancehall artists and fans for being. I would point out, however, that the perspective with which these leaders approach gospel dancehall is one of safeguarding the church and Truth. As such, they consider their task one of authorized policing, and they appeal to Scripture and tradition for guidance in this task. Their frustration here lies in that surveillance and policing—as well as propaganda and polemic—are ineffective against the enthusiastically evangelistic gospel dancehall artists. The frightening prospect here is that the leadership, well intentioned as it no doubt is, finds itself using discourse centered on ethics in an attempt to maintain the politico-religious status quo and to prevent change from occurring too rapidly. The artists themselves, however, believe that the style they have chosen is both good for them and right for the times—a level of conviction which may offer one reason for their persistence in the face of criticism.

One of the multiple ironies of this situation is that both church leaders and gospel dancehall artists appeal to Scripture for authority. Thus, church leaders will quote passages such as Romans 12:2 and interpret it as God's direct message to gospel dancehall artists. "Do not conform any longer to the pattern of this world, but be transformed by the renewing of your mind. Then you will be able to test and approve what God's will is—his good, pleasing and perfect will" (New International Version). Yet gospel dancehall artists and their fans cite this exact verse as one of the passages that inspires them to live counterculturally and to bring the transforming power of the gospel to the world. Or consider the passage in 2 Samuel 6:12–23 that describes King David's dance of praise before God. Gospel dancehall artists consider this text a validation of their unorthodox music, dress, and dance styles.[44] Church leaders, however, respond with passages such as Romans 14:13–23, which stress the importance of living a life that does not cause other Christians to stumble.[45] They then point out that King David's dance caused his wife, Michal, to despise him and led her to stumble into a sinful attitude. Both sides, thus, spiral tightly around this vicious hermeneutic circle, dizzying each other but coming to no clear answers or consensus.

Fear, lack of control, and the gradually eroding cultural base of one generation are, thus, misinterpreted as clear indications that something is fundamentally wrong with the cultural expressions (dancehall culture) of another generation. I believe that this underscores an important aspect of discourse about music in the Trinidadian Full Gospel community, for it illustrates that "ethics" can indeed be enlisted in a struggle quite unrelated to ethical concerns. Full Gospel criticism of dancehall culture in Trinidad provides a case study for the application of theological and moral discourse to musical aesthetics (at best) in order to secure the interests of power. This discourse is, in the final analysis, political. And this state of affairs brings forcibly to mind Alain Badiou's concerns regarding the legitimizing role of ethics within political systems. He writes:

> The modern name for necessity is, as everyone knows, "economics." Economic objectivity—which should be called by its name: the logic of Capital—is the basis from which our parliamentary regimes organize a subjectivity and a public opinion condemned in advance to ratify what seems necessary. Right from the first moment in the constitution of contemporary subjectivity (as "public opinion"), ethics has duly played its accompanying role. For from the beginning it confirms the absence of any project, of any emancipatory politics, or any genuinely collective cause. By blocking, in the name of Evil and of human rights, the way towards the positive prescription of possibilities, the way towards the Good as the superhumanity of humanity, towards the Immortal as the master of time, it accepts the play of necessity as the objective basis for all judgments of value. The celebrated "end of ideologies" heralded everywhere as the good news which opens the way for the "return of ethics" signifies in fact an espousal of the twistings and turnings of necessity, and an extraordinary impoverishment of the active, militant value of principles.[46]

I believe that Badiou's focus on governmental politics can be shifted to the leadership structures of church communities and that necessity, which he describes as the "logic of Capital," can also be understood as the necessity of maintaining power in the face of challenges to the status quo. If this is the case, then gospel dancehall artists are suffering through the "twistings and turnings" of the Full Gospel community's necessity—an espousal that can be understood as a very serious attempt to normalize the "noise" that this style has introduced into the public life of the community. I suggest that this concept can fruitfully be extended to other genres and styles as well. By way of example, consider the harsh indictment by conservative church leaders, when it first appeared during the 1930s, of the gospel blues.[47] Moving beyond the specifically sacred, might not the ethics of style also be useful in analyzing the reception histories of musics such as heavy metal, race records, tango, rave music, and jazz, to name only a few?

It is in this sense that scholars' objections to working in the register of ethics are well taken, for the goal of this discourse is often oriented toward maintaining the status quo and not toward reaching new insights and working toward new meanings. Alain Badiou, John Caputo, and Marjorie Garber, to mention just a few concerned voices, are then quite right to be wary of ethics as it is often used and implicated within politics and religion. I would argue, however, that the bending of ethics to serve as a tool for securing a political or religious will—cynical and common as this undoubtedly is— might be balanced against and countered through the freedom that individuals are able to exercise when facing style and that impossible choice which is placed before them. Put otherwise, the artists who are pursuing gospel dancehall within Full Gospel Trinidad are finding freedom in spite of the systematic attempts at repressing their musical style. I am also convinced that individual members of the Full Gospel community, hailed as they are by these discursive formations, are in the process of identifying (or disidentifying) with gospel dancehall and are, as such, also participating in an essentially ethical process, and this in spite of the discourse seeking to discipline and normalize this noise (dancehall).

If, as I have attempted to illustrate here, the underlying issue facing church leaders is related to their political reservations regarding gospel dancehall and to safeguarding their power interests (necessity), then it is appropriate to conclude this chapter with a few additional thoughts penned by Attali: "Noise carries order within itself; it carries new information. . . . Noise does in fact create a meaning . . . because the very absence of meaning . . . frees the listener's imagination. The absence of meaning is in this case the presence of all meanings, absolute ambiguity, a construction outside meaning. The presence of noise makes sense, makes meaning."[48]

The challenge for gospel dancehall artists, however, remains one of finding a place within the church community while simultaneously exploring, building up, and maintaining a community outside of church walls which functions as an alternative sphere. It strikes me that they will not be able to remain critical of their church community indefinitely, but will need to begin finding strategies for transplanting their own poetics of conviction into the church. A recent song by Sherwin Gardner suggests that this idea is very much on the mind of gospel dancehall artists. This song, "Trendsetters," puts lyrical feet on DJ Space's assertion that the time has come for the young to lead the old.

> We set the trends now
> Following God's steps now.
> Everywhere he goes we go
> He take the lead and we will follow.
> We set the trends now
> Following God's steps now.
> We just want the world to know
> This is the way Flow Masters flow.

God create the music Satan wah pollute it.
Everything God made Satan wanna thief it.
But from the beginning of time
The devil was always behind.
Now he wanna take front ah the line.
Mister Satan you get left behind cause
Everything, everything God created.
Everything, everything!
So when I say we set the trends
I talking to the church and dem.
Cause we and Satan nah no friend.
We got to take our place as the leaders once again . . .
David dance because he was a leader.[49]

But just how Sherwin aims to take his place as a leader remains somewhat uncertain. This process will remain a difficult challenge in the face of the criticism that continues to be directed at the style, for the ethics of style illustrates, in this case, just how deeply ethics has been embedded into political processes in Full Gospel Trinidad. The biggest question, an answer to which only time will reveal, centers around whether these artists will capitulate, compromise, or otherwise give in to this pressure or continue insisting on their own reading of the ethics of style—on living out their own poetics of conviction—until such time as the character of the critical discourse changes to incorporate their interpretation.

6 Jehovah's Music

Jammin' at the Margins
of Trinidadian Gospel Music

> Wherever the revolution begins, is there I want to be
> Tell me are you ready, ready for the revolution?
>
> Sheldon Blackman

In the preceding chapters, I have suggested that the artists and genres under discussion find themselves marginalized within the nation (by belonging to the Full Gospel community) and, to varying degrees, under the umbrella of the Trinidadian Full Gospel community. Those artists who perform primarily North American gospel music are, thus, generally welcomed in their church communities. Gospelypso artists, on the other hand, find themselves in a different space. Their placement might usefully be thought of as doubly marginalized, for they are marginalized within the nation (by their membership in the Full Gospel community) and, subsequently, within the church (by choosing to perform this controversial style). Gospel dancehall artists, for their part, have located themselves with one foot firmly inside and the other tentatively outside of the Full Gospel community. Neither fully rejecting nor entirely embracing their respective congregations, they are exploring the merits of alternative spheres for performance, worship, and community. In short, they remain part of but also somewhat removed from the Full Gospel community. The artist under discussion in this chapter, however, occupies the most radically different space within the nation and in relationship to the Full Gospel community, for this other voice of gospel music in Trinidad remains deliberately and ambiguously in-between the Full Gospel community and the nation, operating at the peripheries of both and fully at home in neither.

The late Ras Shorty I, formerly known as Lord Shorty, is a figure of mythic proportions, and his was a career fraught with multiple paradoxes and radical disjunctures. He is considered the father of soca and is still known as the Love Man by those who followed his career in the 1960s and 1970s. Subsequently, however, he became one of the principal critics of the genre, writing songs such as "Latrine Singers" in order to call attention to what he believed were the dangers related to soca's penchant for sexually oriented lyrics. During the course of about ten years, he adopted an increasingly spiritual approach to his lyrics and lifestyle, calling his compositions from the 1980s onward jamoo music (Jehovah's music).

Ras Shorty I is (in)famous for having experimented with and ultimately incorporated East Indian instruments and rhythms into his music. Much ink has been spilled documenting his lack of sensitivity when writing about East Indian women in songs such as "Indrani." His song entitled "Om Shanti" also generated scandalous attention for what East Indians considered a frivolous use of a Hindu prayer. That criticism did not, however, deter him from later writing a chutney song entitled "Respect Women" or from mixing Rastafarian and Christian ideas as well as Hindi-inspired vocables into his song "Conscious Chutney."

Whereas he was once a commanding personality in calypso circles, he came to be regarded with a measure of skepticism by that group of artists. Prior to his professed conversion to Christianity, the Full Gospel community considered him the poster child of what was wrong with Trinidadian society and calypso. Hard as some tried, the Full Gospel community would, thereafter, never be able unequivocally to accept him into its midst. Ras Shorty I thus remained, for the last twenty years of his life, on the peripheries of both the secular and sacred communities in Trinidad and was not fully accepted by either. And yet he never articulated any clarifications of his position, never defended himself to either group. As I will suggest in the pages that follow, he willingly and deliberately remained entrenched at the outskirts of these two spheres of Trinidadian life, hoping that this strategy might afford him greater influence in both.

This chapter, then, explores the life and music of Ras Shorty I with the goal of coming to a better understanding of how the ethics of style might be brought to bear on analyses of the racial imagination and the poetics of conviction in Trinidad. I also analyze the role that the ethics of style plays in Ras Shorty I's negotiation of nonorthodox evangelical faith at the margins of the nation-state as well as its implication in his appeal to diasporic narratives within postcolonial Trinidad. Before delving into these issues, however, I should like to offer a brief overview of Ras Shorty I's career.

"HOLD ME JESUS, HOLD ME IN YOUR ARMS"

> Another hero is gone, another great loss to mourn.
> But in our memories you live on.
> Sheldon Blackman, "Another Hero Is Gone"

It was a festival of song, an exploration of one man who lived every facet of life and had many talents. Ras Shorty I's funeral service . . . yesterday attracted about 3,000 people dressed in a myriad [of] light colours.

Kim Boodram, *Trinidad Express*

There is perhaps no better place to begin such an overview than with the funeral services held for Ras Shorty I on Wednesday, July 19, 2000. The state-sponsored televised service at the National Cathedral in Port of Spain paid tribute to an artist whose at times controversial career had nevertheless changed the sound and style of music in Trinidad. "Shadow, the calypsonian whose black attire has become his trademark, wore white for Ras Shorty I. So did the hundreds who packed the Holy Trinity Cathedral yesterday for the late singer's funeral."[1] So wrote a journalist from *The Guardian,* who had joined calypsonians, government ministers, representatives of the United Nations, and many others gathered in the Anglican cathedral to celebrate Ras Shorty I's life.

Members of the Trinidad Unified Calypso Association performed the hymn "What a Friend We Have in Jesus."[2] They also provided vocal accompaniment to current and former members of Ras Shorty I's Love Circle as they sang several of their late father's most famous compositions. Super Blue offered tribute by exclaiming, "What Bob Marley was to reggae, Ras Shorty I was to calypso."[3] He then called Ras Shorty I's wife, Claudette Blackman, to his side and sang Bob Marley's "No Woman No Cry."[4] Drumming from Mawasi Experience accompanied the arrival and departure of the casket as well as all of the musical numbers in between.

The cathedral's cantor offered a homily, and the government ministers offered the secular equivalent, announcing that Ras Shorty I's "Watch Out My Children" would be enshrined at the Carnival Institute. This announcement came in response to Prime Minister Basdeo Panday's request that "the necessary steps be taken to ensure [that] Shorty's rich musical legacy [would] be nationally secured."[5] In addition, the resident United Nations representative, Hans Geiser, announced that this same composition was to serve as the theme song for the organization's global drug prevention program. As I attended the two-hour service, I could not help but notice the healing effect that Ras Shorty I's funeral was having on the racial, political, and religious wounds of the nation. For the moment at least, the country was reflecting on the life and work of this artist and rethinking the unifying and spiritual messages that he had expressed in song.

A JAMOO JOURNEY

> Often the good is the enemy of the best. When we knew him
> as Lord Shorty, he was a good man, and the music he sang was
> good. And then, when he moved to the forest and gave his life to
> God, he was the best.
>
> Cantor Winston Joseph

The life and career of Ras Shorty I present an interesting conglomeration of fact and legend—they have, in short, become mythical.[6] Born to Conrad and Nihil Blackman on Sunday, October 5, 1941, Garfield Blackman (Shorty) spent his childhood in Lengua Village, Princes Town. He and his cousin, Herbert Christopher, joined the Lengua Youth Movement around 1959, where they performed with the Southern Harlemites Steel Orchestra, which had been founded by Joseph "Stretch" Collymore. Herbert Christopher remembers, "Shorty was one of the tenor players but he was so talented that in a short space of time, he was playing every pan. Collymore was also a tuner and he tuned the pans in Shorty's presence. Shorty became a tuner himself and also became the arranger when 'Stretch' left."[7] During his years as an active member of the Lengua Youth Movement, Garfield Blackman also began writing calypsos and performing them at the organization's internal competitions.

It did not take long, however, for Garfield Blackman to make a statement on the national calypso scene. In 1961 he appeared as Lord Shorty in the Victoria County Fair at Princes Town.[8] He followed this appearance by writing "Sixteen Commandments" in 1963, and in 1964 he made a strong impression with the song "Cloak and Dagger." By 1965 he was performing for the first time with the Original Young Brigade Tent. The following year, he composed "Long Mango" and the popular song "Indian Singer," and 1968 found him performing as a finalist in the National Calypso Monarch Competition. He followed this success with a semifinalist finish in the 1969 National Calypso Monarch Competition. In 1970 he was crowned the calypso king of San Fernando (south) for his performance of "Mouth Is She Business (Don't Chock She Mouth)."

In 1972 he sang two highly controversial calypsos in the Original Young Brigade Tent. The first was "The Art of Making Love," which he performed with educational choreography. At a Dimanche Gras show attended by Prime Minister Eric Williams, along with Prime Minister Michael Manley of Jamaica and his wife, Dr. Williams took offense at the explicit nature of Lord Shorty's performance. He subsequently initiated a legal inquiry with the attorney general in which he explored censorship options.[9] His second calypso of that season, "Indrani," caused outrage among members of the East Indian community who felt that Lord Shorty was ridiculing the sexuality of East Indian women. He nevertheless won the South Calypso King Competition with these two compositions and sang as a finalist in the National Monarch Competition that year.

Between 1973 and 1978 he was responsible for a string of hits and a radical innovation in the rhythms and instrumentation of calypso. He called the new style "sokah" and incorporated instruments associated with East Indian musical styles, such as the *dholak, dhantal,* and mandolin. In an interview with Roy Burke in 1979, Lord Shorty offered this assessment of his contribution:

> I was trying to find some thing because the talk was that calypso was dying and reggae was the thing. I thought the musicians in the country had a right to get together and use their minds to renew or improve calypso somewhat. Everybody was putting it down. . . . Calypso was dying a natural death. And to come up with a new name and a new form in calypsoul was what Sparrow was trying to do all along. Sparrow tried to add a lot of things to calypso and it didn't work. I felt it needed something brand new to hit everybody like a thunderbolt. . . . I came up with the name soca. I invented soca. And I never spelt it s-o-c-a. It was s-o-k-a-h to reflect the East Indian influence.[10]

Indeed, the idea of using East Indian musical materials had been of particular interest to Lord Shorty for quite some time prior to the release of his seminal sokah compositions. He had, for example, experimented with East Indian materials as early as 1966, the year he composed and performed "Long Mango." His first album-length experiment with sokah was the 1974 release *The Love Man,* which featured Robin Ramjitsingh on the *dholak* and Bisram Moonilal on the mandolin. And yet the song "Endless Vibrations," included on his 1975 album of the same name, is commonly referenced as the first "soca" composition. This might be because it is the first composition in which Lord Shorty abandoned his experiment with East Indian instruments, transferring the rhythmic functions of the *dholak* to the drum kit and substituting a triangle for the sounds of the *dhantal.* In so doing, he arguably assembled the signature sound that has marked soca ever since.[11]

The year 1979 witnessed the release of the album *Soca Explosion,* which included the hit "Om Shanti" and the song "Higher World of Music," his musical tribute to friend and composer Maestro, who had died in an automobile accident earlier in the year. By this time, Lord Shorty was already well on the road to becoming Ras Shorty I. In 1977 he had taken to wearing his hair in dreadlocks and to wearing togas and sandals. In the liner notes to

his album *Children of the Jamoo Journey,* he makes the following statement: "God first called me to service in 1976 while [I was] touring as 'Lord
Shorty & The Vibration International.' I, however, was so immersed in my
folly that I did not give heed to the call. Again in 1977 he touched me even
stronger while on the verge of suicide in Toronto. And by his grace I said,
'Lord, this cannot be life. Oh God, if there is a better way of life show me
and I shall follow you.' He did show me, and I followed."

The spiritually oriented lyrics of songs such as "Om Shanti" and
"Higher World of Music" provide further indication of the significant
change of direction that Lord Shorty was taking in his life. These developments eventually culminated, in 1980, with Lord Shorty's decision to
change his name to Ras Shorty I. He continued to surprise the calypso world
when, in 1981, he moved his family to Piparo and withdrew from tent performances for several years. And it is at this moment of relative uncertainty
and momentous change that the legend and myth of Ras Shorty I began to
grow. By way of example, consider some of the interesting things that jour-
nalists have written about Ras Shorty I's life after about 1980. Here are
some thoughts from a contributor to *Vox Magazine:* "In his testimonies this
acclaimed calypsonian said he had a 'personal revelation' that motivated
him to give up the glamour of the entertainment industry. Together with his
family, he left the debauchery of the urban jungle to lead a more natural life
in Piparo. . . . Convinced that artistes were corrupting the minds of the
masses with dirty lyrics, he vowed to reclaim the music for God. Hence,
Jamoo music—Jehovah's music—was born."[12]

The move to Piparo is here framed as a sacred journey, a pilgrimage that
takes Ras Shorty I away from the "urban jungle" and back to nature. It is
interesting, incidentally, to think about the movement that at this same
time (the late 1970s and early 1980s) was gaining strength in the Bahamas.
By the late 1970s the "stay in the bush" movement began to draw Baha-
mians toward reidentifying and reappropriating those practices and symbols
that might assist them in creating and maintaining a distinct cultural identity.[13] This included dress, music, cuisine, use of language, and a withdrawal
from the urban centers. The idea was to look toward the family islands for
guidance and identity in post-independence Bahamian society.[14]

Ras Shorty I's decision to remove himself, along with his family, to a
remote area of the country—to the bush—is usefully thought of as a sacred
journey. This is especially true since he himself refers to life after his conversion to Christianity as a "Jamoo Journey."[15] It is important, furthermore,
to realize that Piparo has gained a certain currency among Trinidadians as a
place of remove. And I mean this both physically—for it is certainly out of

the way and relatively difficult to get to—and spiritually. As such, Piparo can be considered a sacred center, albeit in a more limited sense than traditional pilgrimage sites. I shall return to this concept in the final section of this chapter.

And yet, lost in many of the narratives of Shorty's conversion and removal to Piparo are the rather stark financial realities that confronted the family at the time. Shorty had recently invested a large sum of money in the production and release of his album *Soca Explosion* (1979), and it had not sold well enough to allow him to recover his loses, rendering him bankrupt and in need of a new start. According to Claudette Blackman, these circumstances, combined with his new sense of spiritual direction, left him with "no choice but to move."[16] This new financial start was also the perfect opportunity to chart a new course as a musician and to develop as a new man of faith. It was, therefore, a conglomeration of factors that led to the move and to the myth that grew around Piparo.

Financial considerations notwithstanding, most accounts of this move focus on the spiritual dimensions of the story, as evidenced by an obituary written for a major British newspaper, which offers the following perspective on Ras Shorty I's sacred journey:

> Few life conversions have been more spectacular than that of the Trinidadian calypsonian and father of soca music, Ras Shorty I. . . . As the notoriously free-living "Lord Shorty," he was the classic Port of Spain "saga boy" in the 1960s and early 1970s, taking part in what he later described as an "orgy of the flesh;" as the self-styled "Love Man," he had a prodigious appetite for women, drink, and drugs. Then, in the late 1970s, he found religion, renounced worldly pleasures and moved deep into the remote Piparo forest in southern Trinidad, 50 miles from Port of Spain. There he built a house, changed his name to Ras Shorty I, grew dreadlocks and lived quietly for the rest of his life with his wife, Claudette, and their 14 children. In Piparo, after a period of Rastafarian-inspired reflection and establishing a new-found faith in Christianity, he gathered together some of his talented children to form his own musical group, the Love Circle, and devoted himself to writing songs about spiritual matters and the dangers of hedonism.[17]

The spiritual side of the man people began to call Ras Shorty I clearly generated some confusion among both secular and sacred communities in Trinidad and, for that matter, around the world. Was this man of Rastafarian persuasion, or did he have a "saving" relationship with Jesus? Did his new-found spirituality necessitate this radical rejection of society, its institutions, and its celebrations? Ras Shorty I, however, consistently leveraged this ambiguity to his advantage, thereby winning fans of decidedly different backgrounds and maintaining a popular currency that would have evaporated had he clarified his position. An excellent example of his ability to walk between and remain equivocal in his theological and ideological convictions can be seen in the unqualified use of the word "spiritual" in many of the editorials that were published around the time of his death. Here is a particularly striking example of this type of writing:

> By the turn of the 1980s Shorty became disenchanted with the very image and music he had created, saying that soca was being used to celebrate the female bottom, rather than uplift the spirits of the people. . . . He turned away from the bright lights, going back to nature. He became Ras Shorty I, *a spiritual person* and took to wearing robes. He also took his children out of school . . . on the premise that the system was not teaching them useful things. He moved into the Piparo forest and began a crusade against the very things for which he had become famous. It is still his campaign.[18]

This excerpt from an article by Terry Joseph of the *Trinidad Express* illustrates just how slippery Ras Shorty I's religious convictions remained to the public, even during his final battle with cancer. Ras Shorty I was "conscious," concerned with morality, and yet somehow there always seemed to be more to his life than that—but exactly what that something was remained rather difficult to define. This deliberate, even studied ambiguity is a major marker of Ras Shorty I's career after 1980, and the music that he composed and performed during these years strengthens this sense of ambiguity. Music is in fact a key factor in Ras Shorty I's pilgrimage, for soon after moving to Piparo, Ras Shorty I began to write and perform with some of his children in a band that he initially called the Home Circle. He coined the term "jamoo" to describe his new emphasis on spiritual matters and to indicate to whom he dedicated this music (Jehovah's music). And even here, a confluence of Judeo-Christian and Rastafarian theology and terminology is evident (ja[h]moo).

This confluence—perhaps juxtaposition is a better word—is also in evidence in a definition of jamoo given by Sheldon Blackman, Ras Shorty I's son and the new leader of the Love Circle following his father's death: "Calypso is the root and foundation of T & T music, which is traditionally an African expression. Soca is the soul of calypso and the combination of East Indian and African rhythms. Rapso is the poetry of calypso and the rap of soca. And Jamoo is *born-again* calypso, soca and rapso and the *consciousness* of Trinidad music and expression."[19] Ras Shorty I soon began calling his family band the Love Circle, and by 1984 he was writing for and performing extensively with the group. Several important songs emerged during the 1980s and '90s, among which are "Watch Out My Children," "Latrine Singers," and "Change Your Attitude." He performed with the band until several months before his death, when he was hospitalized for more intensive medical treatment.

This brief overview of Ras Shorty I's career brings several important themes to the surface. For the purposes of this chapter, these include the politics attendant to naming or labeling genres, the contentious cultural politics within Trinidad, the ambiguous place that Ras Shorty I occupies with regard to popular perceptions of his spirituality, and the accompanying idea of sacred journey. In the pages that follow, I examine each of these themes in order to illustrate the degree to which the ethics of style might usefully be invoked in its analysis.

MUSIC LABELING, OR THE POLITICS OF NAMING

Ras Shorty I twice coined terms intended to describe and label the music that he was creating and performing. More to the point, he was able, twice over, to dictate to his audiences what it was that he was singing and playing. The politics of naming is, at root, informed by issues related to power and legitimacy of one sort or another—by the will to power. Robert Neville observes, "The rhetorical function of names . . . is to lay claim to the legitimating weight of genealogy."[20] Elaborating on the process of naming from a slightly different perspective, David Hall makes the following point: "Reinforcing the weak legitimizing effect of naming, there is the fact that mere persistence tends to legitimate. If we continue telling the same old story [or playing the same new style] we will presume the importance of the tale even if we ourselves are not engaged in it. Inertia is a law of life. What hangs about has authority."[21]

The immediate effects of naming and then performing in a given style might thus take the form of creating a unique niche in the market or achieving semantic, and therefore real, separation from competitors. A new style might also generate controversy, as was the case with sokah, and this controversy translates nicely to publicity. Shannon Dudley reminds us, "The rise of soca incurred a debate, for one thing, about the perils of losing the calypso tradition, and particularly about whether soca singers should be allowed to participate in the adjudicated calypso competition at carnival time."[22]

As time passes, however, Hall and Neville both suggest that the genealogy of the name itself freights the artist's initial efforts with legitimacy. And while the short- and long-term benefits of music labeling are both evident in Ras Shorty I's case, other less obvious issues also seem to be at stake in his creation of the term "sokah" as well as in his invention of the term "jamoo." I should like, therefore, to investigate each of these naming projects in turn, focusing analytical attention, through the ethics of style, on the undercurrents produced in and through the process of naming.

Sokah/Soca

Ras Shorty I has consistently claimed that his main objective in creating soca was to produce a music that blended East Indian and African musical traditions and rhythmic conventions in such a way as to create a music that could usefully and inclusively be called Trinidadian. Born and raised in Lengua Village, which was demographically primarily East Indian, he had from childhood cultivated an affinity for the rhythms and instruments that marked East Indian musics. Even his early calypsos like "Long Mango" (1966) were influenced by East Indian materials. The text concerns Ras Shorty I's advances toward an East Indian girl named Kilwal. The chorus of the song runs as follows: "Ay Kilwal, come and meet me under the mango tree, me ma gone, me pa gone, down dey the mango long."[23]

But apart from obvious textual references such as those in "Long Mango" and from using musical instruments associated with East Indian practices, as was the case with Ras Shorty I's work on *The Love Man*, it is very difficult to provide strong evidence in support of his claim. This difficulty stems from the fact that, although both the lyrics and the sonic textures of East Indian instruments are audible as part of the surface structure of the music, Ras Shorty I has consistently maintained that the deep structure of soca is driven, in part at least, by East Indian rhythmic influences. This assertion has presented significant challenges for scholars studying the rise of soca, its relationship to calypso, and its musical characteristics. Shannon Dudley summarizes the dilemma as follows:

> The exact nature of this [East Indian] influence is difficult to pinpoint. Lord Shorty (now called Ras Shorty I) says that he changed the calypso rhythm by using the rhythms of the East Indian *dholak* drum. Ahyoung is less specific, suggesting that the "pulse anticipation pattern," which often characterizes the kick drum or bass in soca, was likely borrowed from East Indian "chutney" music. However, chutney band leader Ashmead Baksh (of the *Carib Mellow Bugs*) told me that soca predates chutney music and that this *soca* rhythm was borrowed by soca musicians from the moslem East Indian *tassa* drum tradition, a possibility that is also acknowledged by Ahyoung. It remains unclear, then, what rhythmic influence East Indian music had on soca, and in fact the East

Indian influence in soca is much less commonly discussed nowadays
than it was in the early years of soca. . . . Nonetheless, the claim that
East Indian music played an important role in soca's genesis is something
of which most Trinidadians are aware.[24]

Two important points emerge from this passage. First, Dudley makes it
clear that most experts and practitioners cannot trace with any confidence
the actual East Indian sources of Ras Shorty I's inspiration. A brief review
of soca's reception history will illustrate why the ambiguity surrounding
the East Indian influences is so significant. *The Love Man,* released in 1974,
constitutes Ras Shorty I's first album-length exploration of sokah, and it
features East Indian musicians and instruments, placing them prominently
in the mix. Sokah did not create much excitement, however, until after
"Endless Vibrations" was released in 1975, and Ras Shorty I would wait
until his "Sweet Music" became a hit in 1976 before finally shepherding the
style to widespread popular support.

This chronology is important in the narrative of sokah's development because Ras Shorty I introduced a major change to the sonic texture of sokah
between 1974 and 1975. Significantly, the ensemble with which Ras Shorty
I recorded and performed "Endless Vibrations" no longer included East
Indian musical instruments. The rhythmic functions of the *dholak* and the
dhantal were, instead, transferred to instruments already present in the
standard calypso rhythm section, including drum kit and percussion. The
mandolin, moreover, was simply abandoned. Starting in 1975, Ras Shorty I
replaced these sounds and textures with stylistic borrowings from North
American soul and funk, and these are evident in both the arrangements
and the lyrics. This added stylistic material could not help but overshadow
the remaining East Indian elements that he had shifted to the drum kit.
Additionally, Jocelyne Guilbault has pointed out, "According to Ras Shorty
I, some of the musicians, including the keyboard and conga players, found it
too difficult to play the new rhythms and reverted to those they knew
best—the traditional calypso patterns."[25]

These changes, occurring freely during the recording and performing
process, further distanced the sonic qualities of sokah from the compositions
that Ras Shorty I had included on *The Love Man.* And yet the cumulative
effect of these changes led to the widespread acceptance of a new development in calypso—a feat that Shorty had been unable to accomplish with
The Love Man. Guilbault puts it this way: "The mixture of the new
rhythms combined with the traditional ones on *Western* musical instruments not only stopped the controversy about Shorty playing Indian, but

also proved to be a commercial success for his album named *Endless Vibrations.*"[26] The commercial success of this new sound, however, reflects back upon *The Love Man*, raising questions regarding the underlying reasons for that project's lack of commercial viability.

That the word "soca" has consistently been spelled in direct opposition to Ras Shorty I's "sokah" provides an additional avenue toward understanding the critical failure that he experienced with his early experiments in the new style. I am convinced that sokah's lack of commercial success is an indication of the ideological difficulty that Trinidadians had in coming to terms with the East Indian elements that Ras Shorty I had introduced to the music and embedded within the name itself. "Sokah," as defined by Ras Shorty I, is a contraction that fuses Calypso ("so") and the syllable "kah," which represents the first consonant in the Hindi alphabet. The spelling of that label, however, was to change, reflecting the influence of North American soul and funk on the music. Guilbault, discussing the timing of this change, makes the following observation: "It is interesting to note that it is precisely at the time when the changes of instrumentation took place that the spelling of 'sokah' was changed to 'soca' by a journalist who, according to Ras Shorty I, began his story with the headline: 'Shorty is doing soca.' In the process, the interpretation of the term 'soca' no longer made reference to the East Indian contribution, and instead proposed to see the term so-ca as the contraction of the musics believed to be at its foundation, namely, the fusion of soul (so) and calypso (ca)."[27]

Accordingly, the musical roots of soca, from about 1975 on, have consistently been misread as soul and calypso.[28] This misreading suggests that Ras Shorty I may have indeed struck a fault line within Trinidadian society. I maintain that North American influences on the musical style were more easily assimilated into the racial imagination of audiences in Trinidad than East Indian elements. It is also interesting to realize that this misreading occurred just at the moment that "Endless Vibrations" became a hit, paving the way for a groundswell of public support by removing the racialized obstacle from the name itself. Ras Shorty I, finally realizing some critical acclaim for his work and clearly deviating to some degree from his initial project, did not object to the new spelling, thereby allowing soca to become the standard label for the genre that he had initiated.

This misreading goes a long way toward illustrating a point that Ahyoung makes in his discussion of soca's reception history, for he suggests that the primary reason for soca's acceptance stems from its close conformity to the African aesthetics of local music producers and the general population: "The calypso tradition has a dominant African base, and if these traits [soca rhythms] were indeed rekindled by East Indian influence, they were only accepted because of their similarity to familiar African traits, and their ability to be incorporated in the African conceptualization underlying the tradition."[29]

Thus, any elements of East Indian origin were, according to Ahyoung, necessarily subsumed under an African umbrella, thereby relegating them to a less than equal share in the rhythmic and musical base that makes soca work as popular music. And this brings to the foreground a serious inequity of value residing at the heart of the Trinidadian music industry, one which Ras Shorty I claimed to be addressing with sokah and yet did not manage to solve. Soca, moreover, provided him a means musically of sidestepping this inequity while continuing to claim he was addressing it. I will return to this dilemma in the following section.

The second point that Dudley's summary brings to the surface is the simple fact that most Trinidadians are *aware* of the "claim that East Indian music played an important role in soca's genesis."[30] So, in spite of the ambiguous and ill-defined status of East Indian rhythmic materials and the deliberate silencing of East Indian genealogy in the misreading of sokah as soca, Trinidadians are generally aware of this claim. I consider this general understanding as evidence that the genealogy of naming has taken effect in the form of legitimacy. Put differently, Shorty told the "same old story" long enough to legitimize it and then moved the style into a new phase, not only by his own example in "Endless Vibrations" but also by allowing the misreading of the genre's name to stand without protest. His own compositions do indeed stake out both the original, East Indian-influenced sokah and the more comfortable, North American–inspired soca.[31]

This is the precise point at which the ethics of style becomes important to the discussion, for Shorty's original claim is enough to project the style into an entirely different discursive framework. The claim itself sets the style apart as, if nothing else, an attempt at an ethical project driven by his own poetics of conviction. And this brings to mind some additional thoughts penned by Jocelyne Guilbault:

> What is needed . . . is to look at music labels as "devices which are used . . . to produce statements through which other objects are constructed, and hence, other sets of issues are addressed." In other words, we must look at music labels not only in relation to the musical practices they attempt to describe and prescribe, but also in relation to the other statements that are made through them. . . . Indeed, to talk about music labels means to talk about much more than commercially marketable musical categories . . . in many cases it means to talk about the

promotion of a philosophy, the vindication of a principle, or the claim to a public space; and . . . through the expression of these various positionings, it means to talk about the setting into motion of particular social relations, networks and alliances, as well as the emergence of cleavages and resentment.[32]

So, while Ras Shorty I's efforts did not succeed immediately in stabilizing the racialized fault line along which he initially conceived sokah, he did stake out the geography of a project to which he would later return. Although soca took on a life of its own beginning in the second half of the 1970s, there continues to be a strong sense that the genealogical roots of the genre are grounded in Ras Shorty I's attempt to propose a new approach to social and racial relations among Trinidadians. As I will illustrate below, Ras Shorty I's attempts at making this a reality, at times in poor taste and occasionally misunderstood, were often greeted with controversy. Toward the end of the 1970s, however, Ras Shorty I began seriously to struggle with spiritual matters and progressively to withdraw from his former life as the Love Man. It was during this time that he also began to work toward framing his ethical project differently, and it is to a brief exploration of this process that I now turn.

Jamoo

Jamoo is Ras Shorty I's second attempt at music labeling, and the most interesting aspect of this project is that it finds him returning to themes that he was working with during the early sokah years. Before I illustrate the parallel nature of early sokah and jamoo, a bit of definition is necessary. I turn first to the thoughts of Sheldon Blackman:

> It seems as if we've lost the sense of what music is really for. The music only directs us to jump up. It makes us feel everything is OK, so have a good time. It doesn't tell us about our life, what is going on, where we are to go. It keeps us in a state of sleep. My call is for other young people to unite and change what is happening. . . . We have problems in this country, but the music must encourage us to face them, not just prance and charge all over the place.[33]

The purpose of jamoo, then, is directed at generating social activism. But there is more to the project: "We found that youths and the elders have gotten caught up in Jamaican and American music and have forgotten about our music, thinking that it is only for carnival. We are saying that our music is for us and the rest of the world for all time. We must love and respect it. We have to recognize that we can express ourselves spiritually, with praise to God."[34]

These words are very reminiscent of the sentiments that Ras Shorty I offered in his 1979 *Carnival* magazine interview with Roy Burke. The recurring theme is a concern for a local and locally appreciated musical style, and this concern seems to have engendered jamoo in much the same way as it originally led to the creation of sokah. Sheldon Blackman told me, "Shorty never stopped playing soca. He found the spiritual aspect of soca and blended it to create jamoo."[35] There is a sense in which jamoo can be read as a revisiting of old themes, as a new attempt at recovering the same project. And this revisiting is cast in spiritual terms in a short definition offered by Sheldon: "[Jamoo is] born again rapso, calypso and soca. It is the conscious aspect of the music of Trinidad and Tobago."[36] The spiritual rebirth of Ras Shorty I is, thus, linked to his postconversion approach to music, social concerns, and cultural politics. This is the approach that I wish to analyze for the remainder of the chapter.

While Ras Shorty I does not use East Indian instruments in jamoo, the texture of the musical sound is altered significantly from that of soca. For example, the jamoo sound is somewhat unique in that it places an acoustic guitar at the center of the rhythm section. This treatment of the guitar stands in contradistinction to contemporary soca, which utilizes an electric guitar in that role. By using an acoustic guitar, Ras Shorty I not only creates a distinctively roots-oriented sonic quality but also puts in mind the role of the acoustic guitar in the music of the early calypsonians. There are several other characteristics of jamoo music that should be mentioned here. First, the call-and-response structures between lead singer and chorus are emphasized in this style, recalling specifically African performance practices. Second, the bass guitar is free to explore rhythmic patterns that extend beyond the conventions of soca style.[37] The bass guitar lines are, moreover, quite melodic in character, performing countermelodies and exploring a wider range of possibilities than do conventional soca and calypso bass lines. This allows Ras Shorty I to introduce a wide range of styles, including reggae, jazz, rapso, and chutney into his jamoo compositions. Finally, because of the great flexibility that Ras Shorty I builds into jamoo, jamoo might best be understood as an approach to music making rather than a clearly defined performance style. It is, in Sheldon's words, "the conscious aspect of music in Trinidad." This flexibility allows Ras Shorty I to carve out a great deal of space within which to respond to the other gospel musics circulating in Trinidad and to the calypso scene that he has left behind.

When compared to the other styles of gospel music in Trinidad, jamoo is unique in that it rejects as irrelevant the ethical concerns that occupy the various genres discussed earlier. This is accomplished through a combination of several stylistic choices. First, jamoo delegitimizes the claims of North American Pentecostalism through an emphasis on African and Caribbean musical and cultural heritage, making an explicitly historicist claim in the process (in other words, "we were here long before you were"). Second, jamoo places regional musics like dub and reggae alongside a number of other stylistic influences, thereby illustrating that it is not a primary influence or even a secondary concern but rather a style (like any other) to be used in the creation of local music. Finally, Ras Shorty I attempts to broaden the scope of what can or should be considered local through a deliberate focus on East Indian musical materials. To that end, both of his jamoo albums include at least one chutney composition. He also gravitates toward emerging styles. For example, both of his albums include at least one rapso composition, a relatively recent style of soca (at the time) that utilizes rapped lyrics.

The most revealing aspect of this vision of gospel music in Full Gospel Trinidad, however, is the careful balancing of the spiritual and spatial/physical dimensions of life that Ras Shorty I achieves, first through deliberately referencing African heritage and then by clearing space for a larger conception of the local. The implicit critique of the artificial separation of these dimensions in the other musical approaches coupled with Ras Shorty I's rejection of the very terms of their ethical concerns continues to generate a great deal of intensity within the local gospel music industry. In order to explore these tensions, I turn to a discussion of several of the themes related to jamoo's positioning within Trinidad.

RACIALIZED OTHERS

> Everywhere you turn today you hear of "us" and "them," Afro
> and Indo, one religion against another. . . . We are fiercely divided
> into racial, religious, and political camps. Sometimes it's a com-
> bination of all three.
>
> Vernon Ramesar

Ras Shorty I has consistently chosen to incorporate East Indian elements into his musical performances and, in much the same way as David Hall suggests, Ras Shorty I's use of these materials quite simply remained in the air long enough to begin to lay claim to a certain genealogy of legitimacy.[38] I am convinced that, in spite of his penchant for generating controversy, Ras Shorty I genuinely sought to bridge the racial gaps that he witnessed in post-independence Trinidad. Instead of settling for a version of Dr. Eric William's multiculturalism, which required "no mother India, no mother Africa, no mother China, or mother Syria, but only mother Trinidad" but nevertheless fostered a "mother Trinidad" that was primarily Afro-Trinidadian in both cultural and social terms, Ras Shorty I set out to juxtapose culturalisms of both African and South Asian origin within his own work.[39] The problem with his early attempts at doing this, however, stems from the highly stereotyped manner in which he applied his ideas, for instead of illustrating the value of both African and East Indian culturalisms, Ras Shorty I succeeded only in diminishing the East Indian contributions to Trinidadian culture.

Not surprisingly, this project did not engender positive reactions among either the East Indian or Afro-Creole communities in Trinidad. I offer just a few examples here in order to illustrate this point. Helen Myers observes, "In 1972, the famous Afro-calypsonian, Lord Shorty, scandalized Trinidad Indians by wearing on stage an Indian woman's garment, the *ohdani*, which has special significance as a protector of female privacy—a gambit that could hardly help to achieve rapprochement between the races."[40] To make matters worse, the song that he was singing at the time was "Indrani." Keith Warner points out the following about this song:

> Shorty, who claimed that he had "grown up with East Indians in Lengua Village," angered sections of the Indian community by appearing on stage decked in *ohrni* and other obvious Indian accoutrements. In addition, he was still then [1972] known for his very suggestive, sexually-oriented lyrics, so the calypso ["Indrani"] was seen as yet another attempt to drag the Indian woman down into the gutter. Shorty would later (1979) try to redeem himself with *Om Shanti* but ran into even more trouble because he was seen as desecrating something held in reverence by large sections of the Indian community, specifically the Sanatan Dharma Maha Saba.[41]

The lyrics of "Indrani," much like those of "Long Mango," are humorously stereotyped and, thus, spelled trouble for Ras Shorty I. He writes about an East Indian grandmother's advances on him, implying that they occur mostly after she has been drinking rum:

> She so persistent, like a real spoilt brat.
> Maybe is love she want,
> But I feel she too old for dat.
> But the emphasis on the words "Lay low" to me
> Seem to consist some suggestivity.

The lyrics go on to claim that he has always thought of her as a respectable, religious woman but that her continual demands to "lay low" are making him wonder about her intentions. The chorus, for its part, incorporates Hindi vocables in an approximation of East Indian language patterns. Even though the ensemble that performed this song included East Indian instruments, the content of the lyrics generated controversy. Humor and irony, two of the staples of calypso, were thus derailed by the effects of stereotyping. Michael Herzfeld, discussing the dangers of stereotypes, makes the following observation: "The act of stereotyping is by definition reductive, and, as such, it always marks the absence of some presumably desirable property in its object. It is therefore a discursive weapon of power. It does something, and something very insidious: it actively deprives the 'other' of a certain property, and the perpetrator pleads moral innocence on the grounds that the property in question is symbolic rather than material, that the act of stereotyping is 'merely' a manner of speech, and that 'words can never hurt you.'"[42]

And this is precisely the ground upon which Ras Shorty I initially attempted to include East Indian elements into his music. That his first album-length attempt at sokah was a commercial failure attests to the fact that both Afro-Creoles and East Indians in Trinidad were unable to reconcile the competing claims in his music. On the one hand, there is a clear attempt to create a new sound. This was accomplished with the help of East Indian musicians and musical instruments. On the other hand, however, his lyrics and stage antics traded on stereotypes that undermined the claims to validity of his stylistic innovations. It was, therefore, not until he abandoned the East Indian components of his ensemble that soca was able to attain to popular success. Even so, Ras Shorty I continued to be concerned about social integration and the well-being of post-independence Trinidad. This concern is evident in his composition "Om Shanti" (1979).

This song is the first time that Ras Shorty I used his lyrics to express something positive about—and to assign a high value to—East Indian contributions to Trinidadian society. He accomplished this by writing a song that incorporated the popular Om Shanti mantra. The English translation follows:

> This is perfect, that is perfect.
> Take perfect from perfect,
> The remainder is perfect.
> May peace and peace and peace be everywhere.[43]

Ahyoung summarizes the musical accompaniments, pointing out that he used "an organ solo played in the higher register, with a sound that simulates the harmonium and violin role in the East Indian ensemble. . . . [He also used] unison which creates the presence of homophony . . . microtones and a melismatic Indian singing style."[44] By combining these techniques with the lyrics, Ras Shorty I is able to create a song that privileges East Indian elements. An excerpt follows:

> Life today, unlike yesterday.
> Friendship gone leaving hate and scorn.
> Neighbor living like stranger with neighbor,
> No love, sir, no love, sir for one another.
> To unite people as one ah create a song,
> Ah hope it live on from generation to generation.[45]

Although this song is clearly a much more effective vehicle for achieving the goals that Ras Shorty I articulates—"to unite people as one"—his recent past as the Love Man and his earlier failures with incorporating East Indian elements in his music predictably created significant barriers to the song's acceptance. Hindus in particular were offended by his use of a sacred text in a soca song. And yet this song signals a move toward redefining his approach to East Indian materials. In fact, it constitutes one of his first experiments with the approach that he would take in his later jamoo compositions. This song can, thus, usefully be viewed as the bridge from sokah to jamoo. Ahyoung's assessment of Ras Shorty I's development offers a key to this change: "Shorty began his career with a focus on sexual themes. Then with the advent of soca, he changed to the soca theme and was concerned mainly with advertizing, propagating, or selling his new product as forcefully as possible. Now in this later period when Shorty and the soca style are securely established, his themes tend to focus on universal themes like peace and love."[46]

Ras Shorty I's jamoo compositions, indeed, followed on this trajectory and even took it one step further. While he continued to write songs that specifically referenced East Indian performance genres, such as the song entitled "Conscious Chutney," he also began to realize that this needed to be balanced by compositions that articulated his concern for national unity without recourse to East Indian elements. In other words, he began to separate out his main objective from his abiding interest in East Indian musical elements. In so doing, he began to write songs that expressed these principles without overt East Indian references, a strategy that afforded him the chance to articulate his concerns without generating controversy over the appropriateness of the materials. An example of this type of song is "Ah Love You So," which clearly outlines Ras Shorty I's thoughts about racial unity in Trinidad.[47] A brief excerpt follows:

> It is because of unity, through the love of the Almighty
> Trinidad and Tobago is standing.

Through the length and breadth of the land, Indian, Chinese, and
    African,
Syrian and Caucasian, one nation.
In T&T all of we is one family! Real family!
Trinidad and Tobago, how ah love you so.
Many races and cultures combined together we stand.[48]

Ras Shorty I thus indicates his desire for a unified Trinidad by projecting
it onto the country as if it were already a reality. I maintain that his approach
to dealing with the racial imagination in Trinidad has been refined by the fire
of controversy and through the process of learning to live in-between the
nation and the Full Gospel community, a subject that I take up in the next
section of this chapter. Before doing so, however, I should like to conclude this
portion of the chapter by turning to the words of Ronald Radano and Philip
V. Bohlman. In a discussion of the racial imagination, they make an important point that is borne out in the music of Ras Shorty I: "The power of
musical ownership that is so essential to the racial imagination has an extraordinary global presence. In the most universal sense, the condition whose
presence is the most global is that of authenticity, the assertion that a particular music is ineluctably bound to a given group or a given place."[49]

I maintain that Ras Shorty I initially attempted to accomplish a bridging
of cultures by appropriation, a strategy that failed in rather glorious fashion.
Undeterred, he continued to believe, as do Radano and Bohlman, that
"music has the power to undo the historical aporia of silence."[50] For too
long, Ras Shorty I had witnessed the devastating effects of racial tensions, a
state of affairs that he wished to see changed in Trinidad. This led him to
approach the same issues from a different musical perspective, no longer
working with stereotypical musical materials but instead attempting to raise
awareness regarding what he considered a dangerous racial fault line. In his
jamoo compositions he moved closer to accomplishing this through his carefully written lyrics and his unique subject position within the nation. Unlike
gospelypso, which implicitly posits an Afro-Creole cultural identity for Full
Gospel Trinidad, and in contradistinction to North American gospel music
and gospel dancehall, both of which deflect these difficult questions without
addressing them, jamoo illustrates a sustained attempt at speaking to questions of racial unity and cultural politics in Trinidad.

THE SOCIAL POETICS OF AMBIGUITY

I turn now to a closer investigation of Ras Shorty I's jamoo years. From
1980 until the early 1990s Ras Shorty I was relatively quiet on the national

calypso scene, although he did occasionally perform at carnival tents, often at the request of Hollis "Chalkdust" Liverpool at the Spectakulah Tent. His withdrawal to Piparo in 1981 afforded him the chance to begin working toward a new approach to performance and also distanced him from the calypso scene. Suspicious of denominationalism and its discontents, he never joined a church community—a decision that cast doubt on the validity of his conversion among Full Gospel believers. This decade, then, found Ras Shorty I relatively isolated from and in between both communities. This state of affairs suited Ras Shorty I, for he chose to remain in this liminal space—to perform within what Herzfeld has called a militant middle ground. "Militant because it is forever threatened by our desire for closure and hermetic definition; middle because it struggles to escape the overdetermination of binarism; and ground because it is indeed grounded in the direct, empirical evidence of ethnography."[51] Jamoo defies hermetic definition, struggles against the binarism of nation versus Protestantism, and is grounded in Ras Shorty I's own life.

Even his lyrics suggest that he understood this militant middle ground to be his place within Trinidad. For example, in a song entitled "Sing Anything" he applies a prophetic verse from the prophet Isaiah to himself, saying, "I am the voice of one crying in the wilderness."[52] I should like to illustrate how this studied ambiguity functions in Ras Shorty I's song texts. An excellent example is found in his most celebrated jamoo composition, "Watch Out My Children." The song is an expression of Ras Shorty I's fatherly concern for his children, who in this case include the people of Trinidad. Ras Shorty I is concerned that drug use will lead his country's population to "shame and disgrace." The following is from the song:

> Watch out my children, watch out my children.
> It have a fella called Lucifer with a bag of white powder
> And he don't want to powder your face,
> But to bring shame and disgrace to the human race.

The verses go on to encourage his "children" to be careful in the face of temptations and to encourage them to "sober thinking," which results in righteousness, happiness, and even "spiritual bliss." Important here is that spirituality is brought into play without foregrounding a specific religious paradigm—he is, in short, nurturing the ambiguity surrounding his own spiritual life. The song's reference to Lucifer is easily read as a general symbol of evil, whereas "righteousness" and "spiritual bliss" are both ambiguous enough to evade specific referential character. This studied avoidance of a specific and clear use of Full Gospel terminology allows Ras Shorty I to attain the status of crossover. And this is, of course, precisely what happened with the song. As I pointed out earlier, this song has been enshrined at the Carnival Institute of Trinidad and Tobago, was a radio hit during 1989, and has been adopted for use as the theme song of the United Nations' antidrug campaigns. Ras Shorty I attempted to walk a similar line with other songs. Take, for example, the lyrics of "Blessed Are the Elders," written by Sheldon Blackman for the Love Circle:

> In communities must have babies and elderlies beyond their 50s.
> No lie, no lie!
> And even mommy and my daddy learned from grandpa and granny.
> No lie, no lie!
> They say wisdom come from age and youth with bursting energy.
> Just remember this philosophy. Without the root you don't have a tree.
> You see,
>
> Blessed are the elders for they hold the keys of experience.
> Blessed are the elders for they are like trees of endurance.
> Blessed are they, blessed are they!
> So we appreciate their opinion, we celebrate their wisdom.
> Blessed are they, blessed are they!
>
> When an elder and a youngster work together they bound to prosper.
> No lie, no lie!
> New technology has credibility and experience is maturity.
> No lie, no lie!
> So if you want productivity then we must live in harmony.
> Promote the right of equality and respect for all humanity.[53]

In evidence here is the conscious side of Ras Shorty I.[54] He is clearly concerned about the social health of his nation and expresses it in spiritually charged but ambiguous fashion. He is able, in other words, to make his main point without preaching a sermon. This strategic use of language does not satisfy most Trinidadian Full Gospel believers, who consider it nothing more than social activism. Ras Shorty I, however, made a very deliberate effort to remain in a position of relevance within Trinidadian society, a goal that he could not have achieved had he attempted to satisfy the Full Gospel community.

A final example of Ras Shorty I's use of language is found in the song "One Partner," in which he calls attention to the growing AIDS epidemic sweeping the Caribbean region and offers his suggested remedy. A portion of the text follows:

> When Adam was created one woman was designated.
> Not two not three, only he and she.

We in trouble in the Caribbean, our people facing extinction.
This dreaded HIV destroying we.
One partner, one partner! It's time to consider.

According to Ras Shorty I, there is a misconception of manhood circulating in the Caribbean, the logic of which requires a man to have more than one woman in order to garner respect. He counters this by admonishing the youth of the Caribbean to think of the fact that this misconception could wind up killing them if they contract HIV. When compared to the compositions and lifestyle that earned Ras Shorty I the sobriquet the Love Man, this song might come as a surprise, might even be read as hypocritical. And yet no Trinidadian who knew the Love Man and then watched his transformation into Ras Shorty I could doubt his sincerity. Trinidadian Full Gospel believers, however, feel that the lyrics leave too much unsaid. A typical point of view is expressed by Anthony Moses: "You have to bring the truth of the Word of God to the people. The Word of God saves!"[55] The lyrics of Ras Shorty I's song are, in Anthony's opinion, too concerned with physical health and not concerned enough with spiritual health. This is an interesting assessment when considered against the backdrop of Anthony's own, gnostic understanding of the body (see chapter 4).

This type of criticism from Full Gospel ranks did not, however, deter Ras Shorty I; nor does it seem to matter to his son, Sheldon Blackman, who assumed leadership of the Love Circle following his father's death in July of 2000. The Love Circle continues to sing songs whose lyrics are directed at a broad audience and targeted at social concerns in the hope of creating positive change in Trinidad. A brief example from the band's album *Remember Me* illustrates this well. The song is entitled "Seeking Is My Home":

Seeking is my home, knowledge is my bed.
Wisdom understanding is my pillow, it's where I rest I head.
Seeking is my home, knowledge is my bed.
Wisdom understanding is my pillow, it's where I rest I head.
Ah doh sleep to dream, ah dream to change the world.
Ah doh sleep to dream, ah dream to change the world.[56]

These types of songs make up only a portion of Ras Shorty I's jamoo compositions, but they are representative of the ones that have found their way into public consciousness. Ras Shorty I and the Love Circle have, thus, become associated with conscious lyrics and with concerns that fall into the social as opposed to strictly spiritual realm. A final example is instructive in this regard, for it is clearly more explicitly invested in the spiritual wellbeing of the nation than any of the previous examples. It is entitled "You Push the Creator Out" and deals specifically with the government's decision to remove religious education from the curriculum of government schools.

> All yuh push di creator out.
> Yuh didn't want he name in yuh mouth.
> So yuh take him out of di school curriculum.
> No knowledge of God for your children.

The verses cast the nation's rising crime rate as a direct consequence of the government's decision regarding religious education. They go on to mention that each generation builds on the knowledge of the preceding one and ask Trinidadians to reflect on what exactly their children and grandchildren will be in a position to know spiritually. Even this song, however, does not explicitly reference Full Gospel theology—it merely implies it. Once again, the nation is made aware of an issue that, for Ras Shorty I, constitutes a threat to its spiritual wellbeing. But it is made aware of this issue without recourse to reifying and narrow theological vocabulary. In light of the various examples I have presented, I suggest that Ras Shorty I deliberately played on the ambiguities of language in order to appeal to the greatest possible audience.

And this brings me to the concept of social poetics. Ras Shorty I, by resorting to this strategy, was able to remain at once a member of the community and to assert his own unique place within it. Herzfeld articulates social poetics as a type of action: "Poetics means action, and restoring that etymological awareness would also more effectively integrate the study of language into an understanding of the role of rhetoric in shaping and even creating social relations."[57] But it is action deployed to a specific end. Herzfeld defines it as "the analysis of essentialism in everyday life."[58] Ras Shorty I's ability to insert analysis into the life of the nation by calling attention to the ways in which the cultural politics hinder post-independence community is, in my view, an excellent example of social poetics. That he deployed this analytical tool in musical form and from a position of in-betweenness only served to widen the audience at which he was able to direct it. Ras Shorty I, then, moved from essentialist and stereotyped forms of address to a much more subtle and effective means of communication based on social poetics and predicated on his own ambiguous position within Trinidadian society.

For example, his composition "You Push the Creator Out" can be read by Trinidadians as a complaint against the decisions of the government and is, furthermore, nonspecific with regard to who that creator actually is. Ras Shorty I also ties the lack of religious education in the public schools directly to the increase of violence and crime within Trinidadian society. And yet there is a sense in which the lyrics, by extension, also cry for personal responsibility and action. As such, Trinidadians, irrespective of ethnicity and religious affiliation, are able to identify with his appeal to spirituality and, in so doing, find themselves in a better position to identify with each other. And this stands in direct contradistinction to his earlier work, such as "Indrani," which tended, for obvious reasons, to polarize opinion and hinder progress toward unity or mutual understanding.

SACRED JOURNEY AND THE LIFE OF THE NATION

This brief engagement with the life and music of Ras Shorty I reveals his strategic deployment of music labeling as well as ambiguity in order to achieve certain political goals and to introduce a set of ethical concerns to the nation. A few thoughts about the nature of Ras Shorty I's withdrawal to Piparo provide a means of bringing this chapter to a close. Philip V. Bohlman, in discussing the concept of the sacred journey as it plays out in the pilgrimages of the New Europe, makes the following observations: "In many religions, particularly in the major world religions, pilgrimage is understood generally as a journey from the daily life of the individual, the mundane and quotidian, so to speak, to a sacred world. . . . The sacred journey, when successfully completed, reconfigures time, transforming the timeboundedness of this world into the timelessness of the world beyond."[59]

The previous sections of this chapter have made clear that Ras Shorty I did spend a considerable number of years (from the late 1970s through the early 1980s) coming to grips with his spirituality. By 1980 this spiritual journey had taken him away from Port of Spain (the secular world) and toward Piparo (the sacred remove). It was there that jamoo was conceived and deployed as a new musical style. It was from this base that he drew the strength to remain ambiguously in-between the two communities to which he was addressing his music. It was in Piparo that the transformation from stereotyped and essentialist expressions of the Trinidadian racial imagination, as evidenced in his early calypso and sokah compositions, gave way to a more thoughtful and carefully articulated form of social poetics.

As significant as the removal to Piparo was to Ras Shorty I, it was equally important for the nation. Without this withdrawal, it would have been even more difficult for Ras Shorty I to distance himself from his reputation as the Love Man. In the absence of this withdrawal, there would have been very little interest in Ras Shorty I's spiritual journey. Pilgrimage as spectacle and event, pilgrimage as life-changing movement, is therefore at the heart of the public's belief in Ras Shorty I's conversion. It is part of his testimony—a physical and visible exclamation of his spiritual struggle.

As such, his music takes on an interesting position within the Trinidadian Full Gospel community. I have already illustrated the reasons for Full Gospel skepticism with regard to Ras Shorty I's faith, but the very nature of pilgrimage music suggests another, deeper cause for suspicion. Bohlman puts it as follows: "Essential to the power of song texts in pilgrimage is their non-liturgical character; pilgrimage songs do not fit easily into the usual services of the religious calendar or within its dominant institutions. Not only do pilgrimage songs fail to lend themselves to use within liturgy, but they may challenge the order and power of liturgy to serve as the text for central ritual."[60]

Jamoo can, I believe, be understood as pilgrimage music.[61] This assertion is underscored by Ras Shorty I's song "Long Road." The lyrics caution that "it's a long, long road climbing up ahead," and that "people are walking the road but with a double line. They say it's too rough, it's too hard for them, they want an easy road to walk in. But I told them already it's a long road and you must have faith you must be strong." This song, which serves as a narrative of pilgrimage as well as for the Christian life as a whole, can be made to stand in for the position that jamoo occupies in Full Gospel Trinidad.

By refusing to affiliate himself with a denomination, by deliberately writing to a broad audience and refusing to limit his lyrics in specifically Full Gospel ways, Ras Shorty I ensured that jamoo would fulfill the role of pilgrimage music. On the one hand, it is indeed nonliturgical, and it most certainly illustrates his resistance to dominant institutions. On the other hand, however, it is placed within the precise domain that Ras Shorty I wished to influence. For jamoo finds itself in the popular religious sphere and, as such, attracts its share of pilgrims. The ethics of style here reveals Ras Shorty I deploying music in order to confront both nation and Full Gospel community with an alternative range of ideas and meanings, a range that challenges their respective positions and entrenchments and forces listeners to reconsider long-standing social, religious, and political patterns.

In some respects, it remains to be seen what Sheldon Blackman will do with jamoo. During the years since his father passed away, he has worked in between Trinidad and Europe, and because of his long absences, he turned leadership of the Love Circle over to his younger brother Isaac in 2002. Sheldon's follow-on work to *Remember Me*, however, seems to indicate that he aims to remain firmly rooted at the outskirts of both Trinidad and

Europe and to continue moving about at the edges of formal religious institutions. Not afraid to "jam" away at the margins of Trinidadian gospel music, he is writing conscious lyrics, of which a good example is his recent song "Anything":

> We can do anything we want, we just have to want to do it.
> Never underestimate the power of your mind.
> Never underestimate the power of your will, oh no!
> Never underestimate the power of your mind.
> Never underestimate the power of choices.
> We have the greatest power dwelling in our hands.
> Never put a limit to the things you can achieve.
> Never ever doubt yourself you just have to believe.
> Never put a limit to the things you can achieve.
> Never ever doubt the gift of life you have received.[62]

Isaac, for his part, produced his first Love Circle album, *Home Grown*, in 2003, and his work with the band remains firmly in the tradition set by his father. By way of example, the band included a previously unreleased composition by Ras Shorty I entitled "One Day Congotay." Sung by Claudette Blackman, the lyrics address the difficult issue of spousal abuse in Trinidad:

> The way some men does treat women makes me wonder
> If they fall from the sky or if they born from a mother.
> They beating the woman as if she's some beast of burden.
> No love no consideration no kind of reason.

The lyrics then go on to promise that the man will pay one day (that is the definition of the word "congotay") and to remind the man that his pattern of horrible mistreatment could, in the future, be repeated—that even his little daughter is a potential victim of this type of abuse. It is a call to responsibility. The lyrics illustrate further Ras Shorty I's concern over the health of his community.

Isaac's own solo work is experimental, combining jamoo with a wide variety of sounds and styles (including hip-hop, urban, neo-soul, and alternative feels). In an important sense, however, this remains entirely in the spirit of his father's own explorations and faithful to the open approach that jamoo instantiates. His first solo project, *In Your Eyes*, provides a glimpse into future possibilities for jamoo, and he has also worked on collaborative projects with his friend Sherwin Gardner and his brother-in-law, Mark Mohr of Christafari, in an effort to launch the jamoo sound beyond the borders of his family and the Love Circle.

The ethics of style, here, is bound up in the convictions that Ras Shorty I lived out in his daily life. Because he removed himself from and maintained such an ambiguous relationship to institutionalized religion, the discourse surrounding jamoo never reached the critical levels that gospel dancehall and gospelypso experienced. His career, moreover, illustrates a reversal of the trend I pointed out in chapter 4—a trend that also generated very little critical discourse, but in this case because North American gospel music was accepted into Trinidadian practice relatively easily. Ras Shorty I found a means of remaining just far enough removed from the Full Gospel community to avoid the storm of discourse that faces gospelypso and gospel dancehall artists, a strategy that allowed him to pursue his own agenda by applying his poetics of conviction to the social and spiritual concerns he wished to address in Trinidad.

7 Reenvisioning Ethics, Revisiting Style

I am sitting on Roddie's front porch in Fanny Village, Point Fortin, participating in an intense debate that does not appear to be coming to a close anytime soon. The participants include Roddie, his son Kevin, and myself. Kevin is twenty-five years old and works as a structural engineer for a company based in San Fernando. Although he lives in San Fernando, he still considers Mt. Beulah Evangelical Baptist Church his spiritual home, and he makes the forty-five minute trip to Point Fortin every Sunday.

We have just finished consuming a massive Sunday dinner and are settling in for an evening of studied nonaction when Kevin makes the grave error of mentioning the Stitchie concert (gospel dancehall) he attended the previous night. Within minutes Roddie and Kevin are sparring with each other and soliciting my support for their respective points of view. A once-casual conversation has been transformed into a full-fledged debate, thanks in part to a marvelous three-sentence pivot. Sentence 1: Kevin informs his father that the dancehall concert he attended last night was worshipful. Sentence 2: Roddie dismisses the concert as nothing more than entertainment. Sentence 3: Kevin points out that the concert was more worshipful than today's service at Mt. Beulah had been. The evening ends on a strained note.

The previous chapters have explored the several different styles of popular sacred music that are circulating within and around Trinidad's Full Gospel community—musics that extend from the local to the global and back again. The ethics of style has served as the unifying analytical thread throughout this book—as a means of thinking through the discourses that these musics engender and the subject positions that they imply. It remains for me, however, to reconnect the ethics of style to individual congregations to illustrate the important role that these local instantiations of the Full Gospel community fulfill in the Trinidadian gospel music scene. That these musical styles are themselves considered problematic and that they are under discussion with the goal of arriving at some version of community consensus—ideally, unity—is clear and certainly evident in the conversation I just described. It remains necessary, however, to offer an assessment of how this discourse actually plays out at the congregational level and to illustrate the changes that this process effects with regard to the musical dimensions of congregational life, a task toward which I turn in this chapter.

I return to the congregation because it constitutes, for the majority of artists and fans, the institutional locus of authority and legitimacy. This remains true for Full Gospel communities because of their commitment to observing the following admonition of Paul: "Let us not give up meeting together, as some are in the habit of doing, but let us encourage one another—and all the more as you see the Day approaching."[1] Indeed, regardless of whether artists want their music performed in worship services, the community's opinion of their style is articulated and then reinforced at the congregational level. Whether a given style is ultimately incorporated into worship services, then, is less significant than is the fact that the conclusions reached at the local congregational level directly influence discourse surrounding the style. The congregation is, in other words, a primary forum within which believers work toward that ever-elusive consensus.

In this chapter, I illustrate the ways that congregations provide an anchor around which artists and fans explore these various styles. I do so by invoking the ethics of style as an analytical tool in the process of offering a close ethnographic reading of the community that worships together at Mt. Beulah Evangelical Baptist Church, Point Fortin. I choose to use a Baptist church rather than a Pentecostal congregation because it affords me the opportunity to illustrate both the tensions that congregations are facing as they work through articulating their own approach to the ethics of style and the ways in which the Pentecostal worship paradigm is increasingly becoming entrenched in the practices of communities of faith that predate the paradigm itself. I will follow this close reading with some concluding reflections on the ethics of style, revisiting each style and reenvisioning the extent to which ethics might contribute to a more nuanced understanding of these musics and their role(s) within Full Gospel Trinidad.

"THIS LITTLE LIGHT OF MINE"; OR, THE BEACON ON WARDEN ROAD

My family and I lived in the basement of Mt. Beulah Evangelical Baptist Church during the ten-month period within which I conducted the majority of the fieldwork for this book (January–October 2000). We became intimately connected to the community during our stay and were privileged to enter into many wonderful friendships. The following pages are, accordingly, a deeply personal remembrance of time spent with loved ones. They are also, necessarily, a focused examination of the ways in which smaller communities of faith are coping with the demands that gospel musics and the increasing Pentecostal presence in Trinidad are placing on them.

As such, this moment in the book has caused me some discomfort, primarily because it confronts me most thoroughly with the problem of representation. This is the case not least because two of the most polarized voices in this discourse belong to my dear friend Roddie and to his son Kevin. In order to contextualize the discussion that follows, I should like, just briefly, to trace the history of Mt. Beulah Evangelical Baptist Church. I do so because the spiritual journey of the congregation illustrates beautifully the complex ground upon which evangelical, Full Gospel congregations are constituted, often coming to occupy this space by way of unlikely twists and turns. Michel-Rolph Trouillot, moreover, points out that subjects "do not succeed a past; they are its contemporaries," and this fact necessarily significantly influences the ways that these "subjects" interact with the present.[2]

Mt. Beulah Evangelical Baptist Church, Point Fortin

In early May of 2000, I spent a few delightful afternoons in conversation with Deacon McKellar and Mother Joseph. As their honorific titles indicate, they are two of the oldest and most spiritually mature members of Mt. Beulah, having spent the majority of their lives as members of the community. They told me the story of their church and of its charismatic founding pastor.[3]

The life of Mt. Beulah Evangelical Baptist Church is directly connected to the life and work of Mohan "Teach" Nyack. Teach was born into a Seventh-Day Adventist family in 1930. Yet by the time he was nine years old, he had made a deliberate change to the Divine Army of New Creation. He became a baptized member of the church in the same year (1939) and was mentored by Leader Baptiste. Although Teach received his early spiritual instruction under Baptiste, he soon became convinced that the Spiritual Baptist faith held more truth. At the age of fifteen, he parted ways with Leader Baptiste, became a Spiritual Baptist, and began to go on missions (evangelistic journeys) and to preach wherever he could receive an invitation to do so.

During these early postwar years, he benefited from the loyal support of Mother Tyson, Mother Marshall, Mother Hilda, and Elder Pierre. The next fifteen or twenty years (from approximately 1945 to 1965) found Teach strengthening his reputation as a gifted teacher. He taught anywhere he could and was often seen walking along the roads of southern and central Trinidad looking for places to preach. Around 1965 Leader Baptiste offered Teach the use of his church building in Siparia, for he had taken ill and his congregation of the Divine Army of New Creation had dwindled to the point of no return. Teach accepted the invitation and founded the Mt. Beulah Spiritual Baptist Church in Siparia. The church was affiliated to the West Indian United Spiritual Baptist Sacred Order (WIUSBSO) that year, and the legalities related to ownership of the land and building were finally resolved in 1972.

As a result of his growing reputation, pastors would often invite Teach to lead Bible studies at their churches. One such pastor was Rev. John Cudgoe of Penal, who invited Teach to come and hold Bible studies at Mt. Nebo Spiritual Baptist Church in 1968. Teach accepted the invitation and began to teach the people of Mt. Nebo. As a result of his search for spiritual truth, however, he had by this time begun to move away from some of the traditions and doctrines that the Spiritual Baptists held dear. This fact became obvious at a painfully embarrassing Bible study during which Teach, arguing against one of these traditions, declared that men should not wear hats during worship. Present at the meeting was Harvey Glaud, one of the trustees of the WIUSBSO, who, incidentally, never failed to observe this tradition. Predictably, this offense led to Teach's dismissal from the Bible study at Mt. Nebo.

Several members of Mt. Nebo Spiritual Baptist Church, however, sought him out for further instruction. Once their numbers reached thirty and they had found a place to meet, Teach once again began to travel to Penal to lead a Bible study there. He continued to teach in Penal from 1969 to 1975, and the group grew to number approximately eighty people. By 1972, however, it was clear that he could no longer, in good conscience, continue to pastor a congregation of the WIUSBSO, and he took steps to affiliate his church in Siparia to the Independent Baptist Missionary Union of Trinidad and Tobago. Meanwhile, membership in his congregation in Siparia had gradually increased, and in 1975, when the group from Penal began to participate regularly in the services at Siparia, church membership consistently numbered somewhere between two hundred and two hundred and fifty people.

The years between 1975 and 1983 found the church in Siparia very active. In 1976 the church began a mission Bible study in Point Fortin. This was followed, in 1978, by Sunday services held in the Eagle Hall of Point Fortin. Members of the Siparia church began a project in 1979 to replace their existing building with a larger church on the same property. Based on the growth of the congregation in Point Fortin, a building project was also initiated there in 1980. By 1981 the building in Siparia was completed and dedicated, and the membership had grown to approximately five hundred people. Internal struggles over the leadership of the church in Siparia, combined with jealousies among some of the young preachers, however, eventually led to what Deacon McKellar and Mother Joseph considered "a disgraceful treatment of Teach by the church in Siparia."

In 1983 he was asked to retire and hand over the leadership to the young preachers, but he opted instead to oversee the work in Point Fortin. In his absence ("exile" might be a more appropriate word), however, a series of splits decimated the church, leaving the new building virtually empty by 1985. The church in Point Fortin, by contrast, continued to grow. In 1986 Roddie Taylor was ordained to the pastorate by Teach and began assisting with the pastoral duties at Point Fortin. In 1989, honoring the request of some of the remaining members of the Siparia church, Teach sent Pastor Taylor and Deacon McKellar to steady the situation and to begin the rebuilding process in that church.

By 1991 the church in Siparia was growing again, and the members asked that Teach return to lead the church. He did so, sharing the duties of leading the congregations at Siparia and Point Fortin with Pastor Taylor. Another transition was in the making, however, for Teach had moved away from some of the doctrinal beliefs that the Independent Baptist Missionary Union held. Especially problematic for Teach was the belief that Christians needed to experience dreams (visions) as proof of their readiness for baptism. Pastor Taylor began investigating the feasibility of becoming a completely autonomous church under the Companies' Act in Trinidad during 1994. Teach passed away in December of 1996, leaving a lifetime of teaching, two churches, and countless spiritual children as his legacy. Before his death, he also ensured that Pastor Taylor would be installed as his successor and mandated him to push for autonomy.

Pastor Taylor, after weighing the benefits and drawbacks of the Companies' Act, chose to appeal for incorporation, and in 1997 an act of Parliament granted the churches of Mt. Beulah autonomy. With this act of Parliament, the name of the churches was also legally changed from Mt. Beulah Spiritual Baptist Church to Mt. Beulah Evangelical Baptist Church. Pastor Taylor established a new mission in La Brae in 1997. The churches are currently struggling to find their new identity and vision without their founding pastor, Teach, and under the leadership of Pastor Taylor. Membership in the churches has remained reasonably steady at around eighty in Point

Fortin and between fifty and seventy in Siparia. La Brae is currently meeting with approximately twenty members.

Two important themes emerge from this short history of Mt. Beulah Evangelical Baptist Church. First, it should be clear that Deacon McKellar and Mother Joseph have memorialized Teach through their narrative. They consistently take pains to point out that he was a very strong leader and that he continued to search for truth throughout his entire life. That this search caused Teach to chain himself into the flow of several doctrinal discourses successfully and to manifest these identifications through affiliation with five denominations should illustrate the complexities attendant to the negotiation of religious faith in Trinidad.[4] Three of these denominations, moreover, are not considered Full Gospel—Seventh-Day Adventist, Divine Army of New Creation, and Spiritual Baptist—which sheds some light on the significance that Deacon McKellar and Mother Joseph attach to Teach's continued search for the Truth. Throughout our conversation about Teach, both elders made it clear to me that they believe he led them to a right understanding of the spiritual life and of the Bible. Put otherwise, it was Teach's exceptional ability to discern the Truth that allowed him to shepherd his congregation from its Spiritual Baptist affiliation to the Full Gospel position. Teach's spiritual journey—a journey that, by extension, shaped the spiritual lives of his congregants—accordingly goes a long way toward underscoring the felt need of Full Gospel congregations to distinguish themselves from those congregations that are not, in fact, considered faithful to the Full Gospel.

Second, this narrative illustrates that individuals make choices about their denominational affiliation. In this case, the emphasis is placed on the pastor and his choices, but the congregants have the same freedom to chain themselves to new discourses (to identify themselves with new denominations and congregations). It should come as no surprise that members were not always happy with the choices that their pastor was making and that some even exercised their freedom to find another community within which to worship. And following on this idea, I suggest that music—like doctrine—functions as a polarizing force within congregations, a force that can often influence the identificatory choices of individual members.

The remainder of this section, then, illustrates the powerful influence of music on congregational membership and unity through an analysis of the ways that the members of Mt. Beulah Evangelical Baptist Church approach the popular musics explored in the previous chapters. In order to do this, I introduce a tripartite conceptual model that takes into account not only the

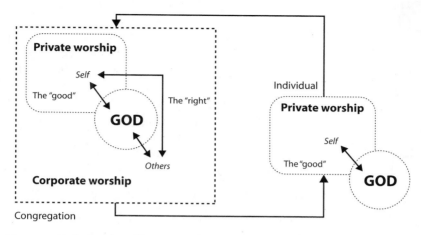

Figure 4. God–church–self.

questions related to ethical and moral discourse that I raised in chapter 2, but also the ways in which Full Gospel believers understand their relationship to God and to each other.[5] This model can be expressed in its most schematic formulation as "God–church–self" and is intended to give some heuristic shape to the normative understanding of an individual believer's experience of God by emphasizing that this experience is mediated through the worship of a given congregation (church). It is not, however, a strictly linear model, for there is a strong commitment among Full Gospel believers to maintaining a personal relationship with God.

The model should be understood as giving some descriptive shape to a cyclical relationship wherein the individual has access to two modes of divine encounter that feed back into each other. One of these is often referred to as devotional, or private, whereas the other is considered corporate and involves participation in congregational services. An individual, thus, willingly identifies herself with a community of believers, remaining individuated from yet becoming united with her fellow believers during worship services. A further refinement of the model involves introducing the questions of the "good" and the "right" implicit in ethical and moral discourse into its fabric. In so doing, the model—heuristic and limited though it is—begins to offer a sense of the interrelationships between individual believers and congregations, between selves and others. These interrelationships might be expressed as shown in figure 4.

What I aim to capture here is the complex interrelationship between private and corporate expressions of worship. Reading from left to right, each believer experiences God within the context of corporate worship. But this experience is mediated and expanded by her experiences with the divine within the realm of her devotional worship. The relationship between these two modes of experience is represented here by the arrows bridging the congregation and the individual believer. These arrows also illustrate the individual's deliberate move (her incorporation) into corporate worship—that individual's identification with a given community and the sense in which the community also embraces and shapes her. Corporate worship thus places the individual into relationship with other believers in a way that opens a window onto another significant mode of divine experience. The individual still experiences the divine through the lens of devotional worship but is also able to participate in the act of communal worship, an activity that offers an experience of God made possible through communion with others. Corporate worship is, then, an interpersonal activity that parallels and augments the individual's personal experience of God. Importantly, the cycle feeds back on itself, changing an individual's own view of personal devotion and affecting the shape of her own relationship to God, her own poetics of conviction.

I have also indicated, following Habermas, the distinction between ethical and moral modes of discourse that might theoretically be mapped onto these relationships (the good and the right). However, I have done so with the intent of illustrating that they become inseparable in practice. Given the extent to which these two modes of worship feed into each other, the ethical and the moral are consistently and continuously blurred into one another through the course of lived experience within a given community, a process that reinforces the more useful approach of considering them to be the same (see chapter 2).

It should come as no surprise that the four styles of music discussed in the previous chapters occupy radically different positions in relation to this conceptual model. On the one hand, gospelypso and North American gospel music are both performed with the express intent of gaining access to and subsequently impacting upon the mediating aspect of the church in the lives of believers. Gospelypso demands a commitment to *local* and expressly Trinidadian forms of expression within the church, whereas North American gospel music performatively engenders a virtual connection to the global church, thereby calling for a deliberately nonlocal affirmation of membership in a larger community. These two spaces within the Full Gospel community are represented in figures 5 and 6.

The creative efforts of gospelypso artists are in general not validated within congregations, whereas those artists pursuing North American gospel musics are much more likely to gain access to congregational spaces.

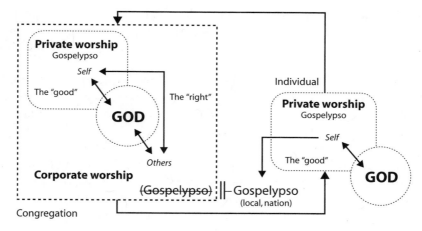

Figure 5. Gospelypso.

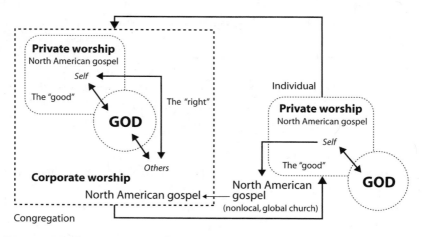

Figure 6. North American gospel.

Now I should be quick to add that things have changed considerably since the 1970s. Although Sean Daniel still laments the lack of support from the church, he has been able to garner a great deal more encouragement and support than did any of the pioneers of the style in their day. This is in part because gospelypso has been around for a relatively long time now. Gospelypsonians have, not unlike Ras Shorty I, been telling the same old story long enough that they have succeeded at least partially in changing the overarching attitudes toward the style. This may also have something to do with the fact that gospel dancehall at the moment represents a far greater threat to Full Gospel identity than does gospelypso. And yet, all things considered, gospelypso still remains in general a style that is performed in places other than church services.

Gospel dancehall and jamoo, on the other hand, subvert the role of the church as mediator, effectively inverting the order of the model so that it can be expressed as God–self–(church). Gospel dancehall accomplishes this by positing an alternate community that stands in for the church, a community that is constituted in and through performance. True corporate worship is, in this case, experienced not at church but at the gospel concert (see figure 7). I represent this by bridging the individual believer and the congregation and by appending a more prominent arrow to that bridge which links the individual to the gospel concerts. The congregation is, thus, still a part of gospel dancehall piety but does not represent the space within which full expression can take place. That space has been fashioned in and through the gospel concerts. Knowing full well that gospel dancehall will not be welcomed in their congregational worship, artists make no effort to legitimize it within that space. Instead, they save their style for mutual encouragement within the gospel concert and look for ways to strengthen the Full Gospel youth. What this sets up, of course, is a great deal of intergenerational conflict and fear regarding the future of the leadership. It also sets up a comparative tension between the two communities within which artists and fans worship.

Jamoo makes the boldest claim of all, simply reducing the model to its most unmediated form: God–self. Ras Shorty I's refusal to affiliate himself with a denomination also signaled his nonparticipation in the normative institutions of Full Gospel faith—in the church portion of the model. Jamoo, thus, explores a strictly devotional version of the model, one in which the community is not necessary for worship (see figure 8).

With this in mind, the broken line between individual believer and congregation is intended to indicate the ambivalence with which Ras Shorty I viewed corporate worship. Whether an individual chooses to engage in it is relatively unimportant because jamoo operates in a space entirely separate from the legitimizing and disciplining power of the congregation. Interestingly, jamoo is the only style that looks to transcend the strictly Full Gospel coordinates of what it means to be in community. As I argued in the previous chapter, the nation, or better yet the spaces between the nation and the church, provides the room that Ras Shorty I requires in order to posit a unity among all Trinidadians. This style, then, explores a much more ambitious ideal of community and does so by negating the specifically Full Gospel marker of the congregation.

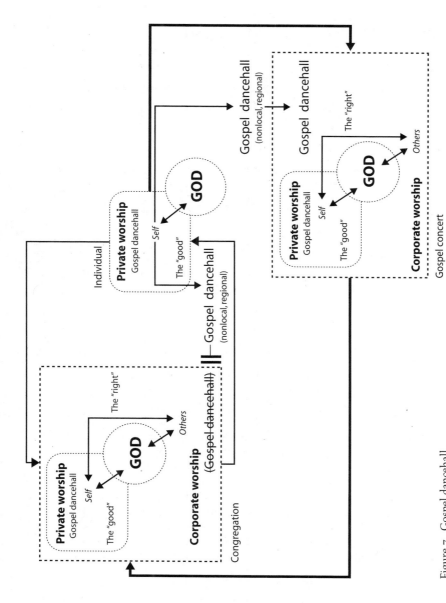

Figure 7. Gospel dancehall.

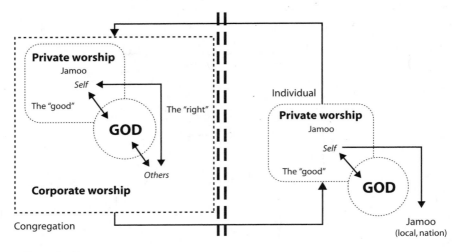

Figure 8. Jamoo.

Naturally enough, opinions vary widely as to the usefulness and appropriateness of these styles in worship services, and it is in the process of negotiating these differences that the ethics of style becomes most visible at the congregational level.[6] I should like, in the following pages, to illustrate some of the key moments of this discourse as it unfolded at Mt. Beulah Evangelical Baptist Church.

NOTES: SUNDAY, JANUARY 23, 2000, WORSHIP SERVICE, POINT FORTIN

The services at Mt. Beulah are held at three o'clock in the evening, and today's musical content included a balance of lined hymns, American choruses, and Trinidadian choruses. Roddie and I had a conversation earlier in the week during which he mentioned that the church is going through a time of transition and that music is inextricably tied up in the process. He believes that the debate rages primarily along generational fault lines and that the lined hymns (read: older generation) are set up against the North American choruses (read: younger generation). Roddie says he is seeking a balance in the services and that the Trinidadian choruses seem to offer a demilitarized zone of sorts, for everyone is comfortable with their inclusion in the worship services.

The transition of which Roddie spoke and which has been in progress since he assumed full leadership of the church in 1996 reflects the influence of the Pentecostal presence in Trinidad. Prior to 1996 very few, if any, North American choruses were being sung at Mt. Beulah. Lined hymns were the standard fare. Roddie, eager to accommodate the wishes of the younger members of his congregation, gradually began to incorporate these choruses into the fabric of Sunday worship, causing no small amount of tension in the process. Mt. Beulah has, nevertheless, adjusted to this accommodation and even seems relatively comfortable with the current balance. The other popular gospel musics in circulation, however, remain a constant strain on the community's unity, dominating the discourse related to the content of worship services.

NOTES: THURSDAY, JANUARY 27, 2000, BIBLE STUDY, POINT FORTIN

Roddie placed the following questions and diagrams on the chalkboard before this evening's Bible study. He did so in order to introduce the themes that he has in mind for the congregational meeting, which is scheduled to take place during carnival week:

Who are we at Mt. Beulah? What is our vision?

GREAT COMMISSION CHURCH? ARE WE OR AREN'T WE?

Great Commission

Doctrinal vision	MANDATE	Degree to which fulfilled
	Evangelism	
	Discipling	
	Fellowship	
	Worship	
	Ministry	
Natural consequences/ blessings	RESULTS	Measuring stick for above
	Numerical growth	
	Spiritual growth	
	Ministries advance	
	Missions	

Once so initiated, the Bible study did not suffer from a lack of participation. In fact, a full hour after its scheduled end, Roddie finally intervened in the debate in order to bring the proceedings to a close. The topic that generated the most heated discussion was that of worship. For one thing, the musical choices of the congregation impact upon the answers that are given to primary questions on the agenda—"Who are we at Mt. Beulah? What is our vision?"—questions which are, after all, explicitly concerned with identity.

As I pointed out in the last section, the community has, since 1996, been coping with the increasing need to adapt its worship to the Pentecostal paradigm (or face the prospect of losing the younger members of its congregation). In the wake of these adjustments, however, it also finds itself faced with strong challenges to its normative conception of worship, primarily but not exclusively by its own younger members. In short, it is no longer enough simply to sing a few North American choruses during the service. Having now opened the door to new sounds and styles, it has become necessary to find justifications for excluding certain styles while embracing others, a task that is proving very tricky indeed.

NOTES: FEBRUARY 27, 2000, WORSHIP SERVICE, POINT FORTIN

> The question of the day relates to my experience at last night's gospel concert, Nicole 2000. The rhetoric that accompanied the entire evening's proceedings leaves no doubt about the fact that the concert organizers, the performers, and the audience viewed this event as worship. If the gospel concert is worship, however, then why is the worship service at Mt. Beulah so different? I have asked several people this question and received some very interesting answers. Roddie, for instance, does not believe that the gospel concerts constitute worship. He maintains, instead, that the concerts represent nothing more or less than a reasonably good form of entertainment. And yet his sons, Kevin and Kervon, along with many of the others who attended the concert yesterday, adamantly maintain that this is a valid form of worship and that they would love to see the styles they heard at the concert become part of the services at Mt. Beulah.

The principal challenge to congregational discourse arising from the ethics of style is rooted in the lack of specific prescriptions and proscriptions about worship in the Bible. The fundamentalist leanings of Mt. Beulah— leanings that lead members to assert that everything of importance for life is found in the Bible—cause the congregation to be caught on the horns of a dilemma, where proponents on both sides of the argument are forced to rely on the same source to legitimize their understanding of worship. They are, in Dick Hebdige's words, caught in a "struggle for possession of the sign [the biblical text]."[7]

While the Bible does offer believers some useful models for worship (for example, Isaiah 6:1–8), these models deal only with the elements that should be included in worship.[8] Activities such as praise, prayer, repentance, forgiveness, and service can all reasonably be expected to impact to varying degrees upon a given worship service. The difficulty lies, then, in that there are no references to the proportions, the genres, or the relative appropriateness of certain styles.

This leads to the uncomfortable realization that almost anything can be legitimized under the idea of worship, that a community must decide for *itself* what its musical vision is. Full Gospel worship is, in other words, not fixed to or limited by a specific place (the sanctuary), a historical moment (nineteenth-century revivalism), or a given cultural frame of reference (missionary activities). Ultimately, the Bible's explicit ambiguity on the subject of worship thrusts each congregation into a more or less constant discourse related to worship, a discourse within which music assumes a most prominent role. Each community must come to terms with its worship style and articulate the styles that it considers an appropriate self-expression of its corporate identity. The local church community, thus, becomes the only arbiter of worship's musical content. In this respect, Full Gospel churches in Trinidad vary widely in their approach to the materials presented in this book. Jesus Ministries in La Horquetta, the congregation which the band Melchizedek Order calls home, for instance, is much more likely to welcome new ideas and sounds and to incorporate what are, for many other congregations, radical and controversial styles than is Mt. Beulah Evangelical Baptist Church.

NOTES: MARCH 18, 2000; SPECIAL MUSIC?

> Just a few days ago Dolores (twenty-one) asked me to help her learn a song that she would like to sing as a special number in the worship service. The song, "Fragile Heart," is performed by Yolanda Adams, a gospel and R&B singer.[9] She purchased the compact disc recording of the song after hearing it on Love 94.1 FM and wants to share the song with the congregation. She told me that she had already played the song for Roddie and that he had given her his blessing to sing it as soon as she felt she was ready. She wants to sing it this coming Sunday.
>
> A few weeks ago Kervon (eighteen), Anna (twenty-six), K. D. (thirteen), and Ayanna (seventeen) sang an a cappella arrangement of "Lean on Me" during the special music portion of the service. This song, performed by Kirk Franklin, is very popular at the moment and is being played a great deal on Love 94.1 FM.[10] Kervon also plans on singing Donnie McClurkin's "Stand" in an upcoming service.[11] Roddie has had nothing but positive and encouraging things to say about these musical choices.

The songs listed in the previous paragraphs, however, are all North American gospel songs of a rather benign nature. In fact, I never heard anything but slow R&B gospel compositions performed in the worship services of Mt. Beulah Evangelical Baptist Church. Conversely, I never heard gospelypso, gospel dancehall, or jamoo performed at any service. *Self*-expression in the church is, at least today, limited to performances of a particular type—specifically to performances of a North American and nonlocal style.

The intersection of self and community, then, is guarded by the discourse surrounding the ethics of style. That North American gospel musics are gradually making their way into the special music of the church illustrates that the ethics of style, and certainly the discourse surrounding it, is generating some new norms in worship services. It is nevertheless clear that the current situation continues to cause a great deal of conflict among those members of the congregation for whom gospel dancehall, gospelypso, and even jamoo constitute important aspects of their devotional worship. I should emphasize that this state of affairs is not unique to Mt. Beulah Evangelical Baptist Church. Mt. Beulah's situation, in fact, typifies the vast majority of congregations in Trinidad. And yet each congregation determines the limits of acceptability for itself.

NOTES: MAY 6, 2000; POPULAR MUSICS AND THE CONTEMPORARY CHURCH?

> "It's all right, the old music, but I like gospel and the [Trinidad] choruses." Sheldon Thompson (thirty-two) is a member of Mt. Beulah Evangelical Baptist Church, and we are discussing the music that he finds important in the context of worship. Long-meter hymns, to which he refers here, are clearly not his favorite form of musical expression. When not in church, he listens to top-forty music from the United States, dancehall, and gospel music. When in church, he would prefer to worship with the same type of energy he experiences in these popular musics.
>
> Kevin Taylor (twenty-five), however, is much more vocal about his belief that church services should reflect the contemporary world and the lives of contemporary Christians. He sees no benefit to singing long-meter hymns and would like to see the congregation allow a wider variety of styles in order to represent the diverse selves that make up the community. "We shouldn't have a better worship experience at a concert than we have at church—but we do. We shouldn't have to look for worship in other places—but we do."[12]

The implicit critique of Mt. Beulah's services is significant in that it signals the identification of individual members with the ethical content of styles such as gospel dancehall. In other words, Kevin is aligning himself with the ethical concerns of gospel dancehall music and its "kingdom reformation" credo. Even though he would like to see gospel dancehall incorporated into worship services at Mt. Beulah, he finds himself supplementing his worship experiences with gospel concerts.

One of the challenges that congregations face with regard to the ethics of style is related to the two modes of divine encounter—the private and the corporate. One of the main reasons that Kevin finds the gospel concert so worshipful is that he is able in that space to reconcile his private, devotional ethics to his corporate, congregational ethics. Put otherwise, the "good" is in this context conflated with the "right." In the environment of a gospel concert, then, the two modes of divine encounter become one, freeing Kevin from the tensions that he routinely experiences during church services at Mt. Beulah. In this context, the impossible choice I have discussed is put at arm's length or, at the very least, deferred for the moment. These styles are readily available in mass mediated formats, which also allows Kevin to imagine himself as part of the wider gospel dancehall community even when he is not participating directly in a gospel concert.

This illustrates, I think, Ulf Hannerz's suggestion that "now that media technology is increasingly able to deal with other symbolic modes . . . we may wonder whether imagined communities are increasingly moving beyond words."[13] Put differently, because the sonically imagined community (as developed through listening to recordings and the radio) is also physically constituted as an extension of the self during gospel concerts, the personal and the corporate are no longer understood as mutually exclusive modes but rather as a potential unity, highlighting again the conflation between moral and ethical modes of discourse. The consequence of these experiences, however, is a heightened awareness of what corporate worship can mean—an awareness that forces some difficult realizations when these concerts are compared with services at Mt. Beulah. It should come as no surprise that Kevin's participation in gospel concerts eventually adds a great deal of pressure to the discourse surrounding the ethics of style at Mt. Beulah Evangelical Baptist Church. This is because Kevin and others like him have experienced the possibility of this type of unity and find it difficult to remain patient with the pace at which the church community arrives at new forms of consensus about style.

Many other members of the congregation, for their part, see no need to conflate the two modes of experience or to move quickly to incorporate the styles under discussion. Roddie, for example, made the following comments in a sermon: "God gives every Christian a song. If you ain't a Christian, then you ain't got no song."[14] When I asked him about this statement and its connection to the ethics of style, he elaborated, saying, "The fact that God gives every *Christian* a song does not mean that that song needs to or even should become *every* Christian's song."[15]

THE ETHICS OF STYLE

I am convinced that the fans of gospel dancehall, jamoo, North American gospel, and gospelypso are, by definition, also implicated in the ethical projects that these styles stake out. Because the style stands in for the discourse, there can be no doubt that Kevin knows exactly what gospel dancehall music means to accomplish in Full Gospel Trinidad. In similar fashion, it is highly unlikely that a person who identifies with jamoo music is unaware of Ras Shorty I's explicit rejection of the normative understanding shared among Full Gospel believers about the need for Christian assembly. Accordingly, the styles that find themselves marginalized within the typical Full Gospel congregation map onto equally marginalized groups within that congregation, groups for whom the styles, nevertheless, best represent their own Christian life-worlds—their own poetics of conviction.

When these relationships are mapped onto the God–church–self model I proposed earlier, it becomes clear that the ethics of style is interchangeable with the ethics of *selves*. For the ethics of style is a reflexive and cyclical process expressed in action through the poetics of conviction. The pioneering gospelypso artists were, after all, searching for an appropriate expression of the ethics of them*selves*. Once they performed themselves as gospelypso, they opened up a new avenue for this type of self-expression to others, and this avenue is now open to new artists as well as fans. In similar fashion, gospel dancehall artists are performing their vision of "kingdom reformation" just as surely as their fans are themselves expressing their affinity for that vision. And yet, these poetics of conviction are tied in important and dynamic ways to identification with the Full Gospel community, and with the exception of Ras Shorty I, none the artists or fans I have discussed throughout this book are willing to break completely from that context. The ethics of style is thus, also, in an important sense about coming to terms with the ethics of community—and this as instantiated by individual congregations, through larger associations, and in the imagined forms of global Christianity.

I have, throughout this book, applied the ethics of style as an analytical tool, the usefulness of which lies in moving past mere moral positioning, thereby taking seriously the convictions and self-expressive processes that shape style. Moreover, I have illustrated the process through which performance of a style such as gospel dancehall comes to stand in for an entire discourse surrounding it. I have consistently refused any separation of the performative aspects of style from the ethical positionality that its performances suggest and have taken at face value the beliefs and convictions of the community. In so doing, I hope that I have suggested a more nuanced approach to dealing with religious experience in a postcolonial Caribbean context.

What emerges out of this book, then, is that Trinidadian Full Gospel believers are constantly negotiating the particularities of their faith and practice, actively engaging with musics of national, regional, and transnational origins and bending them to their own conceptions of the "good." The complexities that these decisions engender, moreover, are mediated not only performatively but also through an active and, at times, painful process of discussion that I have *also* called the ethics of style. Each style I have explored in this book, then—along with other aspects of style like language use, fashion, and even performance context—participates at multiple levels in what I am calling the ethics of style. First, the artist is engaged in a creative identification with the "good" of the style. Ras Shorty I's commitment to jamoo, Sherwin Gardner's conviction about the need for gospel dancehall, Noel "the Professor" Richards's desire to bring gospelypso to the nation, and Michael Dingwell's identification with North American gospel music are all examples of this outward performance of the ethics of style—examples of what I have called the poetics of conviction throughout the book.

Second, the style itself presents members of the Full Gospel community with an impossible choice. Some believers identify themselves with the style, while some choose not to do so. But there is an important dynamic at work here, for the extent to which a musical style is deemed controversial within Trinidadian Full Gospel circles is directly related to this process of identification. Very few members of the Full Gospel community, for example, have difficulty identifying with North American gospel music. It is, as I have argued, the least controversial and most normative of the styles that circulate in Full Gospel Trinidad. Those few individuals who do disidentify with North American gospel music—most notably gospelypsonians—are usually strongly aligned with other styles that preclude their wholehearted identification with North American gospel music. Fans of jamoo, on the other hand, are by and large free to engage in other identifications, and this not least because of the style's essentially devotional character, but also because it has remained essentially a marginal style circulating on the peripheries of the Full Gospel community. The difficult moments, those impossible choices, then, seem to confront Full Gospel believers at the intersections between gospelypso, gospel dancehall, and the more normative North American gospel music. These are, I believe, the points at which the ethics of style becomes most visible, instantiating not only a moment of decision for individual believers, but also finding expression in a discourse about the relative merits of the styles in question.

This ensuing discourse about the efficacy and relative value of style represents the third level at which I invoke the ethics of style. And it should be clear by now that those styles most readily accepted (North American gospel music) or most easily excluded (jamoo) are not discussed in nearly as much detail or with as much urgency by Trinidadians as are those styles that represent potentially viable alternative visions of what it might mean, look, and sound like to be Christian in Trinidad. This is one of the primary reasons why gospelypso and, later, gospel dancehall have generated the most critical reaction from pulpits, in the media, and in general discussions among Full Gospel believers. Gospelypso invokes local materials and memories in an attempt to think about the future of Full Gospel worship in Trinidad—a move that raises too many questions about what it might look like to face the local (including local believers, as opposed to identifying primarily with the global church). Gospel dancehall, for its part, raises the possibility of a regional sound that, as I suggest in chapter 5, is disciplined by what might best be described as a discourse of power. The current worship paradigm—one that is predicated on North America as sound—is valued above gospel dancehall and protected against the poetics of conviction articulated by its artists and fans.

Fourth, as I have already suggested, styles themselves attain an ethical position by virtue of the discourse that surrounds their performance. Interestingly, a style like North American gospel music gains its ethical position within the community in part because it connects in such an "uncomplicated" way the Trinidadian community with global forms of Christianity. This style is, in one sense, legitimized from without—and from a space that still holds an important voice in matters of doctrine and practice (North America)—making a discursive exploration of its merits of secondary concern in relation to the practical matters revolving around finding better ways of incorporating those sounds into local worship services. At the end of the day, then, artists and fans who are practicing and listening to these styles, hailing and being hailed by these competing discourses, are engaged in an ethical project as they determine for themselves the identifications and disidentifications they are willing to make and the spaces that they will occupy in relation to their communities as a result of their choices.

Finally, the task of representing these artists, fans, and believers, of exploring the musical shapes of Full Gospel Trinidad, is also an exercise in the ethics of style. The analytical task, then, is itself an act of identification that implicates me in the ethics of style as well. This not least because I am confronted, as I argued in chapter 2, by the "face of the other," not only in the course of building relationships but also in my listening (which is, using Levinas's words, a "said" implying a "saying"). My identifications thus become, in their own limited way, part of the discourse surrounding style in Full Gospel Trinidad.

By adding the ethics of style to some of the concepts and ideas that Belinda Edmondson has called archetypes of Caribbeanness, by placing this model in dialogue with other approaches, I seek to expand on the vocabulary and theoretical models available to represent the particularities of Full Gospel Trinidad.[16] I desire, furthermore, to approach musical change and theories applied to thinking about musical change—such as hybridity, for example—as secondary symptoms of the deeper, ethical projects that these artists and the communities they live in are pursuing. Much remains to be done to develop the ethics of style into a broadly useful theoretical tool, but I hope that this book has introduced the concept in such a way as to highlight its possibilities for Full Gospel Trinidad in particular and, perhaps, more generally for the region. A refrain penned by Sheldon Blackman is the most fitting conclusion to this book, for it summarizes the primary motivation that drives the artists and fans of each of the styles:

> Generation, generation look the future resting in we hand.
> Generation, generation, wake up the future resting in we hand.
> Backward never, forward we going!
> This generation, make way, we coming!

Epilogue

I am sitting in the balcony of Bethany Independent Baptist Church in St. Madeline. Roddie Taylor was invited to attend this special ordination service, and he brought me along. The street on which this church stands fascinates me, for no less than four churches are nestled within a few hundred yards of each other. At the corner stands a Roman Catholic church, an Open Bible Standard church occupies the opposite end of the block, and a small, independent Pentecostal congregation meets in a private home located immediately next door to the Baptist church. Because the churches are so close to each other, their sonic footprints overlap with one another and, as it happens, all but the Catholic church are holding services today. Accordingly, there are moments during the Baptist service I am attending when the musical content of the other services can clearly be heard.

Intrigued by these overlapping sounds, I slip out and walk down the street, listening as the worship of one congregation rises to prominence only to be merged with and then subordinated to the music emanating from the next church. As I approach the Open Bible Standard church, I notice a car whose owner has chosen publicly to express herself by means of a bumper sticker. The sticker is located on the back window, its background printed in cautionary bright yellow. The boldface inscription is printed in black ink and reads "BOYCOTT HELL—Repent" [see figure 9].

The bumper sticker I photographed that afternoon—a piece printed by the Missouri-based company Testimony Time—foregrounds the shared ground to which all of the artists, fans, and church leaders I have discussed during the course of this book have committed themselves.[1] For starters, it makes explicit the theological imperative that drives the evangelistic zeal so often in evidence throughout Full Gospel Trinidad. This is a battle for souls, and everyone is called to participate. The bumper sticker, furthermore, illus-

Figure 9. Bumper sticker on a vehicle in St. Madeline, Trinidad, 2000. Photograph by Timothy Rommen.

trates the important connections between Trinidadian and North American Christians—connections that are reinforced through a careful attention to North American modes of worship, by keeping up with the latest Christian media offerings, and through frequent travel to and from North America and Trinidad. It is, as such, a visible reminder of Full Gospel Trinidad's participation in the invisible church.

But the three churches, nestled so closely together on the same street in St. Madeline, also serve as a poignant reminder of the challenges that confront Full Gospel Trinidadians with regard to enacting the shared ground given expression through that bumper sticker. The Baptist church remains quite solidly committed to long-meter hymns and Baptist choruses. Unlike Mt. Beulah Evangelical Baptist Church, where accommodation to North American modes of worship is becoming more prevalent, this congregation is still fighting to maintain its unique identity quite apart from and in contradistinction to encroaching Pentecostal paradigms. The Pentecostal congregations, for their part, are avidly incorporating North American gospel music and congregational choruses into their worship. These very different approaches to worship meet, mingle, and merge on the streets of St. Madeline, offering an aural confirmation of the struggles that continue to drive discourse about musical style within Full Gospel Trinidad.

That short walk in St. Madeline crystallized for me the tensions that exist for artists and audiences within Full Gospel Trinidad. There is, on the one hand, a core of shared ground among believers as expressed in the message of that bumper sticker. "BOYCOTT HELL—Repent," then, is a message to which all are committed. The styles through which this message is brought to the nation, on the other hand, vary dramatically from each other and engender controversy among believers who otherwise share the same goal. And it is in this context that the nationalism of gospelypsonians, the determination of gospel dancehall artists, the studied ambivalence of jamoo performers, and the global vision of musicians pursuing North America as sound come to carry the ethical significance that I have traced throughout this book. Each style offers a very different approach to the evangelical concerns of Trinidadian believers, and each promotes a unique sense of what can or should constitute worship. In so doing, these styles provide the musical palette from which individual believers as well as individual congregations construct their own identities.

These pages have traced the struggles of artists, fans, and congregations to sift through and determine the usefulness of these various styles for Full Gospel identity. They have also explored more specifically the difficult and contested process in which Mt. Beulah Evangelical Baptist Church is engaged as members determine for themselves just what they sound like and who they are. And it is in this atmosphere that the ethics of style provides a means of taking seriously the very seriousness of these choices, of foregrounding the deep convictions that drive these discourses, and of analyzing the extent to which musical style is implicated in these fundamentally ethical projects.

Notes

1. The fieldwork that forms the basis for this book was completed over the course of about nine years (1995–2004). I first visited Trinidad in 1995 but did not return again until I conducted predissertation fieldwork in 1998 and 1999. I then spent most of 2000 pursuing my dissertation fieldwork and returned again in 2001 to conduct some follow-up fieldwork. I next returned in 2004 and in 2005 to complete the research for this book. With the exception of my fieldwork in 2000, which lasted ten months, my other fieldwork trips have been between two and four weeks in length. In almost every case, my time in Trinidad has been spent living in the southern town called Point Fortin. Point Fortin is home to Mt. Beulah Evangelical Baptist Church, and its pastor, Roddie Taylor, along with his family, have become some of my dearest friends. During the ten months of my dissertation fieldwork (January–October 2000), my family and I lived in the basement of Mt. Beulah Evangelical Baptist Church, and that community will always hold a special place in our hearts. Participating in the life of Mt. Beulah Evangelical Baptist Church, then, is one of the foundational ethnographic contexts through which I have come to my own convictions about the music and discourses I explore in this book.

2. Belinda Edmondson, ed., *Caribbean Romances: The Politics of Regional Representation* (Charlottesville: University of Virginia Press, 1999), 1 (emphasis mine).

3. Ibid., 2.

4. There are, of course, many exceptions to this trend. Diane J. Austin-Broos's *Jamaica Genesis: Religion and the Politics of Moral Orders* (Chicago: University of Chicago Press, 1997) and Melvin Butler's "Songs of Pentecost: Experiencing Music, Transcendence, and Identity in Jamaica and Haiti" (Ph.D. diss., New York University, 2005) are just two pertinent examples.

5. Michel de Certeau, *The Practice of Everyday Life* (Berkeley: University of California Press, 1984), xiii.

6. Michel-Rolph Trouillot, *Silencing the Past: Power and the Production of History* (Boston: Beacon Press, 1995).

7. Curwen Best, addressing this very question from a pan-Caribbean perspective, has written: "The Center for Black Music Research is clear in its definition. It considers gospel music to be 'African-American Protestant vocal music that celebrates Christian doctrine in emotive, often dramatic ways. . . .' In the Caribbean, though, the meaning of gospel music is not as fixed. Very often in the Caribbean the label 'gospel music' is interchanged with 'Christian music.' Sometimes it refers to the dominant musical style of evangelical assemblies. At other times it is used to define a category of music that approximates the popular style of African-American religious music." Curwen Best, *Culture @ the Cutting Edge: Tracking Caribbean Popular Music* (Kingston, Jamaica: University of the West Indies Press, 2004), 55.

8. The Nicole 2000 concert was sponsored and hosted by the gospel artist Nicole Ballosingh.

9. I have adopted the following approach to incorporating my field notes and experiences into the text: All field notes and field note–inspired materials are presented as extracts. Lightly edited excerpts from my field notes are always accompanied by dates and locations; those passages that I have paraphrased or otherwise rewritten do not include that information.

10. This is a line from Ras Shorty I's song "Sing Anything." It is an adaptation of the text found in Isaiah 40:3.

11. Lyrics reproduced by kind permission of Sheldon Blackman.

1. MUSIC, MEMORY, AND IDENTITY IN FULL GOSPEL TRINIDAD

1. Mt. Beulah Evangelical Baptist Church is one of only a few Baptist churches throughout Trinidad that participates in the Full Gospel associations. Baptist congregations, more often than not, continue to remain separate from Full Gospel circles.

2. Michel-Rolph Trouillot, *Silencing the Past: Power and the Production of History* (Boston: Beacon Press, 1995), 16.

3. The anniversary of this occasion is celebrated in the village of Moruga each year and is a national holiday. Irony notwithstanding, July 31 is referred to as "Discovery Day."

4. Antonio Benítez-Rojo, *The Repeating Island: The Caribbean and the Post-modern Perspective,* trans. James E. Maraniss (Durham, N.C.: Duke University Press, 1996).

5. Kevin A. Yelvington, *Trinidad Ethnicity,* Warwick University Caribbean Studies (London: MacMillan Caribbean, 1993), 4.

6. Bridget Brereton, *A History of Modern Trinidad, 1783–1962* (Portsmouth, N.H.: Heinemann, 1981), 5. Tragically, this story is not nearly as horrific as some histories in the region. For example, the Bahamas was completely depopulated of about twenty thousand people within the first twenty-five or thirty years after Columbus's arrival.

7. Ibid., 5.

8. Dale A. Bisnauth, *History of Religions in the Caribbean* (Trenton, N.J.: Africa World Press, 1996), 21. Bisnauth's observations also illustrate quite clearly the continued decline of the Amerindian population between 1592 and 1644.

9. There were notable exceptions to this pattern of ecclesial complicity during the history of Spanish colonialism. One of the most outspoken churchmen was the Dominican theologian Francisco de Vittoria, who argued that the Amerindians were entitled to liberty, self-government, and property, all of which were being taken from them by Spain. Another example was the Dominican friar Antonio de Montesinos who consistently, and amid great controversy, denounced the cruel way that his parishioners treated the Amerindians in Hispaniola (condensed from Bisnauth, *History of Religions,* 17–18). Bartolomé de Las Casas was also converted to the cause of the Amerindians and wrote extensively on the subject. *A Short Account of the Destruction of the Indies* and *In Defense of the Indians* are two of his more well-known treatises.

10. The accounts of the Arena Uprising were, of course, written by Europeans, who, given that the day's casualties included not only the priests in charge but also the governor, predictably called it the "Arena Massacre." For a thorough exploration of Amerindian histories and the Carib community in Arima, Trinidad (the Santa Rosa Caribs), see Maximilian C. Forte's *Ruins of Absence, Presence of Caribs: Postcolonial Representations of Aboriginality in Trinidad and Tobago* (Gainesville: University Press of Florida, 2005).

11. Yelvington, *Trinidad Ethnicity,* 4.

12. According to Brereton, the irony of the situation was that *British* trading vessels, rather than Spanish ones, frequented Port of Spain during the 1780s and early 1790s and thereby succeeded in dominating the growing export market (see Brereton, *Modern Trinidad,* 18).

13. John Cowley, *Carnival, Canboulay, and Calypso: Traditions in the Making* (New York: Cambridge University Press, 1996), 10.

14. Silvia R. Frey and Betty Wood make the following observation in *Come Shouting to Zion: African-American Protestantism in the American South and British Caribbean to 1830* (Chapel Hill: University of North Carolina Press, 1998), 36: "Most Africans transported from their homeland before the closing of the slave trade in the early nineteenth century subscribed to traditional religious cultures, and they would encounter Christianity for the first time in the Americas. However, the slave ships also included a smattering of people who adhered to their own versions of Islam and Christianity. These religious convictions would also survive the Middle Passage and take their place alongside traditional beliefs and practices in the very different contexts of the New World."

15. Trinidad was formally ceded to Great Britain by the Treaty of Amiens, 1802.

16. For more detailed accounts of these missionary activities, see relevant portions of Armando Lampe's edited collection *Christianity in the Caribbean: Essays on Church History* (Kingston, Jamaica: University of the West Indies Press, 2001); Bisnauth, *History of Religions;* and Eric John Murray's edited col-

lection *Religions of Trinidad and Tobago: A Guide to the History, Beliefs, and Polity of Twenty-three Religious Faiths* (Port of Spain, Trinidad: Murray Publications, 1998).

17. Yelvington, *Trinidad Ethnicity*, 5.

18. In 1813 the governor of Trinidad, Sir Ralph Woodford, requested of the colonial administration that settlers be brought to put undeveloped areas under cultivation.

19. The two northern settlements were located on the plains of Caroni and Laventille.

20. Cited in Murray, *Religions of Trinidad and Tobago*, 217–18.

21. Dick Hebdige, *Subculture: The Meaning of Style* (London: Methuen, 1974), 17.

22. This conflict between London-based missionaries and local believers was repeated elsewhere in the Caribbean as well. In the Bahamas, for example, this same scenario played out a few years earlier. Michael Craton and Gail Saunders have observed, "The chief threat to the independence of the black Baptists in the last years of slavery, indeed, came not directly from the regime but from their need to have white missionary supervisors in order to gain official sanction and respectability. The first official white Baptist missionaries, Joseph Burton and Kilner Pearson, did not arrive in the Bahamas until 1833. . . . Within a few months they had demanded a reformation in the management and practice of the Baptist churches." *Islanders in the Stream: A History of the Bahamian People*, vol. 1, *From Aboriginal Times to the End of Slavery* (Athens: University of Georgia Press, 1992), 334. The Bahamian reaction to this imposition prefigured that of the Trinidadian Baptists. Some church communities accepted this demand while others emphatically did not. One such community rechristened their church "St John's Particular Church of Native Baptists" to reflect their freedom from missionary supervision.

23. For more detailed information on the Baptist presence in Trinidad, see John Milton Hackshaw's *The Baptist Denomination: A Concise History Commemorating One hundred seventy-five Years (1816–1991) of the Establishment of the "Company Villages" and the Baptist Faith in Trinidad and Tobago* (Port of Spain, Trinidad: Amphy and Bashana Memorial Society, 1991).

24. The general misgivings over the practices of Spiritual Baptists are amply demonstrated by the fact that, in 1917, the more established denominations convinced the government of Trinidad and Tobago to pass the Shouters Prohibition Ordinance. This law sought to curb the Spiritual Baptist practice of performing their rites on public streets. Couched in terms of disturbing the peace, the main intent was to reduce the public visibility of the Spiritual Baptists. The law remained in effect until April 29, 1951, when it was repealed by Parliament.

25. Hugh Tinker, *A New System of Slavery: The Export of Indian Labour Overseas, 1830–1920* (New York: Oxford University Press, 1974). This "new system of slavery" was also implemented quite methodically in Suriname and Guyana.

26. For more detailed accounts of the East Indian presence in Trinidad, see

Helen Myer's *Music of Hindu Trinidad: Songs from the India Diaspora* (Chicago: University of Chicago Press, 1998) and Peter Manuel's *East Indian Music in the West Indies: Tan-Singing, Chutney, and the Making of Indo-Caribbean Culture* (Philadelphia: Temple University Press, 2000).

27. Republic of Trinidad and Tobago, Central Statistical Office, 2000 Population and Housing Census. Of the 1,114,772 respondents, 315,408 (28.3 percent) claimed Hindu or Islamic religious affiliation.

28. The Trinidadian Central Statistical Office offers the following percentages: 40.3 percent East Indian, 39.5 percent African, 18.4 percent mixed. For more information, see http://cso.gov.tt.

29. For examples of the increasing importance of migration for communities and nations throughout the Caribbean, see Ray Allen and Lois Wilcken's edited collection *Island Sounds in the Global City: Caribbean Popular Music and Identity in New York* (New York: New York Folklore Society, Institute for Studies in American Music, Brooklyn College, 1998).

30. For a detailed account of the black power movement, see Selwyn D. Ryan and Taimoon Stewart's edited collection *Power: The Black Power Revolution 1970, a Retrospective* (St. Augustine, Trinidad: Institute for Social and Economic Research, University of the West Indies, 1995).

31. A wealth of material has been published on this topic. For a few representative examples, see Ransford W. Palmer's edited collection *U.S.-Caribbean Relations: Their Impact on Peoples and Culture* (Westport, Conn.: Praeger Publishers, 1998); Peter H. Smith's, *Talons of the Eagle: Dynamics of U.S.–Latin American Relations,* 2nd ed. (New York: Oxford University Press, 2000); and Robert A. Pastor's, *Exiting the Whirlpool: U.S. Foreign Policy toward Latin America and the Caribbean,* 2nd ed. (Boulder, Colo.: Westview Press, 2001).

32. The initial founding of the organization is traced from 1912, when the U.S. missionary Rev. Robert Jamieson founded a small church in Montserrat. PAWI currently lists some ninety-three affiliated churches in Trinidad with another fourteen in Tobago. For more information on this organization, see http://www.pawionline.org.

33. See Murray's *Religions of Trinidad and Tobago* for a more detailed Trinidadian perspective on these developments. I have condensed some of this information from the article entitled "Trinidad and Tobago" in *The New International Dictionary of Pentecostal and Charismatic Movements,* ed. Stanley M. Burgess and Eduard M. van der Maas (Grand Rapids, Mich.: Zondervan, 2002). For more information on the rapid expansion of Pentecostalism into Latin America and the Caribbean, see the collection *Between Babel and Pentecost: Transnational Pentecostalism in Africa and Latin America,* ed. André Corten and Ruth Marshall-Fratani (Bloomington: Indiana University Press, 2001), Allan Anderson's *An Introduction to Pentecostalism* (New York: Cambridge University Press, 2004), and David Martin's *Pentecostalism: The World Their Parish* (Malden, Mass.: Blackwell Publishers, 2002).

34. For a thorough study of the tensions that plague Hindu-Christian relations in Trinidad, see Selwyn D. Ryan's *The Jhandi and the Cross: The Clash of*

Cultures in Post-Creole Trinidad and Tobago (St. Augustine, Trinidad: Sir Arthur Lewis Institute of Social and Economic Studies, University of the West Indies, 1999).

35. "Battling for Trinidad's Souls," *Hot Calaloo* (December 2000), www.hotcalaloo.com.

36. The entry on Trinidad and Tobago in the *New International Dictionary of Pentecostal and Charismatic Movements*, for example, lists the combined number of Pentecostalists, charismatics, and neocharismatics at 137,000—a figure that seems to corroborate the claims to rapid growth among Full Gospel believers. This figure, if accurate, would also put Pentecostal membership at roughly 12.3 percent of the total census population, making it the third-largest religious group behind Catholicism (26 percent) and Hinduism (22.5 percent), with Anglicans coming in a distant fourth (7.8 percent).

37. Natasha Coker, "Central Turns Gospel," *Trinidad Express*, August 27, 1998.

38. Harvey Cox, *Fire from Heaven: The Rise of Pentecostal Spirituality and the Reshaping of Religion in the Twenty-first Century* (Cambridge, Mass.: Da Capo Press, 1995), 57.

39. Ibid., 116.

40. Steve Bruce, *Religion in the Modern World: From Cathedrals to Cults* (New York: Oxford University Press, 1996), 22.

41. Roddie Taylor, interview with the author, February 17, 2000. Roddie is pastor of Mt. Beulah Evangelical Baptist Church in Point Fortin. He also serves as president of the local chapter of the Full Gospel association and as president of an interdenominational organization called the United Baptists of Trinidad and Tobago.

42. Charles Wesley and Isaac Watts wrote many popular hymns such as "Rejoice, the Lord Is King" and "When I Survey the Wondrous Cross," respectively.

43. "As the Deer" (1984) and "Lord I Lift Your Name on High" (1989) were written by Martin Nystrom and Rick Founds, respectively.

44. For a detailed account of the musical contributions made by the Company Villages to Protestant Trinidad, see Lorna McDaniel's "Memory Spirituals of the Ex-slave American Soldiers in Trinidad's 'Company Villages,'" *Black Music Research Journal* 14, no. 2 (Fall 1994): 119–44.

45. The self-published *Hymnal of the Open Bible Church* in Cunupia, for example, includes several standard hymns and a great number of North American choruses of the type that are published by Vineyard and Maranatha! but not a single Trinidadian Baptist chorus.

46. I am thinking here of Michael Herzfeld's work in *Cultural Intimacy: Social Poetics in the Nation-State* (New York: Routledge, 1997).

47. Melchizedek Order, "Kingdom Reformation," *Triumph in the Midst of Babylon* (Jesus Ministries, La Horquetta), 1999.

48. Norman C. Stolzoff, *Wake the Town and Tell the People: Dancehall Culture in Jamaica* (Durham, N.C.: Duke University Press, 2000).

49. Jerma A. Jackson, *Singing in My Soul: Black Gospel Music in a Secular Age* (Chapel Hill: University of North Carolina Press, 2004).

2. THE ETHICS OF STYLE

1. "Bad faith" is Sartre's way of expressing that we hold other, perhaps uncomfortable, options and alternatives at bay—sweep them under the rug even—in order to pursue without complications the direction that seems best to us. "Bad faith," in short, names the process by which we deceive ourselves. For a detailed account of this idea, see Jean-Paul Sartre, *Being and Nothingness: A Phenomenological Essay on Ontology*, trans. Hazel E. Barnes (New York: Washington Square Press, 1956).

2. I do not mean to imply here that scholars have been remiss in privileging this approach, but rather to indicate that vocabularies free of at least the most obvious formulations of ethical content have generally found greater acceptance within the academy. Think here, to offer just one obvious example, of the relatively marginal place that moral philosophy occupies within the greater discipline of philosophy.

3. Sherwin Gardner, interview with the author, March 23, 2000.

4. Nathaniel Howard, interview with the author, May 18, 2000.

5. Rev. Vernon Duncan, interview with the author, June 12, 2000.

6. This charge is also fueled by tapping into questions of authenticity. In other words, these artists should be pursuing their evangelistic zeal in styles marked or claimed as explicitly Trinidadian.

7. 1 Corinthians 9:22b, New International Version.

8. Lyrics reproduced by kind permission of Sherwin Gardner. Transcription mine.

9. Taylor articulates the consequences of a failure to explore this type of representation as follows: "But if our moral ontology springs from the best account of the human domain we can arrive at, and if this account must be in anthropocentric terms, terms which relate to the meanings things have for us, then the demand to start outside of all such meanings, not to rely on our moral intuitions or on what we find morally moving, is in fact a proposal to change the subject." Charles Taylor, *Sources of the Self: The Making of the Modern Identity* (Cambridge: Harvard University Press, 1989), 72.

10. Martha Nussbaum calls attention to the curious silence regarding ethics in the field of literary criticism in *Love's Knowledge: Essays on Philosophy and Literature* (New York: Oxford University Press, 1990). Thomas Nagel has also written extensively on the subject of ethics, an example of which is his book *The View from Nowhere* (New York: Oxford University Press, 1986).

11. David Parker summarizes Taylor's concern for an appropriate language of lived experience, articulated in *Sources of the Self*, as follows: "Taylor spends a great deal of time with the question of why we should regard any 'thin' account of ethics, which includes any naturalistic or skeptical reduction of it, as the best account we can give. He asks the question: What ought to trump the

language in which I actually live my life? In doing so, he makes the crucial point that the virtue of this lived 'thick' language is that it expresses our moral intuitions in a way that the 'thin' language does not. His point is that any language that does not allow us to express these is a language about something else, a language which is subtly constraining us to talk about another subject." David Parker, introduction to *Negotiating Ethics in Literature, Philosophy, and Theory,* ed. Jane Adamson, Richard Freadman, and David Parker (New York: Cambridge University Press, 1998), 10. Taylor's contention that "thin" language amounts to a language about something else resonates with my concern that archetypes of Caribbeanness do not, in and of themselves, paint a full portrait of the contexts to which I hope to apply them.

12. Harpham's argument, which is based on a carefully illustrated principle that he calls the "law of return," essentially denies that we are ever in a position to "change the subject" effectively in the first place. He goes on to suggest, "Language, or the partially focused thought of language, has served as a proxy for other issues that resist resolution on their own terms. If the question [Max] Müller asked in 1861—'What is language?'—remains unanswered, that has not inhibited, and has in fact encouraged, the recourse to language as a way of thinking other thoughts and answering other questions. . . . Thus language is the 'critical fetish of modernity.' . . . We have 'looked at' language as a way of refusing to look at humanity 'itself.' " Geoffrey Galt Harpham, *Language Alone: The Critical Fetish of Modernity* (New York: Routledge, 2002), 65–66.

13. Fred Lee Hord and Jonathan Scott Lee, in introducing their volume *I Am because We Are: Readings in Black Philosophy,* single out several themes that unite the many and varied voices they assemble under one cover. They have the following to say about the first of these unifying themes: "The first generative theme constitutive of the black philosophical tradition highlighted herein is the idea that the identity of the individual is never separable from the sociocultural environment. Identity is not some Cartesian abstraction grounded in a solipsistic self-consciousness; rather, it is constructed in and at least partially by a set of shared beliefs, patterns of behavior and expectations. In place of Descartes's 'I think; therefore I am,' we find in this black tradition, 'I am because we are; and since we are, therefore I am.' If individuality is grounded in social interaction, in the life of the community, then that individual's good life is inseparable from the successful functioning of his or her society." Fred Lee Hord (Mzee Lasana Okpara) and Jonathan Scott Lee, introduction to *I Am because We Are: Readings in Black Philosophy* (Amherst: University of Massachusetts Press, 1995), 7–8.

14. With this in mind, Paget Henry argues that Sartre's articulation of "bad faith" works well when applied to the construction of rationality within continental philosophy. He points out that the African willingness to incorporate the spirit is systematically "othered" by the West (as mythic thought) but that it represents nothing less than the metastatic other/alternative possibility that Western thought has denied itself in the pursuit of a rationality that fits its own image. See *Caliban's Reason: Introducing Afro-Caribbean Philosophy* (New York: Routledge, 2000).

15. Ibid., 193.

16. Ibid., 25.

17. While I have not specifically discussed South Asian approaches to spirituality and community here, I should note that East Indians in Trinidad also participate in patterns that can be productively explored from these perspectives. See, for example, Aisha Kahn's *Calaloo Nation: Metaphors of Race and Religious Identity among South Asians in Trinidad* (Durham, N.C.: Duke University Press, 2004).

18. According to Stuart Hall, what is needed in the ongoing discussion about identity is an answer to a question that he asks as follows: "The question which remains is whether we also require to, as it were, close the gap between the two: that is to say, a theory of what the mechanisms are by which individuals as subjects identify (or do not identify) with the 'positions' to which they are summoned; as well as how they fashion, stylize, produce and 'perform' these positions, and why they never do so completely, for once and all time, and some never do, or are in a constant, agonistic process of struggling with, resisting, negotiating, and accommodating the normative or regulative rules with which they confront and regulate themselves. In short, what remains is the requirement to think this relation of subject to discursive formations *as an articulation.*" Stuart Hall, introduction to *Questions of Cultural Identity*, ed. Stuart Hall and Paul duGay (Thousand Oaks, Calif.: Sage Publications, 1996), 13–14 (italics in the original).

19. Alain Badiou, *Ethics: An Essay on the Understanding of Evil*, trans. Peter Hallward (New York: Verso, 2001).

20. Epigraph: John Miller Chernoff, *African Rhythms and African Sensibility* (Chicago: University of Chicago Press, 1979), 125. I use "style" as opposed to "genre" here (and throughout the remainder of the book) in order to suggest the many different types of style that might potentially be addressed (i.e., fashion, speech, gesture, etc.) in the course of thinking about ethics and performance. In other words, I am hoping to keep the ethics of style as open as possible to new contexts, applications, and interpretations.

21. Jean-Jacques Nattiez, *Music and Discourse: Toward a Semiology of Music*, trans. Carolyn Abbate (Princeton: Princeton University Press, 1990). Of interest to me in his account of a semiology of music is his insistence on "reading" both the music *and* the scholar's analysis as "symbolic constructions." Nattiez is very careful to clarify, following Umberto Eco, that semiology is "not the science of communication," and that he is interested merely in "demonstrating the existence of music as a "symbolic form" (34).

22. Ibid., 37.

23. Simon Frith, "Music and Identity," in *Questions of Cultural Identity*, 124. The quotation by Chernoff is in *African Rhythm and African Sensibility*, 125.

24. Ibid., 125.

25. Frith, guarding against any possibility of creating a foundationalist argument, has cautioned: "The question we should be asking is not what does popular music reveal about the people who play it and use it but how does it create them

as people, as a web of identities? If we start from the assumption that pop is expressive, then we get bogged down in the search for the 'real' artist or emotion or belief lying behind it. But popular music is popular not because it reflects something or authentically articulates some sort of popular taste or experience, but because it creates our understanding of what 'popularity' is, because it places us in the social world in a particular way. What we should be examining, in other words, is not how true a piece of music is to something else, but how it sets up the idea of 'truth' in the first place—successful pop music is music which defines its own aesthetic standard" (ibid., 121). While I agree with Frith that we cannot possibly excavate intent, the real, or truth from musical performance, I nevertheless maintain that the context within which Trinidadian gospel music plays out necessitates a discussion that begins with ethics and ends with aesthetics—not the other way around. If this is the case, then Frith's last statement must be taken with a grain of salt, and this not least because the Full Gospel community is bound by a set of doctrinal understandings that constrain believers to orient themselves "in a certain kind of way" toward the world, and this is *prior* to the power of music to "place us in the social world in a particular way." (I have borrowed the phrase "in a certain kind of way" from Antonio Benítez-Rojo's book *The Repeating Island: The Caribbean and the Post-modern Perspective,* trans. James E. Maraniss [Durham, N.C.: Duke University Press, 1996.]) The ability of popular music to "define its own aesthetic standard" is, in other words, competing with an equally powerful framework for judgment within Full Gospel Trinidad.

26. This subheading and the next play on the title of Steven Hendley's book *From Communicative Action to the Face of the Other: Levinas and Habermas on Language, Obligation, and Community* (New York: Lexington Books, 2000).

27. Jürgen Habermas, *Religion and Rationality: Essays on Reason, God, and Modernity* (Cambridge: MIT Press, 2002), 160.

28. Habermas goes on to say that "the evidence of my relation to a theological heritage does not bother me, as long as one recognizes the *methodological difference* of the discourses; that is, as long as the philosophical discourse conforms to the distinctive demands of justificatory speech. In my view, a philosophy that oversteps the bounds of methodological atheism loses its philosophical seriousness" (ibid., 160; italics in the original).

29. Habermas defines discourse ethics as follows: "Discourse ethics replaces the Kantian categorical imperative by a procedure of moral argumentation. Its principle postulates . . . only those norms may claim to be valid that could meet with the consent of all affected in their role as participants in a practical discourse. While retaining the categorical imperative after a fashion, discourse ethics scales it down to a principle of universalization (U). In practical discourses (U) plays the part of a rule of argumentation: (U) For a norm to be valid, the consequences and side effects of its general observance for the satisfaction of each person's particular interests must be acceptable to all." Jürgen Habermas, *Moral Consciousness and Communicative Action,* trans. Christian Lenhardt and Shierry Weber Nicholsen (Cambridge: MIT Press, 1990), 197.

30. William Rehg, *Insight and Solidarity: The Discourse Ethics of Jürgen Habermas* (Berkeley: University of California Press, 1994), 102.

31. Ephesians 4:2–3a, New International Version.

32. Sarah Thornton, *Club Cultures: Music, Media, and Subcultural Capital* (Hanover, N.H.: University Press of New England, 1996), 163–64.

33. In light of the context I have briefly mapped out, I should like to suggest two ways in which my thought diverges from Habermas's. First, I am convinced that the irrational aspects of ethical discourse, what Habermas refers to as mythic thought, are necessary ingredients of rationality in Full Gospel Trinidad. In other words, I do not think that Habermas's postmetaphysical reliance on pure procedural ethics allows for enough breadth in this Trinidadian context. I agree with Paget Henry that Habermas's discourse ethics would work better if this aspect of thought were included rather than systematically excluded. "In Habermas, myth plays a . . . negative role in the construction of Western rationality. It is the category of human thought that Habermas has refused to rescue from scientistic and technocratic oblivion. It constitutes the liminal, irrational category against which communicative rationality is defined. . . . [But] Habermas needs the reconciliatory rationality of myth as an ally. He needs the special powers of this rationality to overcome the bad-faith strategies that empower the blind one-sidedness of the project of technocratic reason . . . Habermas need[s] to transform this liminal other into an ally" (Henry, *Caliban's Reason*, 180 and 194). Second, I am convinced that the ethical and moral modes of discourse that Habermas is at pains to keep separate from each other are, in fact, inseparable—at least in practice. Put otherwise, the ambiguities to which Habermas and Rehg admit are inevitable, unavoidable, constituent parts of what it means to be in relationship.

34. Taylor, *Sources of the Self*, 3.

35. It is helpful here to consider the work of Emmanuel Levinas, who, in contrast to Habermas, grounds his ethics of obligation in the good rather than the right. It is also a theory that privileges relationship through language, focusing on the irreducibility of the act of "saying something" to the fact of the "said." In other words, every "said" implies a much more complexly interconnected "saying," the purpose of which is expressly relational. Steven Hendley, offering a Levinasian reading of this idea, writes, "It is only as my interlocutor, if not in fact then at least in principle, that the other shows me her/his face as one to whom I am obliged to give a kind of consideration that, in some contexts, can only be characterized as moral" (Hendley, *From Communicative Action*, 4). He goes on to discuss the sense in which texts—and I would include music here as well—implicitly posit the face of the other as a "sayer" of the said. "But to recognize that meaning is dependent on, at the very least, a virtual conversational relation with an other I imagine as my interlocutor is to recognize that linguistic meaning would be inaccessible for anyone who was not competent with a conversational use of language, who was not familiar with what it means to defer to an interlocutor and so was not capable of reproducing that sense of deference even when there is no interlocutor to whom to actually defer—that the position of the pure observer, even as only an occasional rather than a permanent possibility, is incoherent, and no interpretation of language is possible that would completely abstract from our conversational competencies as genuine participants in a linguistic community" (10).

36. Emmanuel Levinas, *Totality and Infinity: An Essay on Exteriority*, trans. Alphonso Lingis (Pittsburgh: Duquesne University Press, 1969), 212–13.

37. Unlike John Caputo, for whom obligation simply happens, Levinas is careful to illustrate the relationship that language—the communicative act—establishes between individuals. John D. Caputo, *Against Ethics: Contributions to a Poetics of Obligation with Constant Reference to Deconstruction* (Bloomington: Indiana University Press, 1993). More important, he points to the ways through which this obligation might lead to the possibility of communion (for Habermas, perhaps solidarity), not merely community. In my view, this is the key point that Levinas's work adds to the conceptualization of the ethics of style.

3. NATIONALISM AND THE SOUL

Epigraphs: Eric E. Williams, "Independence Day Address," in *Eric E. Williams Speaks: Essays on Colonialism and Independence*, ed. Selwyn R. Cudjoe (Amherst: University of Massachusetts Press, 1993), 266. Sean Daniel, interview with the author, August 14, 2003.

1. Sean Daniel was attached to the Generation Next Kaiso Tent in 2006.

2. Iwer George and Super Blue are two of the top soca performers in contemporary Trinidad. "Waving" refers here to the Trinidadian (and pan-Caribbean) habit of waving a rag, a piece of clothing, a flag, and so forth at concerts, sporting events, and other public festivals. Lyrics reproduced by kind permission of Andrew O'Brien.

3. For an excellent retrospective analysis of the political, economic, and social climates that fueled the black power movement, see Selwyn D. Ryan and Taimoon Stewart's book *Power: The Black Power Revolution 1970, a Retrospective* (St. Augustine, Trinidad: Institute for Social and Economic Research, University of the West Indies, 1995).

4. Eric Williams, "The Chaguaramas Declaration," in *Eric E. Williams Speaks*, 92.

5. Stuart Hall, introduction to *Questions of Cultural Identity*, ed. Stuart Hall and Paul duGay (Thousand Oaks, Calif.: Sage Publications, 1996), 4.

6. I should mention that am not using the term "gnostic" in a pejorative sense here. I am, rather, making an attempt to highlight the radical dualism that is maintained between God and creation and, by extension, between human beings and their world in gnostic thought. Addressing the problem of evil by removing God from all responsibility has remained a popular solution within Christian circles from the earliest *gnostikoi* ("those who know"), such as Valentinus and Marcion. I remain convinced that a hierarchical understanding wherein the spiritual takes pride of place over the physical—a hierarchy often evident in Pentecostalist worship and worldview—is a contemporary continuation of the same system of thought.

7. Philip J. Lee, *Against the Protestant Gnostics* (New York: Oxford University Press, 1987), 10.

8. For more information on the impact of Yoruba religious culture on Trini-

dad, see Maureen Warner-Lewis's *Trinidad Yoruba: From Mother Tongue to Memory* (Kingston, Jamaica: University of the West Indies Press, 1997) and *Central Africa in the Caribbean: Transcending Time, Transforming Cultures* (Kingston, Jamaica: University of the West Indies Press, 2003). See also Frances Henry's *Reclaiming African Religions in Trinidad: The Socio-political Legitimation of the Orisha and Spiritual Baptist Faiths* (St. Augustine, Trinidad: University of the West Indies Press, 2003).

9. Earl Phillip, interview on radio FM 94.1 with Noel "the Professor" Richards, February 2, 2001 (emphasis mine).

10. The Mystic Prowler performed with the Original Young Brigade Tent starting in 1966 but, starting in the 1970s, increasingly focused his attention on sacred songs. In the early 1990s, however, he returned to the calypso tents and won the Calypso Monarch Competition in 1998 with the songs "Look beneath the Surface" and "Vision of T&T in the Year 2010." He passed away on September 20, 2003.

11. Baptists have been a part of the Protestant landscape in Trinidad since the arrival, between 1814 and 1816, of 781 freedmen (and their families) who fought for Great Britain during the War of 1812. These ex-soldiers were given property and settled in six Company Villages. It is commonly held that they continued to practice the Baptist faith that they encountered as slaves in the United States.

12. Simon Frith, "Music and Identity," in *Questions of Cultural Identity*, 124.

13. This chorus might also fruitfully be read in connection with Max Weber's articulation of the Protestant ethic in *The Protestant Ethic and the Spirit of Capitalism* (London: George, Allen, & Unwin, 1976).

14. It is, of course, not surprising to find that some of the choruses claimed as Baptist choruses have lives outside of Trinidad in places like Jamaica and Barbados. Some have, undoubtedly, entered the repertory from sources outside Trinidad. But the question of ownership is, in this context, not a strictly historical one, but rather concerns the sense of the place that this body of songs occupies within Trinidad's religious landscape. I am, thus, not attempting to make a historical claim, but only to illustrate the local character of this body of songs.

15. Leyland Henry, interview with the author, July 26, 2000.

16. Dale A. Bisnauth, *History of Religions in the Caribbean* (Trenton, N.J.: Africa World Press, 1996), 196–97.

17. Roddie Taylor, interview with the author, February 17, 2000.

18. Hollis Liverpool, *Rituals of Power and Rebellion: The Carnival Tradition in Trinidad and Tobago, 1763–1962* (Chicago: Research Associates School Times, 2001), 202–3. For a detailed exploration of African religious practices in Trinidad, see Henry's *Reclaiming African Religion in Trinidad.*

19. Noel "the Professor" Richards, interview with the author, June 26, 2001.

20. Lyrics reproduced by kind permission of Noel Richards.

21. Calypso Rose released an album of gospelypso, entitled *Jesus Is My Rock*, in 1999 (Rose Records), and the Mystic Prowler released a compilation of songs entitled *Spiritual Songs* in 2000 (Electro Sounds). Even though he is gen-

erally credited for having written the first gospelypso, he has not been able to win support among members of the Full Gospel community because of his decision to sing secular calypsos in the tents since the 1990s.

22. "Jump for Jesus," recorded in 1993, is the first gospelypso radio hit, and it did not go unnoticed that this hit was generated at the hands of an East Indian woman who has generally performed more North American than Trinidadian music. While no gospelypso artist would ever openly criticize her work, her estimation within that artistic community can be measured by the simple fact that her name was never mentioned in a four-hour forum on radio FM 94.1 entitled "Gospelypso through the Years."

23. Taylor, interview.

24. Lyrics reproduced by kind permission of Noel Richards.

25. Marilyn "Destiny" Joseph, interview with the author, June 14, 2000.

26. Lyrics reproduced by kind permission of Noel Richards.

27. I should be quick to add here that there are, of course, many church leaders, pastors, and laypeople who choose to identify with gospelypsonians and their project. In addressing the general trends within the Full Gospel community, I certainly do not mean to suggest that the prevailing interpretation of gospelypso holds uniformly or even strongly in all quarters.

28. My articulation of the poetics of conviction is related in some respects to what Homi Bhabha has called the poetics of identification. According to Bhabha, the poetics of identification "strives to represent the process through which intercultural relations in-between class, gender, generation, race, religion, or region are articulated as hybrid identifications." Homi Bhabha, "On Cultural Choice," in *The Turn to Ethics,* ed. Marjorie Garber, Beatrice Hanssen, and Rebecca L. Walkowitz (New York: Routledge, 2000), 190. In other words, the poetics of identification is useful for analyzing the linkages that make these processes visible.

29. I'm thinking here of choruses such as "Let's Just Praise the Lord," "Amen," "More Precious Than Silver," and "As the Deer."

30. Think of the necessary "openness" of a nonlocal music (its lack of local, historicized contexts) as sharing some essential aspects in common with the act of learning a new language. In the process of acquiring the vocabulary, we turn to a dictionary, which gives us a few definitions and usages for a given word. In practice, we have no choice but to accept these definitions as the range of meanings for the word. But if we were to run our findings by a fluent speaker who had grown up with the language, we would not be surprised to find out that the word can mean a multitude of other things depending on inflection, context, idiomatic usage, and so forth. It is in this sense that the nonlocal is less "bound" by context and history than the local.

31. Phillip, interview.

32. Helen Baylor is a gospel artist of international reputation, and Larry Harewood is a four-time winner of the gospelypso competition as well as a prolific composer of gospelypso music.

33. Michael Herzfeld, *Cultural Intimacy: Social Poetics in the Nation-State* (New York: Routledge, 1997), 6.

34. Earl Lovelace, "Views of Earl Lovelace," interview by Victor Questal, *Caribbean Contact* 5, no. 3 (1977):15–16. Cited in Stefano Harney, *Nationalism and Identity: Culture and the Imagination in a Caribbean Diaspora* (Atlantic Highlands, N.J.: Zed Books, 1996), 35 (emphasis mine).

35. For more detailed information about the early history of carnival and calypso in Trinidad and Tobago, see Liverpool's *Rituals of Power and Rebellion*.

36. Herzfeld, *Cultural Intimacy*, 21.

37. Ibid., 26.

38. The scorecards were broken down into the following criteria for judging: lyrics, 30 points; melody, 20 points; performance, 25 points; rhythm, 15 points; audience response, 10 points. This information was condensed from Phillip, interview.

39. Leyland Henry, interview with Noel "the Professor" Richards on radio FM 94.1, February 2, 2001.

4. TRANSNATIONAL DREAMS, GLOBAL DESIRES

1. Excerpts from a conversation with Anthony Moses and Sean Friday, June 23, 2000.

2. The idea of the invisible church was initially articulated by John Calvin in his *Institutes of the Christian Religion*, book 4, chapter 1.

3. This is, of course, not an isolated phenomenon, for musicians are constantly wrestling with the extent to which local and more globalized voices should and can participate in coming to terms with Christian worship in a given place. Gregory Barz illustrates this well in a compelling exploration of Gideon Mdegella's musical life as a Lutheran choir director and composer in Tanzania. Barz has included this material in his book *Music of East Africa: Experiencing Music, Expressing Culture* (New York: Oxford University Press, 2004).

4. For more detailed explorations of cosmopolitanism, see Kwame Anthony Appiah's *Cosmopolitanism: Ethics in a World of Strangers* (New York: Norton, 2006); Pheng Cheah and Bruce Robbins's edited collection *Cosmopolitics: Thinking and Feeling beyond the Nation* (Minneapolis: University of Minnesota Press, 1998); and Steven Vertovec and Robin Cohen's edited collection *Conceiving Cosmopolitanism: Theory, Context, and Practice* (New York: Oxford University Press, 2002).

5. For an excellent treatment of the racial imagination, see Ronald Radano and Philip V. Bohlman, eds., *Music and the Racial Imagination* (Chicago: University of Chicago Press, 2000).

6. Because North American gospel music has generally not created much controversy within the Trinidadian Full Gospel community, I rely to a greater extent on field notes and interviews in this chapter than I do elsewhere in the book. There is simply much less need to justify or argue the applicability and usefulness of North American gospel music in this context—a state of affairs that leads to very little exposure in various media outlets. The discourse about North American gospel music, then, surfaces in comparison to other musical

styles and upon reflection, but not as a necessary companion to the musical style (as is the case with gospelypso and gospel dancehall).

7. Steve Bruce, *Religion in the Modern World: From Cathedrals to Cults* (New York: Oxford University Press, 1996), 22.

8. For other studies on the tensions created by denominationalism, see Steve Bruce's "Authority and Fission: The Protestants' Divisions," *British Journal of Sociology* 36 (1985): 592–603, and *A House Divided: Protestantism, Schism, and Secularization* (New York: Routledge, 1989).

9. The various Baptist groups in Trinidad maintain an organization that was, until recently, called the Trinidad and Tobago Baptist Fellowship. The organization's name was changed to the United Baptists of Trinidad and Tobago in 2002.

10. Jonathan Boyarin, "Space, Time, and the Politics of Memory," in *Remapping Memory: The Politics of TimeSpace*, ed. Jonathan Boyarin (Minneapolis: University of Minnesota Press, 1994), 26.

11. It is not coincidental that the Nazarite Steelband was founded by Rev. Leyland Henry and is housed in his church in San Juan.

12. Experiments with services commonly referred to as "traditional" (primarily hymns and congregational readings) and "contemporary" (dominated by choruses and often incorporating drama and interpretive dance) have, on the whole, been rather polarizing, leading many worship leaders and music ministers to search for more palatable alternatives. Blended services are an attempt to accommodate the broadest possible range of musical tastes within a single service. For a more elaborate treatment of this trend, see Robb Redman's book *The Great Worship Awakening: Singing a New Song in the Postmodern Church* (San Francisco: Jossey-Bass, 2002).

13. Ulf Hannerz, *Transnational Connections: Culture, People, Places* (New York: Routledge, 1996), 91–92.

14. Jacques Derrida, "Faith and Knowledge: The Two Sources of 'Religion' at the Limits of Reason Alone," in *Religion: Cultural Memory in the Present*, ed. Jacques Derrida and Gianni Vattimo (Stanford, Calif.: Stanford University Press, 1998), 11.

15. Philip V. Bohlman, "World Musics and World Religions: Whose World?" in *Enchanting Powers: Music in the World's Religions*, ed. Lawrence E. Sullivan (Cambridge: Harvard University Press, 1997), 69 (emphasis mine).

16. Earl Phillip, interview on radio FM 94.1 with Noel "the Professor" Richards, February 2, 2001 (emphasis mine).

17. This is, of course, a generalization. There are many fine examples of North American choruses that exhibit the praise-oriented qualities that I just attributed to Trinidadian choruses. Significantly, however, Trinidadian worship leaders tend to make good use of the large number of North American choruses that exhibit the more worship-oriented characteristics I discuss here.

18. We might also think of the concept of *jouissance* in this connection. Lacanian readings of desire as a longing for that which remains, by definition, always already unobtainable are not entirely dissimilar to the desire for God expressed through these sentimentally charged choruses.

19. Michael Herzfeld, *Cultural Intimacy: Social Poetics in the Nation-State* (New York: Routledge, 1997), 56–57.

20. Derrida, "Faith and Knowledge," 4.

21. Hollis Liverpool, *Rituals of Power and Rebellion: The Carnival Tradition in Trinidad and Tobago, 1763–1962* (Chicago: Research Associates School Times, 2001), 416.

22. The Apostles 5, *'Tis So Sweet* (1976), excerpted from the liner notes.

23. Love 94.1 FM was sold and reconstituted as Isaac 98.1 FM. Isaac remains the sole Christian station on the FM band in Trinidad. Jamie's most recent role is as the DJ of a gospel music slot on 195.5 FM, a station dedicated primarily to talk and news radio.

24. The album is entitled *Thankful* and was released by Sony (CTDP 100249) in 2000.

25. Jamie Thomas, interview with the author, June 3, 2000.

26. I want to be clear. I am in no way directing this criticism at Arjun Appadurai, whose work I find immensely helpful. Rather, I am adding my voice to those of scholars who are working toward a more critical and nuanced use of theoretical constructs in the Caribbean. An excellent collection of such material, as I've already indicated elsewhere in this book, is found in *Caribbean Romances: The Politics of Regional Representation,* ed. Belinda Edmondson (Charlottesville: University Press of Virginia, 1999).

27. Stuart Hall, introduction to *Questions of Cultural Identity,* ed. Stuart Hall and Paul duGay (Thousand Oaks, Calif.: Sage Publications, 1996), 6.

28. Rex Nettleford, *Inward Stretch Outward Reach: A Voice from the Caribbean* (London: Macmillan Press, 1993), 129.

29. It is also the first line of the chorus to "Awesome God," a very popular North American chorus composed by Rich Mullins.

30. Catherine Hall, "Histories, Empires, and the Post-colonial Moment," in *The Post-colonial Question: Common Skies, Divided Horizons,* ed. Iain Chambers and Lidia Curti (New York: Routledge, 1996), 65.

31. This quote is excerpted from the Nicene Creed, penned during the first ecumenical council, convened in 325. Most Full Gospel churches in Trinidad are wary of creeds and do not accept extrabiblical materials as authoritative in any way. It is nevertheless interesting to consider the ideal penned in 325 and to juxtapose it to contemporary realities.

32. Matthew 25:31–46 (New International Version) reads as follows:

> When the Son of Man comes in his glory, and the angels with him, he will sit on his throne in heavenly glory. All the nations will be gathered before him, and he will separate the people one from another as a shepherd separates the sheep from the goats. He will put the sheep on his right and the goats on his left. Then the King will say to those on his right, "Come, you who are blessed by my Father; take your inheritance, the kingdom prepared for you since the creation of the world. For I was hungry and you gave me something to eat, I was thirsty and you gave

me something to drink, I was a stranger and you invited me in, I needed clothes and you clothed me, I was sick and you looked after me, I was in prison and you came to visit me." Then the righteous will answer him, "Lord, when did we see you hungry and feed you, or thirsty and give you something to drink? When did we see you a stranger and invite you in, or needing clothes and clothe you? When did we see you sick or in prison and go to visit you?" The King will reply, "I tell you the truth, whatever you did for one of the least of these brothers of mine, you did for me." Then he will say to those on his left, "Depart from me, you who are cursed, into the eternal fire prepared for the devil and his angels. For I was hungry and you gave me nothing to eat, I was thirsty and you gave me nothing to drink, I was a stranger and you did not invite me in, I needed clothes and you did not clothe me, I was sick and in prison and you did not look after me." They also will answer, "Lord, when did we see you hungry or thirsty or a stranger or needing clothes or sick or in prison, and did not help you?" He will reply, "I tell you the truth, whatever you did not do for one of the least of these, you did not do for me." Then they will go away to eternal punishment, but the righteous to eternal life.

33. Rev. Vernon Duncan, personal communication with the author, facilitated by Noel "the Professor" Richards, April 10, 2006.

34. Theodor Adorno, *Minima Moralia: Reflections from Damaged Life*, trans. E. F. N. Jephcott (New York: Verso, 1978), 127.

35. Hannerz, *Transnational Connections*, 4.

36. For some excellent studies on ethnicity in Trinidad, see Kevin A. Yelvington's edited collection *Trinidad Ethnicity*, Warwick University Caribbean Studies (London: Macmillan Caribbean, 1993); Peter Manuel's *East Indian Music in the West Indies: Tan-Singing, Chutney, and the Making of Indo-Caribbean Culture* (Philadelphia: Temple University Press, 2000); Aisha Kahn's dissertation "Purity, Piety, and Power: Culture and Identity among Hindus and Muslims in Trinidad" (Ph.D. diss., City University of New York, 1995); and Selwyn D. Ryan's *The Jhandi and the Cross: The Clash of Cultures in Post-Creole Trinidad and Tobago* (St. Augustine, Trinidad: Sir Arthur Lewis Institute of Social and Economic Studies, University of the West Indies, 1999).

37. "I Sings" is included on Mary Mary's album *Thankful*; "Let's Dance" is included on Hezekiah Walker's album *Family Affair* (Verity J2 3132, 1999).

38. Lyrics reprinted by kind permission of Sherwin Gardner.

5. REGIONALISMS

1. "Living Dangerously," editorial insert, *Trinidad Express*, February 9, 1997, 19.

2. Felicia Marion, "Drink," included on *Compassion* (Friends in Fellowship 0006, 1997).

3. V. S. Naipaul, *Guerrillas* (New York: Vintage Books, 1975), 125. "The

Loudest Island in the World" is the title given to the section devoted to Jamaican music in *World Music: The Rough Guide* (New York: Penguin Books, 1994), 521. I use it here because it is ambiguous enough to allow for both positive and negative readings. In other words, it encapsulates the predicament of dancehall in Jamaican culture.

4. Gage Averill, *A Day for the Hunter, a Day for the Prey: Popular Music and Power in Haiti* (Chicago: University of Chicago Press, 1997), 1.

5. Norman C. Stolzoff, *Wake the Town and Tell the People: Dancehall Culture in Jamaica* (Durham, N.C.: Duke University Press, 2000), 6.

6. This is, of course, also a story about the ethics of style.

7. Belinda Edmondson, "Trinidad Romance: The Invention of Jamaican Carnival," in *Caribbean Romances: The Politics of Regional Representation*, ed. Belinda Edmondson (Charlottesville: University Press of Virginia, 1999), 67–68.

8. Ibid., 72.

9. Ronnie McIntosh, "Why Dance Hall Is Such Powerful Stuff," interview by Jean Fairweather, *The Gleaner*, April 24, 1994, cited in Stolzoff, *Wake the Town*, 5.

10. Joan Rampersad, "Ronnie: Jamaican Influence Ruining Soca," *Trinidad Express*, February 5, 1999 (emphasis mine).

11. The moral outrage of Trinidadians is most often reserved for and directed at calypsonians. For example, David Rudder was accused of "preaching the gospel of sexual permissiveness" by Professor Courtenay Bartholomew, a leading AIDS researcher (Terry Joseph, "Rudder Defends His Song: It's the Trini Way," *Trinidad Express*, July 26, 1999). I believe that this trend is a direct by-product of the negotiation of proximity.

12. Believer in Christ, "Keep the Devil Out of Church" *Trinidad Express*, September 2, 1992.

13. Stolzoff recognizes this critical perspective among Jamaican Protestants as well, noting that most "devout Christian members of the black lower class are morally opposed to dancehall." Stolzoff, *Wake the Town*, 232.

14. As quoted in Celia Sankar, "Dub for Christ: Youngsters Get the Gospel Message, but Older Evangelists Query the Medium," *Trinidad Express*, June 14, 1992, 10.

15. As quoted in ibid.

16. "Gospel Takes on Reggae, Dancehall Rhythms: Here Comes Melchizedek Order," *Trinidad Express*, July 11, 1999, 30.

17. Christian artists have also found ways of incorporating these lyrical themes into heavy metal, hip-hop, and alternative music (including bands like Whitecross, D.C. Talk, and the Newsboys, respectively). And while these bands effectively explore lyrics involving violence—as in Stryper's "To Hell with the Devil" and Whitecross's "Holy War"—these genres are not as widely popular in the Caribbean as dancehall. It is for this reason that artists like Sherwin Gardner and Spiritual Ninja tend to channel their lyrics through dancehall and, to a lesser degree, through R&B and hip-hop.

18. Stolzoff, *Wake the Town*, 172.

19. Curtis "Spiritual Ninja" Miller, interview with the author, June 28, 2000.

20. The obvious reference to Bob Marley's "Exodus" and Rastafarian imagery (i.e., I-ance, Babylon system, etc.) is here mixed with biblical metaphor and constitutes another important aspect of Full Gospel dancehall. I take this up a bit later in the chapter. Lyrics reproduced by kind permission of Lyndon R. Sterling (a.k.a. Tiko).

21. The text was composed by Issac Watts in 1707, and it was set to music in 1867 by Robert Lowry.

22. Lyrics reprinted by kind permission of Sherwin Gardner.

23. Lyrics reproduced by kind permission of Lyndon R. Sterling.

24. A Concerned Believer in Christ, "Why Use Dub Music?" *Trinidad Express,* July 31, 1992, 9.

25. Lyrics reproduced by kind permission of Sherwin Gardner.

26. Lyrics reproduced by kind permission of Ancil Valley.

27. Margaret Toussaint, interview with the author, March 13, 2000.

28. Anthony "Space" Williams, interview with the author, July 8, 2000.

29. I do not want to imply, however, a community of artists that is happily sharing all successes. There are, of course, rivalries among the artists, but the Full Gospel context within which they are acted out does not allow for open hostility. Furthermore, none of the artists would admit that they even *dislike* another artist, as this would be considered a sinful and prideful attitude. Finally, the community is small enough that it still maintains a familial atmosphere.

30. The epigraph is from A Concerned Believer in Christ, "Why Use Dub Music?"

31. Lyrics reproduced by kind permission of Ancil Valley.

32. What can and should be said of these lyrics, however, is that they clearly contribute to the most unforgiving and negative view of women—a view that serves only to reinforce the trope of the male's spiritual susceptibility to and victimization by the "evil" woman. The lyrics also go on to offer proof (in the third verse) of the male's physical dominance. While this song addresses one of the charges facing dancehall artists—slackness—it unfortunately raises a series of very important gender-related concerns that are left entirely unaddressed.

33. Darryl Ramdhansingh, "Jumping for Jesus or the Devil?" *Trinidad Express,* April 20, 1993, 9.

34. The expression "salt and light," used by many Full Gospel believers in Trinidad, is a condensed reference to the sayings of Jesus as recorded in Matthew 5:13–15.

35. Rev. Vernon Duncan, interview with the author, June 12, 2000.

36. Carolyn Cooper, *Noises in the Blood: Orality, Gender, and the "Vulgar" Body of Jamaican Popular Culture* (Durham, N.C.: Duke University Press, 1995).

37. Ibid., 87–95.

38. One could even extend this into a North American context and think about the ways that Ebonics has been received and debated in recent memory.

39. Cooper, *Noises in the Blood,* 2.

40. John P. Homiak, "Soundings on Rastafari Livity and Language," in *Rastafari and Other African-Caribbean Worldviews,* ed. Barry Chevannes (New Brunswick, N.J.: Rutgers University Press, 1995), 175.

41. Roddie Taylor, interview with the author, March 14, 2000.

42. Mikhail Bakhtin, *The Dialogical Imagination: Four Essays by M. M. Bakhtin,* ed. Michael Holquist (Austin: University of Texas Press, 1981), 293.

43. Jaques Attali, *Noise: The Political Economy of Music* (Minneapolis: University of Minnesota Press, 1985), 33.

44. 2 Samuel 6:12–23 (New International Version) reads as follows:

Now King David was told, "The Lord has blessed the household of Obed-Edom and everything he has, because of the ark of God." So David went down and brought up the ark of God from the house of Obed-Edom to the City of David with rejoicing. When those who were carrying the ark of the Lord had taken six steps, he sacrificed a bull and a fattened calf. David, wearing a linen ephod, danced before the Lord with all his might, while he and the entire house of Israel brought up the ark of the Lord with shouts and the sound of trumpets. As the ark of the Lord was entering the City of David, Michal daughter of Saul watched from a window. And when she saw King David leaping and dancing before the Lord, she despised him in her heart. They brought the ark of the Lord and set it in its place inside the tent that David had pitched for it, and David sacrificed burnt offerings and fellowship offerings before the Lord. After he had finished sacrificing the burnt offerings and fellowship offerings, he blessed the people in the name of the Lord Almighty. Then he gave a loaf of bread, a cake of dates and a cake of raisins to each person in the whole crowd of Israelites, both men and women. And all the people went to their homes. When David returned home to his household, Michal daughter of Saul came out to meet him and said, "How the king of Israel has distinguished himself today, disrobing in the sight of the slave girls of his servants as any vulgar fellow would!" David said to Michal, "It was before the Lord, who chose me rather than your father or anyone from his house when he appointed me ruler over the Lord's people Israel—I will celebrate before the Lord. I will become even more undignified than this, and I will be humiliated in my own eyes. But by these slave girls you spoke of, I will be held in honor." And Michal daughter of Saul had no children to the day of her death.

45. Romans 14:13–23 (New International Version) reads as follows:

Therefore let us stop passing judgment on one another. Instead, make up your mind not to put any stumbling block or obstacle in your brother's way. As one who is in the Lord Jesus, I am fully convinced that no food is unclean in itself. But if anyone regards something as unclean, then for him it is unclean. If your brother is distressed because of what you eat, you are no longer acting in love. Do not by your eating destroy your brother for whom Christ died. Do not allow what you consider good to be spoken of as evil. For the kingdom of God is not a matter of eating and drinking, but of righteousness, peace and joy in the Holy Spirit, because anyone who serves Christ in this way is pleasing to God and approved by men. Let us therefore make every effort to do what leads to peace and to mutual edification. Do not destroy the work of God for the sake of food. All food is clean, but it is wrong for a man to eat anything that causes someone else to stumble. It is better not to eat meat or drink wine or do anything else that will cause your brother to fall. So whatever you believe about these things keep between yourself and God. Blessed is the man who does not condemn himself by what he approves. But the man who has doubts is condemned if he eats, because his eating is not from faith; and everything that does not come from faith is sin.

46. Alain Badiou, *Ethics: An Essay on the Understanding of Evil*, trans. Peter Hallward (New York: Verso, 2001), 31–32.

47. For a detailed study of this genre and its reception history, see Michael W. Harris's *The Rise of Gospel Blues: The Music of Thomas Andrew Dorsey in the Urban Church* (New York: Oxford University Press, 1994). Also see Jerma A. Jackson's *Singing in My Soul: Black Gospel Music in a Secular Age* (Chapel Hill: University of North Carolina Press, 2004).

48. Attali, *Noise*, 33.

49. Lyrics reprinted by kind permission of Sherwin Gardner.

6. JEHOVAH'S MUSIC

1. Natasha Ofosu, "Hail 'Marley' of Calypso," *Trinidad Guardian*, July 20, 2000, 1.

2. The Trinidad Unified Calypso Association choir included Super Blue, De Fosto, Pink Panther, Chalkdust, Karega Mandela, and Calypso Kerr and was led by Sean Daniel.

3. Ofosu, "Hail 'Marley' of Calypso," 1.

4. Super Blue's musical tribute was not well received by most calypsonians or by Ras Shorty I's family. Most felt that he should have performed a hymn or one of Shorty's compositions. Super Blue later issued an apology, claiming that he had intended to sing Psalm 23 and was caught off guard when the Love Circle sang it just before he was to perform. An article in the *Trinidad Express* entitled "Don't Blame Super Blue for 'No Woman No Cry'" (July 20, 2000) quoted Super Blue's manager, Alvin Daniel, who said, "This [turn of events] embarrassed him [Super Blue] greatly and he had to think up an alternative on the spur of the moment."

5. Wayne Bowman, "State Help for Shorty Funeral," *Trinidad Guardian*, July 14, 2000, 2.

6. The information presented in this section has been condensed from various sources, including several interviews with Ras Shorty I's family, various newspaper articles, biographical information available online, and a particularly helpful article by Jocelyne Guilbault entitled "The Politics of Labelling Popular Musics in English Caribbean." This article is available online as part of the e-journal *Transcultural Music Review* 3 (1997), http://www.sibetrans.com/trans/trans3/guilbault.htm.

7. Keino Swamber, "Shorty a Boxer?" *Trinidad Express,* July 19, 2000, 32.

8. This name was intended to point out in humorous fashion that Garfield Blackman, who stood well over six feet tall and was an imposing figure onstage, was anything but short.

9. Lord Shorty responded to Dr. Williams's actions in classic style at the 1973 national Calypso King finals, singing "The PM Sex Probe." In the song, he claimed that he had only tried "to educate my people" and, reflecting on the prime minister's reaction to this noble effort, realized that he must have "touched him where he is most lacking." He also went on to include the song on his album *The Love Man,* released in the following year.

10. As quoted in Selwyn E. Ahyoung, "Soca Fever: Change in the Calypso Music Tradition of Trinidad and Tobago" (master's thesis, Indiana University, 1981). Excepts from an interview with Lord Shorty by Roy Burke, published in the 1979 carnival magazine.

11. One important change to this instrumentation is the substitution of the iron from the steelband for the triangle after about 1978.

12. Charis, "Songs of Praise," *Vox Magazine,* June 7, 2001.

13. The "stay in the bush" movement was spearheaded by Eric Minnis, a popular and well-respected performer in the Bahamas.

14. The family islands are considered the antithesis of the urban and cosmopolitan Nassau. The idea was to look toward the rural, small town, agricultural aspects of Bahamian life and to construct from them a post-independence authenticity that could then be used to convey Bahamianness.

15. Quoted from the liner notes to *Children of the Jamoo Journey,* 1997.

16. Claudette Blackman, interview with the author, September 11, 2004.

17. Peter Mason, "Ras Shorty I: Calypsonian Who Found Religion after a Life of Sex and Drugs," *Guardian,* July 15, 2000.

18. Terry Joseph, "Ras Shorty I: Ras Shorty Comes Full Circle," *Trinidad Express,* May 15, 2000, 48 (emphasis mine).

19. Sheldon Blackman, interview with Dennis Taye, *Trinidad Guardian,* October 24, 1999 (emphasis mine).

20. Robert Neville, "Sketch of a System," in *New Essays in Metaphysics,* ed. Robert Neville (Albany: State University of New York Press, 1989), 272 n. 3.

21. David L. Hall, *Richard Rorty: Prophet and Poet of the New Pragmatism* (Albany: State University of New York Press, 1994), 23.

22. Shannon Dudley, "Judging 'by the Beat': Calypso versus Soca," *Ethnomusicology* 40, no. 2 (Spring/Summer 1996): 285. Many calypsonians wrote songs expressing their views regarding the emergence of soca, and Ahyoung's "Soca Fever!" presents numerous excellent examples.

23. As quoted in Ahyoung, "Soca Fever!" 94.

24. Dudley, "Judging 'by the Beat,'" 286–87.

25. Guilbault, "The Politics of Labelling Popular Musics."

26. Ibid. (emphasis mine).

27. Ibid.

28. In using this term I am thinking of the "strong misreading" that Harold

Bloom posits as the only avenue toward creativity in poetry in *The Anxiety of Influence*, 2nd ed. (New York: Oxford University Press, 1997). As such, I do not use it with negative intent but consider the misreading of "sokah" as "soca" one of the principal reasons for soca's historical development and popularity in Trinidad.

29. Ahyoung, "Soca Fever!" 250.

30. Dudley, "Judging 'by the Beat,'" 287.

31. A good example of this trend is the title of Lord Shorty's 1977 album, which conflates both of these ideas into a single phrase: *Sokah Soul of Calypso*.

32. Guilbault, "The Politics of Labelling Popular Musics."

33. As quoted in Gillian Moore, "A Jamoo Journey through the Carnival Jam," *Trinidad Express*, March 6, 1998.

34. Blackman, interview, October 24, 1999.

35. Sheldon Blackman, interview with the author, June 30, 2001.

36. As quoted in Moore, "A Jamoo Journey."

37. For a thorough discussion of rhythm in soca and calypso, see Dudley, "Judging 'by the Beat.'"

38. The epigraph by Vernon Ramesar is from "Wake Up, My People," *Trinidad Express*, July 19, 2000, 17.

39. Cited in Selwyn D. Ryan, *The Jhandi and the Cross: The Clash of Cultures in Post-Creole Trinidad and Tobago* (St. Augustine, Trinidad: Sir Arthur Lewis Institute of Social and Economic Studies, University of the West Indies, 1999), 37.

40. Helen Myers, *Music of Hindu Trinidad: Songs from the India Diaspora* (Chicago: University of Chicago Press, 1998), 375.

41. Keith Q. Warner, "Ethnicity and the Contemporary Calypso," in *Trinidad Ethnicity*, ed. Kevin A. Yelvington, Warwick University Caribbean Studies (London: Macmillan Caribbean, 1993), 287.

42. Michael Herzfeld, *Cultural Intimacy: Social Poetics in the Nation-State* (New York: Routledge, 1997), 157.

43. Translation printed in Ahyoung, "Soca Fever!" 208.

44. Ibid.

45. Ibid., 207.

46. Ibid., 209.

47. This song was written by Ras Shorty I's son Sheldon Blackman while he was being prepared to take over leadership of the Love Circle.

48. Lyrics reproduced by kind permission of Sheldon Blackman.

49. Ronald Radano and Philip V. Bohlman, introduction to *Music and the Racial Imagination* (Chicago: University of Chicago Press, 2000), 36.

50. Ibid., 37.

51. Herzfeld, *Cultural Intimacy*, 170.

52. The text is adapted from Isaiah 40:3: "A voice of one calling: In the desert prepare the way for the Lord; make straight in the wilderness a highway for our God." This verse is generally understood as a prophetic description of John the Baptist, a reading made explicit in Matthew 3:3, where this verse is invoked as part

of the narrative of John the Baptist's life. In applying this verse to himself, Ras Shorty I claims for himself an analogous space in the "wilderness" of Trinidad.

53. Lyrics reproduced by kind permission of Sheldon Blackman.

54. Importantly, Sheldon Blackman was apprenticing under his father at the time he wrote this song. Given that Ras Shorty I still had complete creative and artistic control over the Love Circle, the song reflects, by its inclusion on the album, its usefulness to Ras Shorty I's project.

55. Anthony Moses, interview with the author, May 2, 2000.

56. Lyrics for "Seeking Is My Home," printed in the liner notes of Sheldon Blackman and the Love Circle's *Remember Me* (Shorty Music Publishing, 2000). Lyrics reproduced by kind permission of Sheldon Blackman.

57. Herzfeld, *Cultural Intimacy*, 145.

58. Ibid., 31.

59. Philip V. Bohlman, "Pilgrimage, Politics, and the Musical Remapping of the New Europe," *Ethnomusicology* 40, no. 3 (Fall 1996): 386–87.

60. Ibid., 391.

61. While Full Gospel believers do not generally go on pilgrimages, I believe that jamoo fulfills certain functions within Full Gospel Trinidad that can be understood from this point of view.

62. Lyrics reproduced by kind permission of Sheldon Blackman.

7. REENVISIONING ETHICS, REVISITING STYLE

1. Hebrews 10:25, New International Version.

2. Michel-Rolph Trouillot, *Silencing the Past: Power and the Production of History* (Boston: Beacon Press, 1995), 16.

3. Deacon McKellar and Mother Joseph, interviews with the author, May 7 and 8, 2000.

4. This is a paraphrase taken from ideas penned by Stuart Hall in his introduction to *Questions of Cultural Identity*, ed. Stuart Hall and Paul duGay (Thousand Oaks, Calif.: Sage Publications, 1996), 6.

5. I introduce this model hoping that it will be understood only as a heuristic device and not as a structure of belief. I am merely offering a slightly different visual perspective on the ideas presented here.

6. These varying opinions about the usefulness of a given style also go a long way toward illustrating the provisional and heuristic nature of the diagrams I offer here. Again, it is my hope that they will not be read as an attempt on my part to engage in a structuralist or essentialist representation of these musical practices, but rather as a means of engaging with and then complicating some of the prevailing approaches to these styles within Full Gospel Trinidad.

7. Dick Hebdige, *Subculture: The Meaning of Style* (London: Methuen, 1974), 17.

8. Isaiah 6:1–8 (New International Version) reads as follows:

In the year that King Uzziah died, I saw the Lord seated on a throne, high and exalted, and the train of his robe filled the temple. Above him were seraphs, each with six wings: With two wings they covered their faces, with two they covered their feet, and with two they were flying. And they were calling to one another: "Holy, holy, holy is the Lord Almighty; the whole earth is full of his glory." At the sound of their voices the doorposts and thresholds shook and the temple was filled with smoke. "Woe to me!" I cried. "I am ruined! For I am a man of unclean lips, and I live among a people of unclean lips, and my eyes have seen the King, the Lord Almighty." Then one of the seraphs flew to me with a live coal in his hand, which he had taken with tongs from the altar. With it he touched my mouth and said, "See, this has touched your lips; your guilt is taken away and your sin atoned for." Then I heard the voice of the Lord saying, "Whom shall I send? And who 1will go for us?" And I said, "Here am I. Send me!"

9. Yolanda Adams, "Fragile Heart," *Mountain High . . . Valley Low* (Electra 62439, 1999).

10. Kirk Franklin, "Lean on Me," *The Nu Nation Project* (Gospo Centric 90178, 2000).

11. Donnie McClurkin, "Stand," *Donnie McClurkin* (Warner Alliance 46297, 1996).

12. Sheldon Thompson, interview with author, May 6, 2000; Kevin Taylor, interview with the author, May 6, 2000.

13. Ulf Hannerz, *Transnational Connections: Culture, People, Places* (New York: Routledge, 1996), 21.

14. Roddie Taylor made these statements during a sermon he delivered as a guest speaker at St. Peter's Spiritual Baptist Church, Point Fortin, February 13, 2000.

15. Roddie Taylor, interview with the author, May 6, 2000.

16. Belinda Edmondson, ed., *Caribbean Romances: The Politics of Regional Representation* (Charlottesville: University Press of Virginia, 1999).

EPILOGUE

1. Testimony Time offers these bumper stickers free of charge. For more bumper sticker texts, see Testimony Time's website at http://www.christian bumpersticker.org.

Selected Bibliography

Adorno, Theodor. *Minima Moralia: Reflections from Damaged Life.* Translated by E. F. N. Jephcott. New York: Verso, 1978.

Ahyoung, Selwyn E. "Soca Fever: Change in the Calypso Music Tradition of Trinidad and Tobago." Master's thesis, Indiana University, 1981.

Allahar, Anton L., ed. *Ethnicity, Class, and Nationalism: Caribbean and Extra-Caribbean Dimensions.* Lanham, Md.: Lexington Books, 2005.

Allen, Ray, and Lois Wilcken, eds. *Island Sounds in the Global City: Caribbean Popular Music and Identity in New York.* New York: New York Folklore Society, Institute for Studies in American Music, Brooklyn College, 1998.

Anderson, Allan. *An Introduction to Pentecostalism.* New York: Cambridge University Press, 2004.

Anidjar, Gil, ed. *Acts of Religion/Jacques Derrida.* New York: Routledge, 2001.

Aparicio, Frances R., and Candida F. Jaquez, eds. *Musical Migrations: Transnationalism and Hybridity in Latin/o America.* Vol. 1. New York: Palgrave Macmillan, 2002.

Appadurai, Arjun, ed. *Globalization.* Durham, N.C.: Duke University Press, 2001.

———. *Modernity at Large: Cultural Dimensions of Globalization.* Minneapolis: University of Minnesota Press, 1996.

Appiah, Kwame Anthony. *Cosmopolitanism: Ethics in a World of Strangers.* New York: Norton, 2006.

———. *The Ethics of Identity.* Princeton: Princeton University Press, 2005.

———. *In My Father's House: Africa in the Philosophy of Culture.* New York: Oxford University Press, 1992.

Attali, Jaques. *Noise: The Political Economy of Music.* Minneapolis: University of Minnesota Press, 1985.

Austin-Broos, Diane J. *Jamaica Genesis: Religion and the Politics of Moral Orders.* Chicago: University of Chicago Press, 1997.

Averill, Gage. *A Day for the Hunter, a Day for the Prey: Popular Music and Power in Haiti.* Chicago: University of Chicago Press, 1997.

Badiou, Alain. *Ethics: An Essay on the Understanding of Evil.* Translated by Peter Hallward. New York: Verso, 2001.

———. *Metapolitics.* Translated by Jason Barker. New York: Verso, 2005.

Bakhtin, Mikhail. *The Dialogical Imagination: Four Essays by M. M. Bakhtin.* Edited by Michael Holquist. Austin: University of Texas Press, 1981.

Balliger, Robin. "Noisy Spaces: Popular Music Consumption, Social Fragmentation, and the Cultural Politics of Globalization in Trinidad." Ph.D. diss., Stanford University, 2001.

Barz, Gregory. *Music in East Africa: Experiencing Music, Expressing Culture.* New York: Oxford University Press, 2004.

Behague, Gérard H., ed. *Music and Black Ethnicity: The Caribbean and South America.* New Brunswick, N.J.: Transaction Publishers, 1994.

Bellegarde-Smith, Patrick, ed. *Fragments of Bone: Neo-African Religions in a New World.* Urbana-Champaign: University of Illinois Press, 2005.

Benítez-Rojo, Antonio. *The Repeating Island: The Caribbean and the Post-modern Perspective.* Translated by James E. Maraniss. Durham, N.C.: Duke University Press, 1996.

Berrian, Brenda F. *Awakening Spaces: French Caribbean Popular Songs, Music, and Culture.* Chicago: University of Chicago Press, 2000.

Best, Curwen. *Culture @ the Cutting Edge: Tracking Caribbean Popular Music.* Kingston, Jamaica: University of the West Indies Press, 2004.

Bhabha, Homi, ed. *The Location of Culture.* New York: Routledge, 1994.

———. *Nation and Narration.* New York: Routledge, 1990.

———. "On Cultural Choice." In *The Turn to Ethics,* edited by Marjorie Garber, Beatrice Hanssen, and Rebecca L. Walkowitz, 181–200. New York: Routledge, 2000.

Bilby, Kenneth. *True-Born Maroons.* Gainesville: University Press of Florida, 2005.

Bisnauth, Dale A. *History of Religions in the Caribbean.* Trenton, N.J.: Africa World Press, 1996.

Bloechl, Jeffrey, ed. *The Face of the Other and the Trace of God: Essays on the Philosophy of Emmanuel Levinas.* New York: Fordham University Press, 2000.

Bloom, Harold. *The Anxiety of Influence.* 2nd ed. New York: Oxford University Press, 1997.

———. *Omens of Millennium: The Gnosis of Angels, Dreams, and Resurrection.* New York: Riverhead Books, 1996.

Bohlman, Philip V. "Pilgrimage, Politics, and the Musical Remapping of the New Europe." *Ethnomusicology* 40, no. 3 (Fall 1996): 386–87.

———. "World Musics and World Religions: Whose World?" In *Enchanting Powers: Music in the World's Religions,* edited by Lawrence E. Sullivan, 61–90. Cambridge: Harvard University Press, 1997.

———, Edith Blumhofer, and Maria Chow, eds. *Music in American Religious Experience.* New York: Oxford University Press, 2006.

Boyarin, Jonathan. "Space, Time, and the Politics of Memory." In *Remapping*

Memory: The Politics of TimeSpace. Edited by Jonathan Boyarin. Minneapolis: University of Minnesota Press, 1994.

Brereton, Bridget. *A History of Modern Trinidad, 1783–1962*. Portsmouth, N.H.: Heinemann, 1981.

———. *Race Relations in Colonial Trinidad, 1870–1900*. New York: Cambridge University Press, 1979.

———, and Kevin A. Yelvington, eds. *The Colonial Caribbean in Transition: Essays on Post-emancipation Social and Cultural History*. Kingston, Jamaica: University of the West Indies Press, 1999.

Bruce, Steve. "Authority and Fission: The Protestants' Divisions." *British Journal of Sociology* 36 (1985): 592–603.

———. *A House Divided: Protestantism, Schism, and Secularization*. New York: Routledge, 1989.

———. *Religion in the Modern World: From Cathedrals to Cults*. New York: Oxford University Press, 1996.

Burgess, Stanley M., and Eduard M. van der Maas, eds. *The New International Dictionary of Pentecostal and Charismatic Movements*. Grand Rapids, Mich.: Zondervan, 2002.

Burton, Richard D. E. *Afro-Creole: Power, Opposition, and Play in the Caribbean*. Ithaca, N.Y.: Cornell University Press, 1997.

Butler, Melvin. "Songs of Pentecost: Experiencing Music, Transcendence, and Identity in Jamaica and Haiti." Ph.D. diss., New York University, 2005.

Caputo, John D. *Against Ethics: Contributions to a Poetics of Obligation with Constant Reference to Deconstruction*. Bloomington: Indiana University Press, 1993.

Chambers, Iain, and Lidia Curti, eds. *The Post-colonial Question: Common Skies, Divided Horizons*. New York: Routledge, 1996.

Cheah, Pheng, and Bruce Robbins, eds. *Cosmopolitics: Thinking and Feeling beyond the Nation*. Minneapolis: University of Minnesota Press, 1998.

Chernoff, John Miller. *African Rhythm and African Sensibility*. Chicago: University of Chicago Press, 1979.

Chevannes, Barry, ed. *Rastafari and Other African-Caribbean Worldviews*. New Brunswick, N.J.: Rutgers University Press, 1995.

———. *Rastafari: Roots and Ideology*. Syracuse, N.Y.: Syracuse University Press, 1994.

Clayton, Martin, Trevor Herbert, and Richard Middleton, eds. *The Cultural Study of Music: A Critical Introduction*. New York: Routledge, 2003.

Cooper, Carolyn. *Noises in the Blood: Orality, Gender, and the "Vulgar" Body of Jamaican Popular Culture*. Durham, N.C.: Duke University Press, 1995.

———. *Sound Clash: Jamaican Dancehall Culture at Large*. New York: Palgrave Macmillan, 2004.

Corten, André, and Ruth Marshall-Fratani, eds. *Between Babel and Pentecost: Transnational Pentecostalism in Africa and Latin America*. Bloomington: Indiana University Press, 2001.

Cowley, John. *Carnival, Canboulay, and Calypso: Traditions in the Making.* New York: Cambridge University Press, 1996.

Cox, Harvey. *Fire from Heaven: The Rise of Pentecostal Spirituality and the Reshaping of Religion in the Twenty-first Century.* Cambridge, Mass.: Da Capo Press, 1995.

Craton, Michael, and Gail Saunders. *Islanders in the Stream: A History of the Bahamian People.* Vol. 1, *From Aboriginal Times to the End of Slavery.* Athens: University of Georgia Press, 1992.

———, eds. *Islanders in the Stream: A History of the Bahamian People.* Vol. 2, *From the Ending of Slavery to the Twenty-first Century.* Athens: University of Georgia Press, 1998.

Cudjoe, Selwyn R., ed. *Eric E. Williams Speaks: Essays on Colonialism and Independence.* Wellesley: Calaloux Publishers, 1993.

de Certeau, Michel. *The Practice of Everyday Life.* Berkeley: University of California Press, 1984.

Derrida, Jacques, and Gianni Vattimo, eds. *Religion: Cultural Memory in the Present.* Stanford, Calif.: Stanford University Press, 1998.

Dudley, Shannon. *Carnival Music in Trinidad: Experiencing Music, Expressing Culture.* New York: Oxford University Press, 2003.

———. "Judging 'by the Beat': Calypso versus Soca." *Ethnomusicology* 40, no. 2 (Spring/Summer 1996): 269–98.

Edmondson, Belinda, ed. *Caribbean Romances: The Politics of Regional Representation.* Charlottesville: University of Virginia Press, 1999.

Floyd, Samuel A., Jr. *The Power of Black Music: Interpreting Its History from Africa to the United States.* New York: Oxford University Press, 1996.

Fojas, Camilla. *Cosmopolitanism in the Americas.* West Lafayette, Ind.: Purdue University Press, 2005.

Foner, Nancy. *Islands in the City: West Indian Migration to New York.* Berkeley: University of California Press, 2001.

Forte, Maximilian C. *Ruins of Absence, Presence of Caribs: Postcolonial Representations of Aboriginality in Trinidad and Tobago.* Gainesville: University Press of Florida, 2005.

Foucault, Michel. *Essential Works of Michel Foucault, 1954–1984.* Vol. 1, *Ethics, Subjectivity, and Truth.* Edited by Paul Rabinow. New York: New Press, 1998.

———. *Essential Works of Michel Foucault, 1954–1984.* Vol. 2, *Aesthetics, Method, and Epistemology.* Edited by James D. Faubion. New York: New Press, 1999.

———. *Essential Works of Michel Foucault, 1954–1984.* Vol. 3, *Power.* Edited by James D. Faubion. New York: New Press, 2001.

Frey, Silvia R., and Betty Wood. *Come Shouting to Zion: African-American Protestantism in the American South and British Caribbean to 1830.* Chapel Hill: University of North Carolina Press, 1998.

Frith, Simon. "Music and Identity." In *Questions of Cultural Identity,* edited by Stuart Hall and Paul duGay, 108–27. Thousand Oaks, Calif.: Sage Publications, 1996.

Garber, Marjorie, Beatrice Hanssen, and Rebecca L. Walkowitz, eds. *The Turn to Ethics*. New York: Routledge, 2000.

Glazier, Stephen, D. *Marchin' the Pilgrims Home: Leadership and Decision-Making in an Afro-Caribbean Faith*. Westwood, Conn.: Greenwood Press, 1983.

Glowacka, Dorota, and Stephen Boos, eds. *Between Ethics and Aesthetics*. Albany: State University of New York Press, 2002.

Gordon, Lewis R. *Existence in Black: An Anthology of Black Existential Philosophy*. New York: Routledge, 1996.

———. *Existentia Africana: Understanding Africana Existential Thought*. New York: Routledge, 2000.

Gossai, Hemchand, and Nathaniel S. Murrell, eds. *Religion, Culture, and Tradition in the Caribbean*. New York: St. Martin's Press, 2000.

Guilbault, Jocelyne. *Zouk: World Music in the West Indies*. Chicago: University of Chicago Press, 1993.

Habermas, Jürgen. *Moral Consciousness and Communicative Action*. Translated by Christian Lenhardt and Shierry Weber Nicholsen. Cambridge: MIT Press, 1990.

———. *Religion and Rationality: Essays on Reason, God, and Modernity*. Cambridge: MIT Press, 2002.

———. *The Theory of Communicative Action*. Vol. 1, *Reason and the Rationalization of Society*. Translated by Thomas McCarthy. Boston: Beacon Press, 1984.

———. *The Theory of Communicative Action*. Vol. 2, *Lifeword and System: A Critique of Functionalist Reason*. Translated by Thomas McCarthy. Boston: Beacon Press, 1984.

Hackshaw, John Milton. *The Baptist Denomination: A Concise History Commemorating One hundred seventy-five Years (1816–1991) of the Establishment of the "Company Villages" and the Baptist Faith in Trinidad and Tobago*. Port of Spain, Trinidad: Amphy and Bashana Memorial Society, 1991.

Hall, Catherine. "Histories, Empires, and the Post-colonial Moment." In *The Post-colonial Question: Common Skies, Divided Horizons*, edited by Iain Chambers and Lidia Curti, 65–77. New York: Routledge, 1996.

Hall, David L. *Richard Rorty: Prophet and Poet of the New Pragmatism*. Albany: State University of New York Press, 1994.

Hall, Stuart. "Negotiating Caribbean Identities." In *New Caribbean Thought: A Reader*, edited by Brian Meeks and Folke Lindhal, 24–39. Kingston, Jamaica: University of the West Indies Press, 2001.

———, and Paul duGay, eds. *Questions of Cultural Identity*. Thousand Oaks, Calif.: Sage Publications, 1996.

Hannerz, Ulf. *Transnational Connections: Culture, People, Places*. New York: Routledge, 1996.

Harney, Stefano. *Nationalism and Identity: Culture and the Imagination in a Caribbean Diaspora*. Atlantic Highlands, N.J.: Zed Books, 1996.

Harpham, Geoffrey Galt. *Language Alone: The Critical Fetish of Modernity.* New York: Routledge, 2002.

Harris, Michael W. *The Rise of Gospel Blues: The Music of Thomas Andrew Dorsey in the Urban Church.* New York: Oxford University Press, 1994.

Hebdige, Dick. *Cut 'n' Mix: Culture, Identity, and Caribbean Music.* New York: Routledge, 1987.

————. *Subculture: The Meaning of Style.* London: Methuen, 1974.

Hendley, Steven. *From Communicative Action to the Face of the Other: Levinas and Habermas on Language, Obligation, and Community.* New York: Lexington Books, 2000.

Henry, Frances. *Reclaiming African Religions in Trinidad: The Socio-political Legitimation of the Orisha and Spiritual Baptist Faiths.* St. Augustine, Trinidad: University of the West Indies Press, 2003.

Henry, Paget. *Caliban's Reason: Introducing Afro-Caribbean Philosophy.* New York: Routledge, 2000.

Herzfeld, Michael. *Cultural Intimacy: Social Poetics in the Nation-State.* New York: Routledge, 1997.

Hill, Donald R. *Calypso Calaloo: Early Carnival Music in Trinidad.* Gainesville: University of Florida Press, 1993.

Homiak, John P. "Soundings on Rastafari Livity and Language." In *Rastafari and Other African-Caribbean Worldviews,* edited by Barry Chevannes, 127–81. New Brunswick, N.J.: Rutgers University Press, 1995.

Hord, Fred Lee (Mzee Lasana Okpara), and Jonathan Scott Lee. *I Am because We Are: Readings in Black Philosophy.* Amherst: University of Massachusetts Press, 1995.

Houk, James T. *Spirits, Blood, and Drums: The Orisha Religion in Trinidad.* Philadelphia: Temple University Press, 1995.

Jackson, Jerma A. *Singing in My Soul: Black Gospel Music in a Secular Age.* Chapel Hill: University of North Carolina Press, 2004.

James, C. L. R. *Beyond a Boundary.* Reprint, Durham, N.C.: Duke University Press, 1993.

Kahn, Aisha. *Calaloo Nation: Metaphors of Race and Religious Identity among South Asians in Trinidad.* Durham, N.C.: Duke University Press, 2004.

————. "Purity, Piety, and Power: Culture and Identity among Hindus and Muslims in Trinidad." Ph.D. diss., City University of New York, 1995.

Korom, Frank J. *Hosay Trinidad: Muharram Performances in an Indo-Caribbean Diaspora.* Philadelphia: University of Pennsylvania Press, 2002.

Kraidy, Marwan M. *Hybridity, or The Cultural Logic of Globalization.* Philadelphia: Temple University Press, 2005.

Lampe, Armando, ed. *Christianity in the Caribbean: Essays on Church History.* Kingston, Jamaica: University of the West Indies Press, 2001.

Las Casas, Bartolomé de. *In Defense of the Indians.* Translated by Stafford Poole. De Kalb: Northern Illinois University Press, 1992.

————. *A Short Account of the Destruction of the Indies.* Translated by Nigel Griffin. New York: Penguin Classics, 1999.

Lawson, Winston A. *Religion and Race: African and European Roots in Conflict—A Jamaican Testament*. New York: Peter Lang, 1996.

Lee, Philip J. *Against the Protestant Gnostics*. New York: Oxford University Press, 1987.

Levinas, Emmanuel. *Entre Nous: Thinking of the Other*. Translated by Michael B. Smith and Barbara Harshav. New York: Columbia University Press, 1998.

———. *Otherwise Than Being, or Beyond Essence*. Translated by Alphonso Lingis. Boston: Kluwer Boston, 1981.

———. *Totality and Infinity: An Essay on Exteriority*. Translated by Alphonso Lingis. Pittsburgh: Duquesne University Press, 1969.

Levinson, Jerrold, ed. *Aesthetics and Ethics: Essays at the Intersection*. New York: Cambridge University Press, 1998.

Liverpool, Hollis. *From the Horse's Mouth: An Analysis of Certain Significant Aspects in the Development of the Calypso and Society as Gleaned from Personal Communication with Some Outstanding Calypsonians*. Diego Martin, Trinidad: Juba Publications, 2003.

———. *Rituals of Power and Rebellion: The Carnival Tradition in Trinidad and Tobago, 1763–1962*. Chicago: Research Associates School Times, 2001.

Lovelace, Earl. "Views of Earl Lovelace." Interview by Victor Questal. *Caribbean Contact* 5, no. 3 (1977): 15–16. Cited in Stefano Harney, *Nationalism and Identity: Culture and the Imagination in a Caribbean Diaspora*. Atlantic Highlands, N.J.: Zed Books, 1996.

Lum, Kenneth A. *Praising His Name in the Dance: Spirit Possession in the Spiritual Baptist Faith and Orisha Work in Trinidad, West Indies*. New York: Routledge, 2000.

Makoni, Sinfree, Geneva Smitherman, Arnetha F. Ball, and Arthur K. Spears, eds. *Black Linguistics: Language, Society, and Politics in Africa and the Americas*. New York: Routledge, 2003.

Manuel, Peter. *East Indian Music in the West Indies: Tan-Singing, Chutney, and the Making of Indo-Caribbean Culture*. Philadelphia: Temple University Press, 2000.

Martin, David. *Pentecostalism: The World Their Parish*. Malden, Mass.: Blackwell Publishers, 2002.

Mason, Peter. *Bacchanal: The Carnival Culture of Trinidad*. Philadelphia: Temple University Press, 1999.

Mbiti, John. *African Religions and Philosophy*. 2nd ed. New York: Oxford, 1990.

McDaniel, Lorna. "Memory Spirituals of the Ex-slave American Soldiers in Trinidad's 'Company Villages.'" *Black Music Research Journal* 14, no. 2 (Fall 1994): 119–44.

Meskell, Lynn, and Peter Pels, eds. *Embedding Ethics: Shifting Boundaries of the Anthropological Profession*. New York: Berg, 2005.

Mintz, Sidney W. *Caribbean Transformations*. Chicago: Adeline, 1974.

———, and Sally Price, eds. *Carribean Contours*. Baltimore: Johns Hopkins University Press, 1985.

Mitchell, Tony, ed. *Global Noise: Rap and Hip-Hop outside the USA*. Middletown, Conn.: Wesleyan University Press, 2001.

Murray, Eric John, ed. *Religions of Trinidad and Tobago: A Guide to the History, Beliefs, and Polity of Twenty-three Religious Faiths*. Port of Spain, Trinidad: Murray Publications, 1998.

Murrell, Nathaniel S., William D. Spencer, and Adrian A. McFarlane, eds. *Chanting Down Babylon: The Rastafari Reader*. Philadelphia: Temple University Press, 1998.

Myers, Helen. *Music of Hindu Trinidad: Songs from the India Diaspora*. Chicago: University of Chicago Press, 1998.

Nagel, Thomas. *The View from Nowhere*. New York: Oxford University Press, 1986.

Naipaul, V. S. *Guerrillas*. New York: Vintage Books, 1975.

Nattiez, Jean-Jacques. *Music and Discourse: Toward a Semiology of Music*. Translated by Carolyn Abbate. Princeton: Princeton University Press, 1990.

Nelson, Eric Sean, Antje Kapunst, and Kent Still, eds. *Addressing Levinas*. Evanston, Ill.: Northwestern University Press, 2005.

Nettleford, Rex. *Inward Stretch Outward Reach: A Voice from the Caribbean*. London: Macmillan Press, 1993.

Neville, Robert, ed. *New Essays in Metaphysics*. Albany: State University of New York Press, 1989.

Nussbaum, Martha. *Love's Knowledge: Essays on Philosophy and Literature*. New York: Oxford University Press, 1990.

Olmos, Marguerite Fernándes, and Lizabeth Paravisini-Gebert, eds. *Creole Religions of the Caribbean: An Introduction from Vodou and Santeria, to Obeah and Espiritismo*. New York: New York University Press, 2003.

———, eds. *Sacred Possessions: Vodoo, Santeria, Obeah, and the Caribbean*. New Brunswick, N.J.: Rutgers University Press, 1997.

Pacini Hernandez, Deborah, Hector Fernandez L'Hoeste, and Eric Zolov, eds. *Rockin' las Americas: The Global Politics of Rock in Latin/o America*. Pittsburgh: University of Pittsburgh Press, 2004.

Palmer, Ransford W., ed. *U.S.-Caribbean Relations: Their Impact on Peoples and Culture*. Westport, Conn.: Praeger Publishers, 1998.

Parker, David. Introduction to *Negotiating Ethics in Literature, Philosophy, and Theory*, edited by Jane Adamson, Richard Freadman, and David Parker, 1–17. New York: Cambridge University Press, 1998.

Pastor, Robert A. *Exiting the Whirlpool: U.S. Foreign Policy toward Latin America and the Caribbean*. 2nd ed. Boulder, Colo.: Westview Press, 2001.

Pinn, Anthony B. *Noise and Spirit: The Religious and Spiritual Sensibilities of Rap Music*. New York: New York University Press, 2003.

Poewe, Karla, ed. *Charismatic Christianity as a Global Culture*. Columbia: University of South Carolina Press, 1994.

Premdas, Ralph R. *Identity, Ethnicity, and Culture in the Caribbean*. St. Augustine, Trinidad: University of the West Indies Press, 1999.

Puri, Shalini. *The Caribbean Postcolonial: Social Equality, Post-nationalism, and Cultural Hybridity.* New York: Palgrave, 2004.

———. *Marginal Migrations: The Circulation of Cultures within the Caribbean.* London: Macmillan Caribbean, 2003.

Radano, Ronald, and Philip V. Bohlman, eds. *Music and the Racial Imagination.* Chicago: University of Chicago Press, 2000.

Ramnarine, Tina. *Creating Their Own Space: The Development of an Indian-Caribbean Musical Tradition.* Kingston, Jamaica: University of the West Indies Press, 2001.

Ramsey, Guthrie P., Jr. *Race Music: Black Cultures from Bebop to Hip-Hop.* Berkeley: University of California Press, 2003.

Rawls, John. *Justice as Fairness: A Restatement.* Cambridge, Mass.: Belknap Press, 2001.

Redman, Robb. *The Great Worship Awakening: Singing a New Song in the Postmodern Church.* San Francisco: Jossey-Bass, 2002.

Reed, Teresa. *The Holy Profane: Religion in Black Popular Music.* Lexington: University of Kentucky Press, 2003.

Rehg, William. *Insight and Solidarity: The Discourse Ethics of Jürgen Habermas.* Berkeley: University of California Press, 1994.

Rohlehr, Gordon. *Calypso and Society in Pre-independence Trinidad.* Port of Spain, Trinidad: G. Rohlehr, 1990.

Rommen, Timothy. "Nationalism and the Soul: Gospelypso as Independence." In *Black Music Research Journal* 22, no. 1 (Spring 2002): 37–63.

———. "Protestant Vibrations? Reggae, Rastafari, and Conscious Evangelicals." *Popular Music* 25, no. 2 (May 2006): 235–63.

———. " 'Watch Out My Children': Gospel Music and the Ethics of Style in Trinidad and Tobago." Ph.D. diss., University of Chicago, 2002.

Rorty, Richard. *Contingency, Irony, and Solidarity.* New York: Cambridge University Press, 1989.

Ryan, Selwyn D. *The Jhandi and the Cross: The Clash of Cultures in Post-Creole Trinidad and Tobago.* St. Augustine, Trinidad: Sir Arthur Lewis Institute of Social and Economic Studies, University of the West Indies, 1999.

———. *The Muslimeen Grab for Power: Race, Religion, and Revolution in Trinidad and Tobago.* Port of Spain, Trinidad: Imprint Caribbean, 1991.

———, and Taimoon Stewart, eds. *Power: The Black Power Revolution 1970, a Retrospective.* St. Augustine, Trinidad: Sir Arthur Lewis Institute of Social and Economic Studies, University of the West Indies, 1995.

Sartre, Jean-Paul. *Being and Nothingness: A Phenomenological Essay on Ontology.* Translated by Hazel E. Barnes. New York: Washington Square Press, 1956.

Savishinsky, Neil. "Transnational Popular Culture and the Global Spread of the Jamaican Rastafarian Movement." *New West Indian Guide* 68, nos. 3–4 (1994): 259–81.

Shepherd, Verene A., and Glen Richards, eds. *Questioning Creole: Creolisation Discourses in Caribbean Culture.* Kingston, Jamaica: Ian Randle, 2002.

Smith, Peter H. *Talons of the Eagle: Dynamics of U.S.–Latin American Relations*. 2nd ed. New York: Oxford University Press, 2000.

Stoll, David. *Is Latin America Turning Protestant? The Politics of Evangelical Growth*. Berkeley: University of California Press, 1990.

Stolzoff, Norman C. *Wake the Town and Tell the People: Dancehall Culture in Jamaica*. Durham, N.C.: Duke University Press, 2000.

Stuempfle, Stephen. *The Steelband Movement: The Forging of a National Art in Trinidad and Tobago*. Philadelphia: University of Pennsylvania Press, 1996.

Sullivan, Lawrence E. *Enchanting Powers: Music in the World's Religions*. Cambridge: Harvard University Press, 1997.

Swed, John F., and John W. Pulis, eds. *Religion, Diaspora, and Cultural Identity: A Reader in the Anglophone Caribbean*. Amsterdam: Gordon and Breach Publishers, 1999.

Sylvan, Robin. *Traces of the Spirit: The Religious Dimensions of Popular Music*. New York: New York University Press, 2002.

Synan, Vinson. *The Century of the Holy Spirit: One hundred Years of Charismatic Renewal, 1901–2001*. Nashville: Thomas Nelson, 2001.

———. *The Holiness-Pentecostal Tradition: Charismatic Movements in the Twentieth Century*. 2nd ed. Grand Rapids, Mich.: William B. Eerdmans, 1997.

Taylor, Charles. *The Ethics of Authenticity*. Cambridge: Harvard University Press, 1991.

———. *Modern Social Imaginaries*. Durham, N.C.: Duke University Press, 2004.

———. *Sources of the Self: The Making of the Modern Identity*. Cambridge: Harvard University Press, 1989.

Taylor, Patrick, ed. *Nation Dance: Religion, Identity, and Cultural Difference in the Caribbean*. Bloomington: Indiana University Press, 2001.

Thornton, Sarah. *Club Cultures: Music, Media, and Subcultural Capital*. Hanover, N.H.: University Press of New England, 1996.

Tinker, Hugh. *A New System of Slavery: The Export of Indian Labour Overseas, 1830–1920*. New York: Oxford University Press, 1974.

Trouillot, Michel-Rolph. *Global Transformations: Anthropology in the Modern World*. New York: Palgrave Macmillan, 2003.

———. *Silencing the Past: Power and the Production of History*. Boston: Beacon Press, 1995.

Turner, Victor. *The Ritual Process: Structure and Anti-structure*. New York: Aldine de Gruyter, 1968.

Vásquez, Manuel, and Marie Friedmann Marquardt. *Globalizing the Sacred: Religion across the Americas*. New Brunswick, N.J.: Rutgers University Press, 2003.

Vertovec, Steven. *Hindu Trinidad: Religion, Ethnicity, and Social Change*. London: Macmillan Caribbean, 1992.

———, and Robin Cohen, eds. *Conceiving Cosmopolitanism: Theory, Context, and Practice*. New York: Oxford University Press, 2002.

Warner, Keith Q. "Ethnicity and the Contemporary Calypso." In *Trinidad Eth-

nicity, edited by Kevin A. Yelvington, 275–91. Warwick University Caribbean Studies. London: Macmillan Caribbean, 1993.

———. *Kaiso! The Trinidad Calypso: A Study of Calypso as Oral Literature.* Washington, D.C.: Three Continents Press, 1982.

Warner-Lewis, Maureen. *Central Africa in the Caribbean: Transcending Time, Transforming Cultures.* Kingston, Jamaica: University of the West Indies Press, 2003.

———. *Trinidad Yoruba: From Mother Tongue to Memory.* Kingston, Jamaica: University of the West Indies Press, 1997.

Weber, Max. *The Protestant Ethic and the Spirit of Capitalism.* London: George, Allen, & Unwin, 1976.

Yelvington, Kevin A. *Trinidad Ethnicity.* Warwick University Caribbean Studies. London: Macmillan Caribbean, 1993.

———, and Faye Venetia Harrison, eds. *Afro-Atlantic Dialogues: Anthropology in the Diaspora.* Santa Fe, N.M.: School of American Research Press, 2005.

Young, Robert C. *Colonial Desire: Hybridity in Theory, Culture, and Race.* New York: Routledge, 1995.

———. *Postcolonialism: An Historical Introduction.* Malden, Mass.: Blackwell Publishers, 2001.

Zane, Wallace W. *Journeys to the Spiritual Lands: The Natural History of a West Indian Religion.* New York: Oxford University Press, 1999.

Zupancic, Alenka. *Ethics of the Real: Kant, Lacan.* New York: Verso, 2000.

Index

Text: 10/13 Aldus
Display: Aldus
Compositor: BookMatters, Berkeley
Printer and binder: Maple-Vail Manufacturing Group